The Hero and the City

The Hero and the City

An Interpretation of Sophocles'
Oedipus at Colonus

Joseph P. Wilson

Ann Arbor

THE UNIVERSITY OF MICHIGAN PRESS

Copyright © by the University of Michigan 1997
All rights reserved
Published in the United States of America by
The University of Michigan Press
Manufactured in the United States of America
⊗ Printed on acid-free paper

2000   1999   1998   1997   4   3   2   1

A CIP catalog record for this book is available from the British Library.

Library of Congress Cataloging-in-Publication Data

Wilson, Joseph P., 1956–
   The hero and the city : an interpretation of Sophocles' Oedipus at
Colonus / Joseph P. Wilson.
      p.   cm.
   Includes bibliographical references and index.
   ISBN 0-472-10796-8 (alk. paper)
   1. Sophocles.   Oedipus at Colonus.   2. Greek drama (Tragedy)—
History and criticism.   3. Oedipus (Greek mythology) in literature.
4. City and town life in literature.   5. Heroes in literature.
I. Title.
PA4413.O53W54   1997
882'.01—dc21   96-45814
                                                          CIP

To my parents,
first and best of all my teachers

Preface

Cedric Whitman observed, in the preface to his *Sophocles: A Study of Heroic Humanism* (Cambridge, Mass., 1951), that "The best excuse for a new book about Sophocles is the number and diversity of those already existing." Since that time, the number and diversity of works on Sophocles have increased dramatically, an increase that lays additional burdens on any author intrepid enough (or foolish enough—I do not wish to suggest that the adjectives are mutually exclusive) to add to the bibliographical surfeit. Put simply, those added burdens are to say something new, or at least useful, and to say it in an interesting manner. I have tried to do both: readers will decide for themselves whether I have succeeded.

As to the new or useful, I have tried throughout to emphasize the importance of Oedipus' heroism, and Sophocles' dramatic treatment of that heroism, as the driving action of the *Oedipus at Colonus*. In my view, Oedipus never "becomes" a hero in this play. Rather, he never ceased to be a hero, even during his darkest moments at Thebes, even during the long years of exile. He arrives at Athens a hero, not (pace Burian) a suppliant, and demands that Athens, Theseus, Creon, and Polyneices treat him accordingly. In so doing, Sophocles engages his compatriots in a dialogue on the nature of heroism and reminds them of the polis' need to create a space for heroes. An Athenian populace that found its beloved city slowly disintegrating under the stresses of the Peloponnesian War could not have missed the point.

As to the interesting, one of the anonymous readers of the manuscript version of this book took exception to my references to *Doonesbury*, to Robertson Davies, to other contemporary authors or events, and to judgments about matters within the play, and about the story of Oedipus itself, that derived ultimately from my own personal experiences and observations. I take this opportunity to offer a brief apologia.

A 1995 issue of *Lingua Franca* (vol. 5, no. 6) included an article entitled "Can Classics Die?" The question should, and probably does, scare every working classicist on the continent. The author, David Damrosch, offered less hope than one might like, although a number of the field's luminaries provided more optimistic analyses of the field's current crises and its potential resilience. I weigh in with my own opinion. Classics will not die. Homer, Sophocles, Vergil, and the rest are far tougher and more durable than the most virulent, number-crunching, classicidal sub-assistant-vice-provost for institutional research can imagine. Classics will not die. But classicists have done less than they should to help themselves and their discipline.

Literary criticism in classics, as now practiced in this country, suffers from two huge liabilities. First, it is seldom accessible to people outside of the field, and second, it is seldom very interesting. Theory-driven, jargon-riddled discourse avails little to narrow the gap between literature and the literate. (The unacknowledged weakness of the current "cutting edge" in criticism is the depressing ease with which it can be joined.) We need to find learned audiences from all fields and engage them, rather than attempt to prove how well we have mastered the latest isms. Toward that end, I have written what I hope to be a learned, intelligent work on the *Oedipus at Colonus* that will prove both accessible and interesting to classicists, nonclassicists, and even learned laypersons. (The latter group of people exists, and many among them are eager for criticism they can read, about authors and works they have read. Classicists should be prepared to enter that arena; why should Harold Bloom and Civil War historians have all the fun?) If some of my references are a bit off the wall, so much the better. Of one thing I am certain: the Athenian audience brought with them to Sophocles' tragedies everything they knew and everything they were. The American critic of the late twentieth century should do no less.

The body of secondary scholarship on this play is vast, and it would not be possible to cite every scholar on every point of agreement or contention. I have confined my notes to areas of significant disagreement and to matters on which other scholars have made singularly salient observations. Disagreement should of course never be confused with disrespect. All translations are my own, with one exception (duly cited in the notes).

I have a number of debts of gratitude to acknowledge, and I do so here with the greatest pleasure. First and foremost, I would like to thank the Research Committee of the University of Scranton, especially its past chairman, Thomas Hogan, and the provost, Richard Passon, for their generous support of my work. The chairman of my department, Bob Parsons, and two colleagues, Len Champney and Len Gougeon, were kind enough to read my initial proposals and made valuable suggestions. Dr. Parsons deserves special thanks, both for introducing me to the joys of word processing and for never mentioning the wear and tear I have caused to the department's laser printer and copier. Joyce Knott provided much valuable clerical assistance. I am grateful to my many colleagues (they know who they are) with whom I have long been in competition, in Hesiod's best type of strife. They have made me better, largely because they are so much better than I am. I want to thank Roger Hornsby, Richard Krill, and my great friend and E-mail correspondent, Joe Hughes, for long friendship and support. I want to thank Mary Ann, who, for reasons fathomable only to her, continues to put up with me. To the dedicatees of this book I can only acknowledge, never repay, my debts.

I also wish to express my deepest gratitude to the University of Michigan Press, to the classics editor, Ellen Bauerle, and her assistant, James Laforest, and to the anonymous readers of the manuscript. Their assistance has been invaluable. For all the contents of my work, I am solely responsible.

Contents

1

Sophocles and Oedipus

Of the three great tragic poets of fifth-century Athens, none commands respect so widely as Sophocles. Reasons can be adduced without difficulty. The Athenians recognized the epiphany in their midst and awarded him twenty-four firsts. Out of 123 plays, 96 took first prize, while he never finished lower than second, an astonishing winning percentage. Indeed, the esteem in which he was held by his fellows led to a modest but respectable political career and to his posthumous elevation to the status of cult hero, in connection with the worship of Aesclepius. The first true literary critic confirmed the judgment of the citizens of an earlier day. For better or worse, thanks largely to the authority of Aristotle's *Poetics*, the *Oedipus Tyrannus* stands as the archetypal Greek tragedy, and the standing of that play has transferred the attendant recognition to its author. That schoolmasters and careerists of a later era may have preferred Euripides to Sophocles tells us more of their shortcomings than of any deficiency, real or perceived, on the part of the poet.[1]

The playwright was destined for a comeback. The pure merit of his work, and the tendency to identify him with "classicism" itself, guaranteed it. The result was a paradox. The identity with classicism, the source of his literary apotheosis, nearly buried him as well. He was to be admired, not studied. The German neo-Hellenists at the close of the eighteenth and the beginning of the nineteenth century were intrigued by Oedipus, but in the main, nineteenth-century critics, particularly the

---

1. This entire question of Euripides' receiving preference in the school curricula is of course very tendentious, relying as it does on a suggestion of Wilamowitz-Moellendorf (U. von Wilamowitz-Moellendorf, *Analecta Euripidea* [1875, reprint, Hildesheim, 1963], 133). However, Wilson and Reynolds, who show no inclination to agree with Wilamowitz-Moellendorf on the matter, are still forced to explain the more frequent presence of editorial remarks and stage directions in Euripides by appealing to his greater popularity, even in the second century B.C. See L.D. Reynolds and N.G. Wilson, *Scribes and Scholars*, 2d ed. (Oxford, 1974), 14, 46–47.

English, all but ignored Sophocles and focused on his younger rival.[2] This was, in Whitman's view, attributable to Sophocles' own greatness. As Whitman remarks, "As a poet, artist, and thinker, Sophocles had all but died of his own magnificent fame."[3] But at last, the poet was restored to his proper status, thanks in part to the work of Nietzsche and Freud; he is acknowledged as the master of Greek tragedy, and since his rehabilitation at the turn of the century his work has enjoyed universal recognition.

His dramatic contemporaries have fared less well. Critics invariably recognize the power of Aeschylus yet wonder at and sometimes apologize for his craftsmanship or his idiosyncratic diction, for Aeschylus is a playwright of ideas, as Winnington-Ingram observed. While Aeschylus' ability to inspire piety and idealism earned the approbation of Aristophanes, the pure difficulty of his style nearly condemned him to oblivion.[4] Euripides, in turn, provides one of the great and most consistently productive mines of information on the historical and mythological world of the Greeks and offers a fairly straightforward and interesting read, although his characters are somewhat melodramatic.[5] Unfortunately, as J.R.R. Tolkien once observed of Shakespeare's plays, Euripides' works "just haven't got any coherent ideas behind them."[6] For his deceptive accessibility he is sometimes praised, sometimes faulted, not always admired (even in his own time), and

---

2. For a good summary discussion of the shifts in popularity endured by the playwright, see R. Scodel, *Sophocles* (Boston 1984), 125 ff., and C.H. Whitman, *Sophocles: A Study of Heroic Humanism* (Cambridge, Mass., 1951).

3. *Sophocles*, 6.

4. Longinus 3.2 gives an idea of how difficult Aeschylus' style can be. I find attractive the suggestion that his work declined in popularity in great part because he was so difficult to read. See L. Spatz, *Aeschylus* (Boston, 1982), 168. For an additional view, see W.B. Stanford, *Aeschylus in His Style: A Study in Language and Personality* (Dublin, 1942), who gives a thorough overview of the ancient criticisms.

5. Euripides, of course, has never lacked detractors, even in those periods when he was most admired. For an account of the hostility toward his work in the nineteenth century, see A.W. Verrell, *Euripides the Rationalist* (1895; reprint, New York, 1962), vii–ix, 1–3.

6. I refer, of course, to the remark preserved in H. Carpenter's *The Inklings* (New York, 1978), 146, in his wonderful re-creation of an "average" Thursday night meeting in C.S. Lewis' rooms (as if such meetings could ever be termed "average").

certainly never granted the literary apotheoses routinely accorded his elder contemporary.[7]

In respect to comparisons with his colleagues, Sophocles, in one sense, at least, has no critics. At this we should not be surprised. Aeschylus wrote of ideas, Euripides of people; Sophocles managed to do both. Few dramatists have managed, as he did, to construct and maintain drama built around the inquiry into the ramifications of an abstract question: the respective rights of, and the tensions between, the *oikos* and the polis in the *Antigone,* or the irreconcilability of fate and free will in the *Oedipus Tyrannus.* Seldom have playwrights even envisioned the characters that Sophocles so brilliantly animated: the chillingly self-absorbed Ajax; the eternally politic, ever deceitful Odysseus; a Deianeira perfectly matched in obtuseness with her Heracles, each character seemingly operating in tandem, neither enjoying any clear understanding of the real state of affairs.

The list of both ideas and characters could be extended, indefinitely perhaps. But over all Sophocles' other creations towers Oedipus, the perennial fixation of classicists, dramatists, and Freudians—the tragic figure who best represents and confounds the zeitgeist, now as in the fifth century B.C. Of all the wonders, as Sophocles states in the *Antigone,* none is so wondrous as man, yet the strongest and cleverest man cannot escape his own self-created destiny, either by intellect or pure force of will.[8] Confronted with the terrifying predictions of Apollo, Oedipus (as most read the story) made the best use of the intelligence and strength with which the gods had endowed him, but both despite and because of these inbred traits, he managed to fall from respected monarch to blind, incestuous parricide in the course of a single day. He stands as the embodiment of Aristotle's *peripeteia,* the classical point of reference for the fall of humankind as a consequence of self-knowledge, and a nightmarish scenario for the operation of Murphy's Law. There, at the conclusion of the *Oedipus Tyrannus,* Oedipus could have remained, a finished hero, blinded, blubbering, paralyzed in the ruin of his own folly, the figure of his ravaged face part memory, part nightmare for every audience that ever saw the play, especially for all viewers who saw themselves in the fallen hero. Sophocles could have left

---

7. His fate in Aristophanes' *Frogs,* as well as the alleged circumstances surrounding his self-imposed exile to Macedon, should be adequately instructive. Moreover, he won only five firsts, one of those posthumously.

8. *Antigone* 332–33.

him demolished by rage, just as he left Ajax frozen in death, a monument to the immutability of self-destruction. But the poet willed things differently. That poetic will we find manifested later in the *Oedipus at Colonus.*

The task of assigning a date to most of Sophocles' plays demands of its assayer a level of recklessness most commonly found in polar explorers and moderately talented undergraduates. I shall not contribute to the glut of imaginative but seldom conclusive scholarship, beyond a fairly safe observation: Sophocles wrote the *Oedipus Tyrannus* sometime in the late 430s or early 420s B.C. and did not return again to his most famous character until very nearly the end of his life.[9] Thus, the *Oedipus Tyrannus,* the ultimate cautionary tale of assumption, presumption, and consequence, he presented to an Athenian audience when Athens was at or near the height of its power, its fleets in control of the seas, its treasury ever enriched by the tribute of its "allies," its city and empire secure from all rivals. According to the tradition, never successfully challenged despite the ingenuity of some scholars, Sophocles then returned to the Oedipus story around 406 B.C. with the composition of the *Oedipus at Colonus.* Athens and Oedipus had both endured a great deal in the interim.

The *Oedipus at Colonus* exercises a particular fascination for us on at least three distinct grounds. First, and most obviously, it is in all probability the last surviving Greek tragedy. At the time of its composition, Aeschylus had been dead for a half-century, Euripides for at least some time;[10] Sophocles himself was nearly ninety. The play, then, is the final work of the best of the dramatists, composed when the author was old enough to know that death, if not imminent, could not be too far away. Hence, the age of the author suggests, if in fact it does not mandate, one approach for interpreting the work. Second, the political circumstances that obtained in Athens as the city labored to the conclusion of the Pelo-

---

9. Jebb makes the best argument for the late date, citing both the tradition and internal evidence in the play; see R.C. Jebb, *Oedipus at Colonus,* ed. E.S. Schuckburgh (Cambridge, 1913), xxx–xxxiii.

10. It is theoretically possible, even given a very late date of composition for the *Oedipus at Colonus,* that Euripides' may have written the *Bacchae* and the *Iphigeneia at Aulis* slightly later, but the tradition is clearly against such dating. Certainly Euripides died sometime before spring 406, or the story that Sophocles led his chorus out in mourning garb at the *Proagon* of the Dionysia has no point.

ponnesian War stand closely allied to the question of the poet's age. By 406 B.C., the imperiled status of military and civil affairs fostered the inescapable conclusion that the city, like the playwright, was running short on time. Finally, the presence of Oedipus, resurrected on the stage of the theater of Dionysus, requires that we consider once more the nature of the archetypal tragic man, in order to weigh thoroughly the significance of his final theatrical epiphany in the dual and apparently paradoxical role as blind beggar and cult hero.

Sophocles and Old Age

No other play of Sophocles, indeed no other Greek play at all, and perhaps no play before *Lear*, speaks so eloquently and so frequently to the concerns of senectitude. A body of town elders comprise the chorus of all three of the Theban plays, but only in the *Oedipus at Colonus* do those old men refer so vividly and so frequently to the difficulties intrinsic to their advancing years. Moreover, in this work, the protagonist is old, as is the primary antagonist, Creon (by his own testimony at 733), and the conflict between Oedipus and his uncle and former brother-in-law, a crucial point in the drama, takes place in the presence of the *gerontes* of Colonus. The choristers, as they witness the confrontation between the two men, evidence the helplessness common to the aged: they cannot assist Oedipus when the Theban representative assaults him; they merely observe and remark on the wrong being done him. Indeed, their powerlessness in the face of Creon's abduction of Antigone testifies to their ultimate inefficacy even better than does their blatant and sometimes tedious lament on the infirmities that attend inevitably on their lengthening years, the theme recurrent in the third choral ode (1211–48).

In augment to the problems encountered by the chorus, the intergenerational conflict between Oedipus and Polyneices, as well as the presence of Antigone and Ismene, compounds and enhances our sense that the articulation of the frustrations of aging is in some sense autobiographical. Youth delineates and defines old age far more clearly in the contrasts that the poet can exploit. Even should we ignore the possibility that Sophocles employed for a dramatic model the problems he encountered with his own son, Iophon, when he created his play, much in the interaction of Oedipus with his children, both in his harsh dealings with Polyneices and his tender though ultimately ineffectual concern for his daughters, rings too true to be coincidental or entirely fictive. The old Oedipus, affectionate and irascible, passive and violent, resembles the young Oedipus in that both push their inclinations to the extreme. As the young Oedipus did so, he became, in the judgment of many critics, the tragic Everyman. Perhaps in his later manifestation he becomes every *gerōn*, and hence as valid a representative of the ninety-year-old poet as anyone else.

The age of the poet alone, however, cannot account for the flavor of the work. After all, the *Philoctetes* antedates the *Oedipus at Colonus* by only three years, and one finds little, if any, interest in the concerns of old men in that play, written by a poet then in his late eighties—old by any standards, ancient among many of his contemporaries. If the infirmities of age confronted the dramatist with additional challenges, those challenges did not overwhelm him. We need not envision a terrified Sophocles lying on his deathbed, one eye permanently fixed on the door, waiting for the final summons. Like the rest of us, until the last moment arrived, he no more knew if he had one day or five years left. Hence, we must be wary of making too facile a connection between the circumstances of the author and the words of his characters. The ode reciting the sorrows of old age feels autobiographical but need not be, for the simple reason that old age may not be sorrowful at all. As Cicero reminds us in the *De Senectute*, Cato enjoyed a vigorous old age. We should recall in this regard Plato's suggestion that Sophocles' considered his declining years rather pleasant.[11]

Instead of positing a straight autobiographical equivalence between playwright and protagonist, we do better to note the apparent preoccupation of both the *Philoctetes* and the *Oedipus at Colonus*, that is, the reintegration of the hero into society.[12] As Whitman puts it:

> It is often said that Sophocles in his later years showed the influence of Euripides in that he began to stage beggared kings and heroes in rags as his protagonists. . . . What Sophocles saw in these crownless and shattered figures was the everlasting contradiction of inner and outer value.[13]

---

11. *Republic* 1.329b–c.

12. Cf. C.P. Segal, *Tragedy and Civilization: An Interpretation of Sophocles*, Martin Classical Lectures, vol. 26 (Cambridge, Mass., 1981), 362.

13. *Sophocles*, 190.

Inner and outer value; appearance and reality—in those terms Whitman expresses a fundamental opposition that the tragedian, in his familiar role as educator of the demos, must clarify and resolve. For Sophocles, in his final play, the presence of so many elderly characters enabled him to offer a more detailed portrayal of the old hero, by contrasting the aged but noble Oedipus both to the chorus of old men from Colonus and to the mendacious Creon. The bumbling incompetence of the choristers, who ultimately prove themselves unable to manage any task without the aid or authority of Theseus, and the treacherousness of the Theban envoy, whose evident goodwill is belied by his methods and his motives, highlight both the weaknesses and strengths of the protagonist, who must both obtain the help and gain the respect of the Athenian king to fulfill the destiny mandated by the oracles of Apollo. At the same time the chorus' own chronic lack of resolve emphasizes the ferocious tenacity of Oedipus, who resists desperately any and all challenges to the heroic stature that he claims by nature (*gennaion*, 8), the right to which he has earned by his suffering, and the guarantee of which Apollo has promised. In turn the Theban *gerōn* Creon, who employs such clever deceit and flattery in his attempt to obtain Oedipus for his own purposes, contrasts sharply with both the straightforward, honorable, and heroic Theseus and the heroic prophet Oedipus. Yet Creon and Oedipus have more in common than we may first appreciate, and it is that latent similarity that renders the difference between the two more striking. Both characters attempt to stand outside conventional notions of morality, Creon in his duplicity, Oedipus in his tireless if somewhat unconvincing defense of his own actions and in his curses on his sons; but Creon lacks the inbred nobility, the *gennaion*, necessary to lay claim to the moral authority that alone can justify his actions.

In this insistence on the acknowledgment of the hero's *gennaion*, an insistence with which Sophocles challenges us throughout the *Oedipus at Colonus*, we see the more likely role that Sophocles' own old age played in his ordering of the drama. No mandated sense of despair appears here. We should focus our attention on the power latent in the protagonist, not on his failing physical strength or on the weakness of will and character that plague the other old men in the play. The famous story of Sophocles' dispute with his sons, preserved in Cicero's own meditation on old age, proves instructive. Sophocles was brought into court by his sons, in order that he might be declared senile and that control of his estate might pass to them. Sophocles read the judges part of the *Oedipus at Colonus* and was acquitted.[14] True or not, this story provides a better sense of the vigorous nature of Sophocles' old age, and it qualifies considerably the gloomy view adumbrated in the pessimistic choral ode. Death awaits, the lone sure and certain inevitability of life. Acknowledged, it may then be safely forgotten. Great things remain to be done; of this Sophocles' tragic hero reminds us just as clearly as does Cicero's Cato.

Sophocles and Athens

The age of the playwright can, with some certainty, be adduced as a factor in the composition of the *Oedipus at Colonus,* but it is hardly the only factor, and perhaps it should not be construed in the pessimistic vein sometimes posited. Issues larger than Sophocles' age or Oedipus' eventual destiny imposed themselves on the dramatic agenda. If the prospect of approaching or impending death cannot automatically account for Sophocles' drama, the attendant decline of his native city may. Knox offers a fair summary of the situation.

> He [Sophocles] died in 406 B.C., two years before the destruction of the Athenian fleet at Aegospotami; he did not live to see the Spartan galleys, their oarsmen paid by Persian subsidies, sail into the Peiraeus and force the surrender of Athens. But he knew already, as all the world must have known, that Athens had lost the war, that it faced certain defeat and, possibly—so greatly was Athens hated—extinction.[15]

Knox's brilliant prose underscores the precarious situation in which the Athenians found themselves. Yet we must not go too far in this direction, and we should resist assigning too much prophetic capacity to the playwright. How much of all this could Sophocles have known? Omniscience was presumably denied to him, and as Knox himself points out, death spared him the repugnant duty of witnessing the final humiliation of Aegospotami. Historians good, bad, and indifferent have warned us against placing too much faith in the past's ability to

---

14. Cicero *De Senectute* 7.22.
15. B.M.W. Knox, *The Heroic Temper* (Berkeley, 1964), 143.

read its future as we do. Still, where proof fails, modest speculation is legitimate. Sophocles had conducted his entire life in the public eye, a life that spanned the great period of Athenian ascendance, domination, and decline. He was born before Marathon, first made a reputation after Salamis, witnessed the birth, growth, and most of the dissolution of the Athenian Empire, and served the democracy as *Hellenotamias, strategos,* and *proboulos.*[16] If he lacked certain foreknowledge of the events that concluded the Peloponnesian War, he still could not have been blind. The fall of Athens should have at least seemed likely to him, though he knew that, as the victory at Cyzicus in 410 had shown, Athens possessed an amazing degree of resilience. But more important, perhaps, to the disillusioned playwright than the military resolution of the war, which still lay ahead as only one probability in an uncertain future (one good battle might have changed the war again or at least diminished the severity of defeat), was the deteriorating situation within the polis itself.

By the end of the Peloponnesian War, the great experiment in democracy had shown pervasive, enduring, and ultimately irreparable structural flaws. A confident, mature state does not succumb to the temptations of the demagogue; an Alcibiades has no brief with an *ekklesia* that has kept faith with itself. The slow metamorphosis from the Delian League to the Athenian Empire (a process encapsulated and immortalized in the Melian Dialogue), the recklessness of the demagogues, the debacle at Syracuse, the flirtation with oligarchy in 411, and the disgraceful behavior of the demos toward the generals in the aftermath of Arginusae exhibit the pathology. The state of Cleisthenes, of Themistocles, and of Pericles was failing. If tragedy were not to fail the state, the aging Sophocles would need to move quickly.[17]

But he could not move directly. The limitations on political discourse in tragedy had been made clear by the object lesson of Phrynichus. In 492, he had written a work entitled *The Sack of Miletus,* with which he reminded the Athenian audience of their sorrows and their failures in the Ionian revolt. The demos promptly rewarded his efforts

---

16. For his term as *Hellenotamias,* see *Inscriptiones Graecae,* vol. 1, editio minor, inscription no. 202; as *strategos,* the anonymous *Vita* and Plutarch's *Pericles* 8 and *Nicias* 9; as *proboulos,* Aristotle's *Rhet.* 3.18.

17. For a superb discussion of the political ramifications of Greek tragedy, see J.P. Eubens' introductory chapter to the collection *Greek Tragedy and Political Theory,* ed. J.P. Eubens (Berkeley, 1986), 1–42.

by fining him one thousand drachmas, effectively guaranteeing that no playwright would ever again risk portraying events so controversial in the national consciousness.[18] In order to perform their customary role as educator of the polis, playwrights henceforth needed to proceed by inference and implication, not didactic.

Sophocles, distressed by the situation in the city but governed by those constraints that inhere in the dramatic form, was doubtless aware of the need to impart some final lessons and to declare once more the strength of his own affections, before it was too late.[19] The dramatist chose to create in his last play an idealized Athens, under an idealized monarch, Theseus. Yet throughout the work he is concerned less with Athens qua Athens than with Attica and Colonus; the city lies off in the distance, and the countryside, represented in the drama by the deme of Sophocles' birth, provides the enduring strength, the *ereisma*, of Athens, the strongest refuge of the land.[20] Sophocles may have invented the story that brought Oedipus to Colonus, and he may have done so for any number of reasons. But the regional loyalty that precipitated his choice should not be underestimated. The detailed portrait of the grove in which Oedipus affirms his heroism—the convincing depiction of both the physical environs of Colonus and the intuited, spiritual "feel" of the landscape—reveals and confirms an affection that the author cannot have counterfeited. He directed those affections toward the permanent, away from the ephemeral world of politics and war. The land would endure, regardless of how arrogantly the government conducted the war, how stupidly the citizens behaved under stress, or how brutally the Spartans and their allies might deal with the Athenians. The Cephisus would still drain the plain of the Academy; the olives would still bloom in the groves of Colonus.

On the other side of the coin, however, Sophocles did not neglect the political tuition of his audience. The brisk dressing-down that Theseus

---

18. Herodotus 6.21.

19. A (somewhat unlikely) literary analogy may clarify my point. One is reminded of a *Doonesbury* cartoon in which the elderly ornithologist Dick Davenport urges his wife to rise from bed far earlier than usual in order to accompany him on a search for the Bachman's warbler. As he puts it, "Don't you see? I'm eighty-three years old; the Bachman's warbler is nearly extinct!" When his wife advises him not to be so melodramatic, he replies, "It's only a matter of time before one of us goes."

20. *Oedipus at Colonus* 58.

addresses to Creon on the proper behavior of rulers and cities, the carefully drawn opposition between Thebes and Athens, and the sorry performance of Oedipus' sons, who will destroy their own city and the citizens whom they claim to honor and serve, all for the sake of obtaining power and confirming their own glory, remind us that Sophocles enjoyed a life of full participation in the service of his state, quite apart from his career as a dramatist. In Theseus' sharp rebukes, the voice of Sophocles, the poet who knew something of the nature of public affairs, can be discerned.[21]

Granting the limitations inherent in retrospective analysis, we sense that the *Oedipus at Colonus* provides an artistic closure to the era of classical Athens, mirroring the political realities that existed near the end of the Peloponnesian War. Personal and political chronology coincide, as perhaps they did not at the time of the authorship of the *Philoctetes*. A work presented in 409 may have reflected the optimism of the restored democracy and the victory at Cyzicus in 410. The seasoned and realistic poet, composing a work in 406 in the wake of Arginusae, took into account the worsening condition of the state and sought for his protagonist the ultimate tragic hero and the ultimate survivor, the man whose internal nobility remained intact despite all the vicissitudes of fortune he suffered.[22]

Oedipus

In his final works, Sophocles focused on the problem of restoring the exile to society. As he worked on a new tragedy near the end of the Peloponnesian War, he looked for a setting for this restoration and discovered it in his own backyard. And he chose a hero: Oedipus. Of all the tragic heroes he could have picked for the task, Oedipus was the best known and least tractable. Whitman made an extremely attractive suggestion, to the effect that the *Oedipus Tyrannus* had divided Attic audiences into different camps, with respect to the

---

21. On Sophocles' political career, see V. Ehrenberg, *Sophocles and Pericles* (Oxford, 1954), 117–40.

22. It is impossible to prove, one way or another, if Sophocles was alive and writing the play at the time of Arginusae, which was fought in the late summer of 406 B.C. Some estimates have placed the poet's death in late 406, others in 405. I believe, in the absence of any compelling evidence to the contrary, that he lived to see Arginusae and its aftermath.

question of Oedipus' guilt or innocence, and that "Sophocles may have wished to settle it once and for all," in the *Oedipus at Colonus*.[23] Whitman adduces no evidence for this remark, and of course none exists; it is simply a suspicion, though one of his suspicions is worth a dozen ordinary articles.[24]

Without question, Oedipus by his very nature poses endless, fascinating difficulties for scholars. He simply defies any attempt to pin him down, as it were. He is both too great and too small for the critics. His incestuous relationship with his mother, a relationship made possible by his patricide, created a family so skewed that to attempt even to discuss it can evoke only horror, even from Oedipus himself: thus in the *Oedipus at Colonus* he refers even to his beloved daughters as his "twin curses" (*duo ata,* 532). Yet no one can doubt the real heroism of Oedipus, his brilliant insight in mastering the Sphinx, and his genuine and altogether appropriate concern for his people when they were decimated by the plague. In his deeds, he is both the most evil and the most worthy of men.

His skewed family is one symptom of the difficulty he presents. There are others, one of which seems to have escaped the notice of other scholars. As Zeitlin points out, Oedipus, by his marriage to Jocasta, has managed to collapse time itself.

Is not incest, after all, the quintessential act of return: Is not incest the paradigmatic act that destroys time by collapsing the necessary temporal distinctions between generations.

The collapse of time, in turn, echoes the response to the famous riddle.

Oedipus' unique ability on the intellectual level to solve the riddle is commensurate on the familial level with his singular acts of patricide and incest. On the other hand, the full interpretation of the

---

23. *Sophocles,* 203.
24. Cf. McDevitt's duly modest comment: "Without ascending with Whitman to the metaphysical heights where weaker mortals grasp for breath in the rarefied air . . ." and so on (A.S. McDevitt, "The Nightingale and the Olive," in *Sophocles,* ed. H. Bloom [New York, 1990], 50). The remark is in a sense outrageous. It is also just about right.

riddle would seem to require that Man must properly be defined in his diachronic dimension.[25]

Zeitlin notes that Oedipus, by killing his father and then committing incest with his mother, has moved outside the ordinary course of time. When he killed Laius, he speeded up the process by which he would take his father's place, and when he marries Jocasta, he effects a totally anachronous return to the womb.[26] Thus Zeitlin makes the necessary connection between the solution to the riddle, the physical movement of humankind, and incest. Vernant makes a similar observation and connection in his essay on Oedipus' lameness.

> Oedipus, *Oidipous,* guesses the riddle; he himself is the dipous, the man with two feet. But his error, or rather the effect of the curse that effects his lame lineage, is that, through solving the riddle, supplying the question with its answer, he also returns to his place of origin, to his father's throne and his mother's bed. Instead of rendering him like a man who walks straight in life, following on directly in his lineage, his success identifies him with the monster evoked by the Sphinx' words: the being who at one and the same time has two feet, three feet, and four feet, the man who, in his progression through life, does not respect the social and cosmic order of the generations but instead blurs and confuses them. Oedipus, the adult with two feet, is the same as his father, the old man who walks with a stick, the three-footed one whose place he has taken as the leader of Thebes and even in Iocasta's bed; he is also the same as his children who crawl on all fours and who are not only his sons but his brothers.[27]

For the current discussion, the point of these extensive quotations gleaned from such formidable scholars is not only that Oedipus' lameness and status as incestuous parricide renders him problematic in the

---

25. F. Zeitlin, "Thebes: Theater of Self and Society in Athenian Drama," in *Greek Tragedy and Political Theory,* ed. J.P. Euben (Berkeley, 1986), 128.

26. Ibid.

27. J.-P. Vernant and P. Vidal-Naquet, *Myth and Tragedy in Ancient Greece,* trans. Janet Lloyd (New York, 1990), 215 (in Vernant's essay entitled "The Lame

extreme. Anyone familiar with the myth would grant that conclusion as axiomatic. Rather, their emphases on the hero's physical condition and the relationship to the riddle lay bare yet another difficulty with Oedipus, another layer to the story that, once explored, will remind us once more of how cautiously we must proceed in dealing with the character or any work about him.

The riddle of the Sphinx essentially asks (with some variations),[28] "What creature goes on two legs, three legs, and four legs?" Oedipus supposedly answered "Man" and thereby vanquished the Sphinx. His rationale was simply that infants crawl about on four legs, while men walk on two in their prime and rely on a staff in their dotage. Nothing here appears too controversial. But Vernant notes that the order of the question as it survives in Diodorus Siculus (4.64) is somewhat reversed, since the adult man comes first, the older man next, and the infant last.[29] Thus Vernant almost poses a question that, had he answered it, would have rendered Oedipus so intractable that no sensible scholar would risk discussing him. Indeed, in another essay, he in fact reaches a conclusion that comes very close to the suggestion made at the end of the following discussion, although he reaches that conclusion on an altogether different basis.[30]

Close examination discloses that the oracle, posed as Diodorus Siculus records it, refers precisely to Oedipus himself and only to Oedipus in his diachronic aspect, at least insofar as Sophocles portrays that character at the crucial junctures of his life. First we must prove the point, then we may consider what it means. Let us start with the hero in his infancy. Oedipus, when he was exposed on Mt. Cithaeron, had both his ankles bound together by his father's command. Toward what end and with what effect was this done? Apparently, it was to prevent the child from crawling away. But why prevent the child from crawling? No child on Cithaeron would be likely to crawl away far enough or fast enough to avoid death. A crawling infant, even at his best speed, remains an easy prey for wolves, dogs, and other carnivores. But bind-

---

28. Vernant gives an account of the variations of the riddle, in ibid., 468 n. 20.
29. Ibid., 468 n. 20.
30. In "Ambiguity and Reversal," the fifth essay in Vernant and Vidal-Naquet, *Myth and Tragedy*, Vernant concludes that Oedipus is not in fact a man but "a creature of confusion and chaos" (138). Vernant here would suggest that Oedipus' collapse of temporal boundaries through incest and patricide makes him, in fact, all three terms of the riddle simultaneously: biped, triped, and quadruped.

ing the feet would achieve the stated end of preventing him from crawling off somewhere. Observe a child crawling. The child needs the locomotion of both legs, working at the knees, in order to move. If you were to deprive the child of the ability to move the legs independently, motion would become impossible. An infant would lack the upper-body strength and coordination needed to generate movement, unless the infant were perhaps trained in some fashion. Even for an adult, it is a learned skill and quite tiring.[31] The binding of Oedipus' two legs created a useless appendage; in fact, it left his legs functionally indistinct from his torso and in effect turned him into a biped (having the use of his arms only). Thus, Oedipus lived out the first part of the riddle, as stated in Diodorus, in absolute opposition to the remainder of able-bodied humanity. Lest this seem too improbable or too facile, we should recall that Sophocles had other choices available in his portrayal of the disability that Laius imposed on his infant son. Aristophanes claims that Oedipus was in fact sealed shut in a jar.[32] But Sophocles preferred the story that the infant's feet were tied together, rendering them altogether useless. At the first crucial point in his life, Oedipus went about on two legs, his arms (the only working appendages available), precisely as the version of the riddle in Diodorus suggests, in a manner quite different from most infants, who crawl on all four limbs.[33]

Now let us proceed to the second part of the riddle (as Diodorus has it), a man on three legs. As a young man, Oedipus, who has been raised

---

31. I have not experimented on infants, nor do I recommend it. I have, however, tried a similar experiment on myself. To crawl with the legs bound together (I did not pierce my Achilles tendons; the demands of research will only take me so far!), I had to bring both knees in and up to my torso while simultaneously doing, in effect, a push-up. I can say that this is not an easy or natural movement. It could, I suppose, be learned. But not by an infant. Crawling for an infant is a reciprocal motion. Given time, an infant could conceivably learn some motion, but not a true crawl, and an infant certainly would not pick up the motion without time and training. I have also consulted with James T. Holton, Jr., R.P.T., of the Wilkes-Barre Veterans Administration, on this point (telephone conversation, 22 February 1995). Mr. Holton informs me that infants with cerebral palsy are sometimes trained to move in exactly the manner I suggest, and that such training is an intensive, laborious process.

32. *Frogs* 1190.

33. Segal makes very much the same point when he observes that the binding of Oedipus' legs had caused him to move outside the ordinary processes of time. However, he does not pursue the matter. See C.P. Segal, "Time, Theater, and Knowledge in the Tragedy of Oedipus," in *Edipo: Il Teatro Greco e la Cultura Europea*, ed. B. Gentili and R. Pretagostini (Rome, 1986), 459–84.

as the child of Polybus and Merope, the king and queen of Corinth, hears a drunken suggestion that he may not be the blood child of his parents. He goes to Delphi to inquire about his parentage, and there Oedipus learns from Apollo his awful destiny and decides to leave Corinth forever. On the journey he meets, argues with, and slays Laius. Sophocles has Oedipus give the following account of the chance encounter.

> As I drew near the place where three roads meet, a herald and a
> man in a colt-drawn chariot—just as you mentioned—met me.
> The leading man and the old man himself tried to run me off the
> road by force. Angry, I struck the driver, and when the old man
> saw this he waited till I was past and struck me squarely on the
> head with a double-pointed whip.
>   I didn't settle for just paying him back. I struck him with my
> staff, with this very hand, and straightaway laid him out, knock-
> ing him from his car. Then I killed all of them. (800–813).

Note the order of events. First the herald and then Laius himself would move Oedipus off the road and out of the way by force (*pros bian,* 805). Words are perhaps exchanged, then blows. Oedipus, how-ever, contrary to what one might consider normal behavior in a fight, does not draw his sword but rather attacks his adversaries with his staff *(skeptrō{i}).* Why? Can we safely assume that he had no sword? This seems unlikely. The scion of the royal house of Corinth, as Oedipus believed himself to be, should have been armed for his journey to Del-phi and for any subsequent travels. Trouble on the road was clearly brewing. But when the fight broke out in earnest, Oedipus' weapon of choice is his walking stick. It is not an obvious choice; the makeshift weapon is not, after all, a medieval mace. Sophocles evidently wanted to emphasize in his portrayal of the myth that Oedipus was using a staff to aid him in walking at this critical juncture in his life, the point at which, as Zeitlin says, he begins the process (through his parricide) of collapsing those generational boundaries violated by his act of incest with his mother. Stating the point bluntly, in terms of the riddle, Sopho-cles' Oedipus, at least, is not Vernant's *dipous* but *tripous,* a man walk-ing about Greece using a staff for his support.[34] Hence, any conclusions

---

34. At the risk of taxing the reader's patience, I use yet another personal ref-erence. Walking sticks, dear to the heart of outdoor magazine photographers

that Vernant reaches about the *dipous* cannot be valid (and, of course, a good pun is wasted as a result).

These two points made, it remains only to consider the last phase of life mentioned in the riddle, the four-legged man. Oedipus, at the end of his life, did not apparently travel about with a staff. He traveled with his daughter, on whom he relied for physical support, as the *Oedipus at Colonus* makes clear. Oedipus moves only with her guidance, which she understands as her natural duty, and when necessary he leans on her.[35] In fact, after Creon seizes Antigone, he taunts Oedipus by boasting, "No more will you travel using these two supports (*toutoin skēptroin*, 848)." Jebb would take the line to refer to Antigone and Ismene both (Ismene has already been kidnapped at this point), but he probably errs. Ismene had not in fact journeyed with Oedipus and Antigone; she appears in the play as a messenger, not a companion to her father. The *toutoin skēptroin* refer to Antigone's two feet. Even should we read *toutoin skēptroin* as Jebb did, the argument is not altered. Oedipus still goes about on four "feet," his own and his two supports, Antigone and Ismene.[36] On either reading, the clear force of the dual number of the noun *skēptroin* is preserved. Therefore, in effect, Oedipus at the end of his life goes about on four feet, his two and Antigone's. Thus he fulfills the oracle (as Diodorus Siculus rendered it), in an extremely idiosyncratic fashion. He also transcends it, for at the very end of the play, Oedipus walks under his own power to the place of his tomb (1520–21).

---

and occasional yuppie aficionados, are, for ordinary hiking, even over great distances, virtually useless to a man with two good legs. In fact, they are a hindrance. During my hikes over the rocky hills of southern Ontario, New York, Pennsylvania, and West Virginia, I never carried a walking stick and never felt the need of one. In all my travels, I cannot think of anyone I ever met on a trail who *was* carrying a walking stick, except for a few older hikers (people well into their late fifties, at least). The average road in mythical, Bronze Age Greece was probably not very good, but I doubt if it was any worse than the Loyalsock Trail. I am also assured by the local ROTC commander that the United States Army does not, ordinarily, issue walking sticks. Quite simply, a young Oedipus should not have had one with him, unless Sophocles wished to emphasize the fact that he required one.

35. See lines 22, 113–14, 173, 188, and especially 199–201, where Antigone says, "Match your steps to mine, lean (*proklinas*) your old body on me."

36. At 1109 of the *Oedipus at Colonus*, Oedipus refers to his daughters as "supports of a man" (*skēptra phōtos*); earlier, however, at 746, Creon himself says that Oedipus travels with "one attendant" (*prospolou mias*), that is, Antigone.

This digression, while dealing with matters that lie for the most part outside the *Oedipus at Colonus* itself, reminds us that we must employ the utmost care in examining both the play and the man. Nothing about Oedipus is ever quite what it seems. A healthy skepticism, even on points that seem self-evident, should be maintained throughout the discourse. For, on this reading of the riddle of the Sphinx, when Oedipus was asked "what goes on two legs, three legs, and four legs" and answered "Man," he erred or at least lacked sufficient insight to know the true ramifications of his answer. The riddle, if worded as Diodorus would have it, referred only to Oedipus himself, and sweeping answers were inadequate. Conversely, if the riddle was asked by the Sphinx in a different way, Oedipus, when he answered "Man," missed the point. We must recognize the moral and not be too hasty in evaluating the hero. The tragic audience must invariably render some kind of judgment on Oedipus. Given the peculiar and problematic nature of the hero, we should not necessarily be seduced into accepting the judgments that Oedipus renders for or on himself. In plain terms, Oedipus often errs. The attentive reader must keep this fact in mind while examining the action of the play and the words of the character. No conclusions on Oedipus can be accepted without very careful consideration. The tangled circumstances of his life disallow that possibility.

Antecedents and Methodology

"I shall not attempt to provide even a sketchy summary of the huge bibliography of *Oedipus at Colonus*."[37] By these words Vidal-Naquet summarizes the difficulty that daunts any sane person who would undertake a project on this play, Sophocles, or Greek tragedy in general. This discussion will cite the major authors on all points of conflict or interest. No more is possible or desirable. But the previous foray into an analysis of the additional problems created by a close study of Oedipus, and the resultant need to keep both eyes open in examining both the hero and the play, lead inevitably to a more detailed acknowledgment of the two works that have suggested the best manner in which to proceed.[38]

---

37. Vernant and Vidal-Naquet, *Myth and Tragedy*, 484 n. 1.

38. I omit here mention of Whitman, who, although cited frequently in the text, is more of an idol than an influence; he has been since I first read the following: "(when) Ajax says that in time things become their opposites, it is clear

To observe chronology, the first work is Linforth's monograph *Religion and Drama in "Oedipus at Colonus."*[39] When Linforth undertook his project, the prevailing critical consensus maintained that the *Oedipus at Colonus* was essentially a religious play. Linforth's account of his perceived opposition merits review, for it reminds us of the difficulties entailed in attacking an entrenched orthodoxy.

There are religious elements in the play which form part of its very texture, and which do much to make it the impressive play that it is. To disregard them or to belittle them would be a fatal falsification. But I venture to question whether these elements are so far predominant as to authorize the general statement that *Oedipus at Colonus* is a "religious play," or to support such views as those that have just been cited. It may be urged that the religious quality is so clear on the face of the play that one must be blind to doubt it. Critics, indeed, who discern this quality and recognize the gods at work everywhere, use this judgment as a major premise and interpret the play accordingly. They will resent an attack on the details of their interpretation on the ground that their opponent does not accept the major premise which is to them self-evident. But the generalization which is adopted as a major premise has been obtained only by a process of induction from the details of interpretation, and it is only by an examination of the details that one can determine whether or not there is a fallacy in the induction.[40]

Once he declares his general purpose, Linforth details some of the specific errors that he intends to extirpate or at least moderate. These include a wholly unsalutary tendency to read the play in light of the

---

that he is resolved to be no more a part of the shoddy flux, but to get out of time, seize Being at a blow and be himself forever" (Whitman, *Sophocles*, 199). I doubt that any sentence has ever so clearly and eloquently summarized Ajax's resolve; and this one occurs in a chapter devoted not to Ajax but to Oedipus. I mentioned McDevitt's acknowledgment of Whitman's mastery earlier (see n. 24). *Inter alios*, one might also note Knox, *Heroic Temper*, 193 n. 3: "It will be clear to the reader how much I owe to Whitman's brilliant and eloquent discussion of the play."

39. I. Linforth, *Religion and Drama in the "Oedipus at Colonus,"* University of California Publications in Classical Philology, no. 14 (Berkeley, 1951), 75–192.

40. Ibid., 76.

legend, instead of focusing on the drama itself; reading the play with reference only to the last scenes; and imposing on the *Oedipus at Colonus* a Judeo-Christian ideology entirely foreign to the Greek habit of thought.[41] In consideration of the last point, he cites claims made in works by such eminent classicists as Campbell and Jaeger and in the translation of Fitzgerald, which suggested that the identity of Oedipus to Christ could virtually be treated as a given.[42]

Having laid his groundwork, he commenced a detailed investigation of those elements in the play that he felt could safely be considered religious: "the oracles of Apollo, the Eumenides and the sacred grove, the conception of a hero, the pollution of Oedipus, the curses which he pronounces, the final miracle."[43] Later he summarizes his specific intent:

> From a study of the items included in this summary account and their implications it should be possible to determine the religious quality of the play. When this has been done, an estimate can be made of its proportional significance.[44]

There follows a lengthy, detailed, sometimes laborious study into the specific items of religious significance mentioned earlier. After

41. Ibid., 76–79.

42. See Linforth, *Religion and Drama*, 78–79. Linforth cites L. Campbell, *Religion in Greek Literature* (London, 1898), 281, who wrote of the Greek experience rivaling the Hebrew, in the discovery of "the blessedness of sorrow." Linforth then takes R. Fitzgerald to task for his use of the extraordinary phrase "human divinity" to describe Oedipus' death and heroization in his translation *Sophocles, Oedipus at Colonus: An English Version* (New York, 1941), 151. But Linforth saves his best comment for W. Jaeger, who, in vol. 1 of his landmark *Paideia*, trans. G. Highet (New York, 1939), 281, had claimed: "From the first the tragic king who was to bear the weight of the whole world's sufferings was an almost symbolic figure. He was suffering humanity personified." Linforth remarks: "Symbolic Oedipus has indeed become in the course of history,—symbolic of many things. But if Sophocles conceived that Oedipus bore the weight of the whole world's sufferings and was suffering humanity personified, in either *King Oedipus* or in *Oedipus at Colonus*, he has effectively concealed it." The absence of such extreme comments as Jaeger's, Fitzgerald's, or Campbell's in later criticism on the play adequately demonstrates the shrewdness of Linforth's judgment.

43. Linforth, *Religion and Drama*, 81.

44. Ibid., 82.

more than one hundred pages of thoroughly considered arguments on
the religious elements in the play, arguments distinguished both for
their clarity and good sense, Linforth reaches some conclusions. On the
oracles, their significance is primarily to supply data for the plot; pollution is largely dismissed.

> Theseus, who has no word to say concerning Oedipus' past mis-
> deeds or any possible effect of them, tacitly receives him as guilt-
> less and harmless. This determines the great issue for the audi-
> ence. No debate, but the action of the play itself, establishes the
> principle that no liability is incurred by unintentional wrongdo-
> ing, and this principle is maintained in the extreme case of a man
> whose wrongdoing has been of the most heinous kind.[45]

Linforth will not allow any great significance to the gods, even to the
Eumenides. And as to heroization, he seems unimpressed.

> There is no process of heroization at the end; Oedipus' death
> closes the action, and his estate as a hero, except in anticipation,
> lies outside the limits of the play.[46]

Hence, divine agency dismissed or limited, Linforth constructs his
own view of the action of the play. For him, Oedipus is not a symbol of
humanity, simply a man who "presents a single instance of human fortune." He is entirely unique. Sophocles' play, in turn, offers a magnificent portrayal of an individual beaten but not broken, generally impen-
itent, vigorous in mind and will, and still liable to the extremes of the
old passions that ruined and nearly destroyed him in his younger manifestation. Linforth finally renders his verdict on his own work, as well
as the *Oedipus at Colonus.*

> This is a limited and imperfect account of the man who comes
> alive in the stirring action of the play. The portrait of him which
> Sophocles paints, sometimes in broad strokes, sometimes in deli-
> cate and revealing touches, is full and rich. Can one not perceive
> the greatness of the drama which presents this man and his final

---

45. Ibid., 184.
46. Ibid., 184–85.

fortunes without imagining an upper stage on which the gods are supposed to play a part, without insisting upon alien implications, and without introducing religious sanctions for which the play offers no warrant?[47]

It is entirely unfair to present a synopsis of the work of any scholar; too much must be omitted, and critics can certainly disagree about the importance of any cited selection. Still, a summary was necessary to this discussion. This citation does not necessarily indicate agreement. Frequently, this book disagrees with Linforth's conclusions. For the present work, Linforth provides the example of method, rather than result. His discussions are narrow and focused, sometimes infuriatingly so; his examination of the oracles of Apollo alone run to seventeen pages in his text (80–97). A slightly polemical strain (the offended scholars might, perhaps, have called it very polemical) runs through his discussion as well. This is to Linforth's credit; ideas that challenge inherent or inherited assumptions sometimes have to fight very hard to maintain themselves in a hostile environment. But the best contribution Linforth makes to the study of the *Oedipus at Colonus* is his insistence on a close reading of the text to justify his conclusions, no matter how tendentious those conclusions themselves may seem.

Extremely close reading of the text distinguishes the other book that influenced this work, Ahl's *Sophocles' Oedipus: Evidence and Self-Conviction*.[48] Whether one accepts Ahl's conclusion—that Sophocles never attempted to present firm evidence that Oedipus committed incest and parricide, but rather Oedipus victimized himself by falling into a rhetorical "trap" sprung for an audience that relies overmuch on assumptions external to the *Oedipus Tyrannus*—his is a great work.[49] And although his book deals only in passing with the *Oedipus at Colonus*, Ahl, like Linforth, suggests a modus operandi.

The rule had been formulated by Dodds, as well as anyone, that "what is not mentioned in the play does not exist."[50] And in some respects, this is a sound principle. But Dodds used this position to cut off or limit discussion about the text by limiting the range of allowable

---

47. Ibid., 185–86.
48. F. Ahl, *Sophocles' Oedipus: Evidence and Self-Conviction* (Ithaca, 1991).
49. Ibid., x and passim.
50. E.R. Dodds, "On Misunderstanding the *Oedipus Rex*," in *Oxford Readings in Greek Tragedy*, ed. E. Segal (Oxford 1983), 180.

questions one should ask. Ahl responds brilliantly: "But can one know which questions the dramatist did not intend us to ask?"[51] His question, of course, is rhetorical: Sophocles left no detailed notes for critics of the late twentieth century. Ahl then proceeds to investigate and challenge every aspect of the play, and in the course of his relentless, scene-by-scene, line-by-line, and sometimes word-by-word examination, and (to oversimplify greatly) in his steadfast refusal to accept the characters' remarks and motives at face value, he forces a familiar text to yield unfamiliar conclusions. Even his introductory remarks on the different versions of the Oedipus myth remind us of how careful we must be in assessing supposed evidence from the play itself.[52] After all, we know that characters in a play sometimes lie; but how can we always know which characters are lying at any given moment? As outrageous as Ahl's conclusion may be, the real basis of his method, like Linforth's, is doubt and an insistence on accuracy. No two scholars have ever read texts of Sophocles so carefully.[53]

Such a procedure need not recommend unthinking obeisance to a particular theoretical approach. Doubt evokes suggestions of skepticism, skepticism in turn deconstruction. But as David Lehman pointed out, there is little to distinguish "close reading" from, as he puts it, "soft-core deconstruction," for it does not take one outside the text, or at least not so far outside that one cannot possibly find a way back to

---

51. *Sophocles' Oedipus*, 5.

52. Ahl's central point, that much of what we assume that we know of Oedipus comes from Seneca's version rather than Sophocles' play, offers an excellent caution to those who attempt an analysis of the Greek play. See especially *Sophocles' Oedipus*, 1–3. On the variant traditions, see especially 6–13.

53. I should point out here that I am not exactly convinced that Ahl is right, although I am convinced that he believes he is right. His skepticism may be extreme. One wonders if, were he to write a similar work on the *Oedipus at Colonus*, he might decide that Polyneices and Creon were in league or that Antigone, wearied by chasing around the Greek countryside with her aged father while her youth slipped away, had conspired with Ismene and Creon to stage her own kidnapping and thereby her release from servitude. These are extreme positions, offered for speculation. But given some of the idiosyncratic (to put it charitably) positions reached by critics in the past, there is no telling what conclusions a scholar of Ahl's intellect and skeptical bent could reach. I have in fact discussed with Professor Ahl the effect his method might have if it were applied to, for example, Shakespeare's *Measure for Measure* or *Winter's Tale*.

it.[54] There is no need here to engage in a lengthy diatribe against the contemporary extravagances and excesses of theory-driven literary criticism. The task would take too long and be too depressing. Suffice it to say that those searching for impenetrable jargon and profound hypotheses on the fate of the always excluded other will need to look elsewhere. The approach taken in the current work very clearly privileges the tragedian, in a capitalist, entrepreneurial model that opposes directly a view of the authorship of Greek tragedy such as that espoused by Longo.

> In other words: the concepts of artistic autonomy, of creative spontaneity, of the author's personality, so dear to bourgeois esthetics, must be radically reframed, when speaking of Greek theater, by considerations of the complex institutional and social conditions within which the processes of literary production in fact took place. These conditions predetermine the possible "creative" area of the individual poet, and they offer a preliminary framework to the coordinates within which admissible poetic trajectories will be plotted.[55]

Longo makes and then manages to miss the essential point. No author is constrained to participate in those "complex institutional and social conditions" any more than an academic author is constrained to write a book on Sophocles. Once entered, existing institutions may present an author with some restrictions, but complete human autonomy has never been more than a myth, and it is a fairly recent, ludicrous and uninteresting one at that. At worst, the restrictions of audience and reception constitute the rules of engagement, and in any case, audiences are usually just intuited by writers. Indeed, great writers create their audiences, not, as so often claimed, vice-versa. But the decision to engage, the choice of weapons, and the order of battle remain in the hands of the individual author, whether she or he labors over a

---

54. D. Lehman, *Signs of the Times: Deconstruction and the Fall of Paul de Man* (New York, 1991), 118–24.

55. O. Longo, "The Theater of the *Polis*," in *Nothing to Do with Dionysus: Athenian Drama in Its Social Context*, ed. J. Winkler and F. Zeitlin (Princeton, 1990), 15. I do not wish to give the impression that I am singling out Professor Longo; the same thoughts have been espoused by many. Longo's version is simply the most articulate.

papyrus scroll or a word processor. With the possible exception of the Bible, no complex of social institutions has ever crafted a great book.

This work takes its methodology from the examples set forth by Linforth and Ahl. A close examination of individual components leads by induction, implication, and inference to conclusions on the nature of Sophocles' last play. First, I consider what type of play Sophocles has left us.[56] The general model ascribed to the work is that of a "suppliant" drama, an idea suggested by Reinhardt, elaborated on expertly by Burian, and now generally accepted by contemporary scholars. Chapter 2 offers a stern corrective to that view, much in the manner that Linforth strove to correct the prevailing orthodoxy of his own day, which considered the *Oedipus at Colonus* a religious drama. Like Linforth, this work insists throughout on the heroic nature of the protagonist. Upon reflection, we see that suppliant and hero are antithetical concepts, and it is Oedipus' identity as a hero that dominates the play. At best, the form of suppliant drama provides a very weak basis for Sophocles' work. The driving idea behind the play is not *hiketeia,* or supplication, but *xenia,* or hospitality, a relationship better suited to heroes.

Chapter 3 deals at great length with one single verse of the play, 637, and with the reading of *empolin* by most editors in preference to the manuscripts' *empalin.* At 637 as it is commonly read, Theseus offers Athenian citizenship to Oedipus. A great number of difficulties obtrude. In the first place, the manuscript reading is not so problematic as to merit correction. Moreover, not a shred of evidence anywhere in the play can be adduced to support the suggestion that Oedipus becomes a citizen in Athens, and the effort by the redoubtable Vidal-Naquet to make *empolin* acceptable without an attendant offer of citizenship ultimately founders. In addition, Theseus' rule in Athens is absolute; he is a hero bound to a polis, but he is not the idealized democrat that appears in other plays. For Oedipus, to become a citizen is to become a subject, and that possibility, like true suppliancy, falls outside of the heroic ideal. A grant of citizenship thus compromises the somewhat paradoxical equality of the relationship between the king and the exile. Hence, *empalin* must be retained.

Chapter 4 assays a detailed study of Colonus, Athens, Thebes, and

---

56. I will not, at this juncture, relate the relevant bibliography. Such an account would simply clog up the brief summaries with useless detail that will have to be repeated anyway.

the characters who represent each place: for Colonus, the *xenos* and
the chorus; for Athens, Theseus; and for Thebes, Creon. In Colonus
Oedipus is revealed as a hero, and only there can his heroic power be
maintained. And by setting the play in Colonus, Sophocles can
accomplish a number of things. He can in vivid terms relate his affection for his native deme; he can make use of the mythological associations of Colonus with Theseus and Peirithous; and he can juxtapose
city and countryside, to demonstrate the strengths and weaknesses of
each, as well as their interdependence. And in Colonus we can see
Oedipus magnified in stature, not through any change on his own
part, but in contrast with lesser characters, particularly the chorus and
Creon. The contrast between Athens and Thebes, in turn, allows us to
understand the nature and the workings of both the good polis and
the bad, while the inevitable comparison of Theseus and Creon accen-
tuates Sophocles' ongoing dialogue on the antithetical relationship
between heroism and cowardice.

Chapter 5 deals with some of the religious issues that run through
the play. On the whole, they are dealt with skeptically. Upon close
examination of the text, it appears that Oedipus is aware of most, if not
all, of his future, well in advance. The oracles that the Thebans had
received concerning their exiled former leader are not "new" oracles in
the sense that they contain any new prophecies regarding the hero.
They are simply the old oracles concerning Oedipus recycled, but they
are improperly understood, since the Thebans lack the ability and
knowledge to read them correctly. As to the question of Oedipus' guilt
or innocence, we find, if we follow Ahl's method and consider very
carefully the types of arguments employed and the order in which they
are presented, that Oedipus' own defense of his actions proves a bit
shaky, particularly his answer to the charge of incest. His facility of
argument, which seems at times to exceed his sincerity, reminds us of
two things. First, as Oedipus is a hero, he stands above the judgments
of ordinary mortals. Second, this is precisely the type of issue where
Dodd's strictures will not work. The question of guilt or innocence has
been raised and answered, and we have every right to examine Oedipus' defense rather than accepting it at face value. In turn, Oedipus'
curses must be examined. They look suspiciously like predictions, and
in fact they are. But they have no efficacious life of their own. Rather,
they are brought to pass by the actions of his sons, actions of which he
is fairly well apprised before he utters even his first imprecation. In fact,

they are prophecies in themselves, oracles produced by Oedipus concerning the fate of his sons, which he can utter because, like Apollo had done long ago in Oedipus' case, Oedipus can "read" his sons.

Finally, chapter 6 considers the death of Oedipus, his status as a cult hero, and the political lessons of the *Oedipus at Colonus*. The ordering may seem disjointed, a discussion of death and translation relevant to the matters discussed in chapter 5. But the question of a state cult leads inevitably to political questions. The view taken here claims that the work is a good deal darker and more antidemocratic in tone than has been recognized. It is darker because, when all is said and done, even his status as a cult hero seems scant compensation for the protagonist. And it is antidemocratic because Theseus comes off far better than his compatriots and because Sophocles has structured his play specifically to make that point. The groundwork has been laid beforehand; the insistence on the heroic nature of king and guest (in contrast to the often sorry display made by the locals) and the emphasis on the land (rather than the city) suggests that the poet chose in his last work to focus on things older and more enduring than the democracy. We are left, then, with a remarkable paradox. The last tragedy of classical Athens (the polis that reinvented itself after the overthrow of the Thirty Tyrants scarcely merits the honorific adjective) is an implicit critique of democracy. The quintessential democratic institution extols the praises of the monarch, though not of the tyrant. Reasons are not hard to find. If the historian's Pericles could boast that Athens was the education of Greece, Athens in turn had been taught some bitter tactical and strategic lessons from Sparta and her allies. The democracy nearly buckled under the strain, falling under the sway of demagogues, betraying itself in 411, and violating its own rules in the aftermath of Arginusae. For Sophocles to fulfill his duty as educator of the polis, he would in turn have to deliver a very strict and severe lesson of his own.

2

Hiketeia or Xenia

In what manner, exactly, should we approach the *Oedipus at Colonus*? Some structure must be at least posited at the outset, to give us a rough idea of how to proceed. Two attractive suggestions have been made by previous scholars. In his chapter on the *Oedipus at Colonus*, Bowra divided the structure of the play into three "movements." The first movement begins with the arrival of Oedipus into Colonus and culminates in his acceptance by Theseus into the city; the second movement consists of the exchanges between Oedipus and his protector, Theseus, and his dual antagonists, Creon and Polyneices; and the third movement describes Oedipus' death and/or reception by the gods.[1] In broad relief, Reinhardt made the same point with his observation that "the beginning is closest to the ending, but the middle part moves furthest away," in effect postulating a ring composition.[2] And although Winnington-Ingram subsequently offered a more detailed, five-part structure to the play, using the arrivals of separate characters (Oedipus and Antigone, Ismene, Creon, and Polyneices) and the departure of the hero from the stage to mark the *discrimina*, his proposal seems ultimately impracticable and forced.[3] Bowra's suggested format offers a more coherent view. Therefore, this analysis proceeds for the most part according to Bowra's general plan of the structure of the play. However, as Winnington-Ingram has correctly perceived, the plot does not move in a straightforward, linear fashion: Sophocles has interwoven his story in too complex a manner to allow for absolute, facile, concrete divisions between sections. He was, after all, crafting one complete story, not attempting to mold three minidramas into one. To get a true

---

1. C.M. Bowra, *Sophoclean Tragedy* (Oxford, 1944), 311.
2. K. Reinhardt, *Sophocles*, trans. H. Harvey and D. Harvey (New York, 1979), 194.
3. R.P. Winnington-Ingram, *Sophocles: An Interpretation* (Cambridge, 1980), 250.

sense of all the elements in the work, a certain amount of doubling back is required.

Once we have decided on a structure, we must then decide what "type" of work Sophocles has left for us, and we must isolate the controlling idea of the play. These are not easy tasks, as the precise nature of the *Oedipus at Colonus* has long provoked dispute and has engendered, to state the case as generously as possible, some rather idiosyncratic criticisms. Among some older notions, now discarded, was Robert's view that Sophocles had added as an afterthought the entire scene in which Oedipus confronts his son Polyneices (1254–1413), in consequence of the legal suit brought by the author's son to have him declared incompetent, an episode recalled in Cicero's *De Senectute* (7.22).[4] Waldock simply contended that the poet had insufficient material for an entire play and was thereby constrained to display considerable artistic ingenuity to create and maintain some dramatic form until he could arrive at his "real" topic, the translation of Oedipus.[5] Perotta regarded the choral ode on old age (1211–48) as a personal lamentation by the poet—ignoring, perhaps, the fact that both Oedipus and the choristers are themselves old—and he seems to view that lone passage as the entire excuse for the play.[6] Finally, to end this representative sampling, Blumenthal suggested that the work anticipates Sophocles' own fate as a recipient of cult worship, a view that assigned a degree of prescience to the poet that most scholars have been unwilling to grant.[7]

Such arguments were rooted in a persistent sense that the *Oedipus at Colonus* suffers from some inherent and irreparable flaw, which must then be ascribed to the poet's old age or declining power.[8] In addition, some critics have claimed that the material itself, while not perhaps insufficient in Waldock's sense, may not be genuinely "dramatic," though how exactly those critics chose to define the term *dramatic* remains elusive. Weinstock argued that only the middle section of the work provided any real drama, apparently ignoring that there is ample

4. C. Robert, *Oidipus: Geschichte eines poetischen Stoffs im grieschischen Altertum* (Berlin, 1915), 470 ff.

5. A.J.A. Waldock, *Sophocles the Dramatist* (Cambridge, 1951), 218–20.

6. G. Perotta, *Sophocles* (Messina, 1935), 602.

7. A. von Blumenthal, *Sophocles* (Stuttgart, 1936), 237. Bowra, *Sophoclean Tragedy*, 307, and P. Burian, "Suppliant and Savior: *Oedipus at Colonus*," *Phoenix* 28, no. 4 (1974): 408–9, record these and other examples of the same type.

8. For a saner view, see Winnington-Ingram, *Sophocles*, 248.

conflict between Oedipus and the chorus in the first part and between Oedipus and his son Polyneices in the third.[9] Reinhardt referred to the work as the "enactment of a cult legend."[10] For Bowra, "the central theme of the play is the transformation of Oedipus into a hero," while the gods prove that they can recompense Oedipus for his sufferings.[11] Whitman, in the best of all modern works on Sophocles, attempted to cover every apparent possibility with his remark that "The *Oedipus at Colonus* is a folk tale, a mystery play, and a national festival piece."[12]

Alas, upon reflection, discontent arises on several counts. A religious pageant, even one that secured the high praise of Norwood,[13] should not make for great drama, and the *Oedipus at Colonus* is certainly great drama. Nor can any serious doubt be adduced concerning the extent of Sophocles' dramatic skills. No less worthy critics than Kitto and Knox insisted on the power and unity of the play and on the virtuosity of the poetry.[14] Moreover, an emphasis solely on the religious aspects of the play, an emphasis expertly rejected by Linforth, required too substantial a focus on the ending, that is, on the hero's death or disappearance (which, upon examination, actually seems rather brief and facile). And such an emphasis fails to account for the significance of the powerful scenes between the protagonist and the chorus, Theseus, Creon, and Polyneices. To state the matter as straightforwardly as possible, a reading of the play that neglected the importance of the first fifteen hundred lines rather suggested that Waldock's highly idiosyncratic analysis was right. Understandably, scholarship explored alternative possibilities and discovered superior interpretations.

Thus Peter Burian countered, in an article that proved a useful corrective to some of the sillier excesses of previous critics,

The dramatic form of the play is not an improvisation, but an adaptation of the pattern of suppliant drama, a pattern of action

---

9. H. Weinstock, *Sophocles* (Leipzig, 1931), 201.

10. *Sophocles*, 194.

11. *Sophoclean Tragedy*, 307–8.

12. *Sophocles*, 191.

13. G. Norwood, *Greek Tragedy* (New York, 1960), 168–72. For Norwood, the *Oedipus at Colonus* is "simple in structure, superbly rich in execution"; he states that "On the purely literary side the *Oedipus at Colonus* is certainly the greatest and the most typical work of Sophocles."

14. H.D.F. Kitto, *Greek Tragedy* (London, 1939), 382; see also Knox, *Heroic Temper*, 142–248.

familiar from Aeschylus' *Suppliants* and Euripides' *Children of Herakles* and *Suppliants.*

For Burian, the play was not a sacred pageant but rather, in an echo of Bowra, a drama in which Oedipus was "to become a hero before our eyes."[15] By postulating the suppliant plays of Euripides and Aeschylus as models for the *Oedipus at Colonus,* Burian followed earlier leads from Reinhardt and Bowra, and he has since found substantial agreement.[16] In the view of these critics, earlier commentators had put far too much stress on the supernatural aspects that pervade the end of the play. An equally significant portion of the "meaning" of the tragedy can be found in the middle section—or, to follow the division proposed by Bowra, at the end of first third of the play—in which Theseus accepts Oedipus into Athens. The key to interpreting and understanding the *Oedipus at Colonus,* then, lies for the most part in our realization that Oedipus undertakes the role of a suppliant of both Athens and the Eumenides and that Sophocles has reworked or even reinvented the form of the suppliant drama in this work.

As to the specifics of Oedipus' reception into Athens, whether or not Theseus actually grants citizenship to Oedipus is an extremely vexed question, better left postponed for a full examination later. For the current inquiry, that question, which depends on the alternative readings of *empalin* or *empolin* in line 637, arises only in passing and only at the end of this discussion. Far more pressing is the need to consider the nature of Burian's claims and to reexamine the supposed nature of the play from the perspective of suppliant drama. This theory concerning

---

15. Burian, "Suppliant and Saviour," 408.

16. See Reinhardt, *Sophocles,* 204–6 (noted by Burian); Bowra, *Sophoclean Tragedy,* 307. For contemporary agreement with Burian, see C.P. Segal, *Tragedy and Civilization,* 362–408; L. Slatkin, "*Oedipus at Colonus:* Exile and Integration," in *Greek Tragedy and Political Theory,* ed. J.P. Euben (Berkeley, 1986), 210–21; J.C. Hogan, *A Commentary on the Plays of Sophocles* (Carbondale, Ill., 1991). L. Spatz, in her discussion of Aeschylus' *Suppliants,* refers to this as a "fugitives received" play (*Aeschylus,* 59)—an unhelpful nuance, since fugitives ought to be fleeing from someone and Oedipus is doing no such thing. Knox, in his introduction to the play in R. Fagles, trans., *Sophocles: The Three Theban Plays* (New York, 1982), indicates that he views Oedipus as a suppliant in his approach to Theseus (266). This list is not intended to be exhaustive, merely representative.

the form or genre of the work, while apparently sound and superficially tenable, needs considerable revision. An investigation of the
specifics of the case suggests that the suppliant dramas provided, at
best, a very tenuous framework for Sophocles' tragedy. Oedipus has
arrived at Athens a hero (albeit an improbable one), not a suppliant.
This play portrays neither any growing awareness of his heroic stature
on his part nor his transformation into a hero, but rather his insistence
on his own heroic stature (despite his sufferings) and the other characters' growing recognition, apprehended more or less readily, of that
stature. An investigation of the works subsumed under the genre of
suppliant drama, and even of the nature of supplication itself, reveals
one certainty: suppliants have been defeated and require help. Oedipus
may need help, but he has never conceded defeat. The conqueror of the
Sphinx has a stiffer spine.

To decide whether the *Oedipus at Colonus* genuinely falls into the cat-
egory of a suppliant drama will require some background work on the
nature of such plays. First, we need to examine the standard components of suppliant drama, as critics of this play have defined them. Second, a close look at the previous suppliant dramas in Greek tragedy is
in order. Finally, then, with these preliminary investigations finished, a
discussion of the *Oedipus at Colonus* can proceed.

Burian, whose detailed investigation of the suppliant aspects of the
work has done the most to influence other scholars, has encapsulated
the traditional nature of the suppliant dramas.

> The suppliant, in flight from a powerful enemy, seeks refuge in a
> foreign land. He must win the support of his host, who, when the
> enemy approaches, undertakes to save him even at the cost of
> war. The battle ends favorably for the suppliant's cause, and his
> safety is assured.

Burian noted that "All of these elements can be traced in the *Oedipus at
Colonus*, but none appears in its straightforward, 'typical' form."[17]

Burian's model for suppliant drama so described fairly closely
approximated that of Reinhardt, although Reinhardt had also stated, in
allowing for a distinction between Aeschylus and Euripides,

---

17. "Suppliant and Savior," 409.

It is not the older form, but this newer form, especially of the younger poet [Euripides], which Sophocles fills with new force, bursts open and overwhelms.[18]

A complementary view of the essentials of suppliant drama can be found in Hogan's commentary on the *Oedipus at Colonus.*

> Suppliant drama always focuses on a victim, but the very nature of the supplication puts the victim under the power of a divinity and thereby lends the helpless suppliant a kind of power. By entering a sanctuary, touching an altar, or otherwise putting himself within the power of the divine, the victim shares that power insofar as violating the person of the victim also violates the power of the god.[19]

Both Burian and Reinhardt are forced to observe an essential truth, that Oedipus' supplication in this play is not in any way typical. The difficulty of positing an atypical supplication, a difficulty that Burian especially overlooked, reveals itself when we see, on a close reading, that no genuine supplication takes place at all, at least in the sense that the Greeks ordinarily understood the word and in view of the examples from other plays. Reinhardt wisely anticipated such a difficulty in a footnote, in which he cautioned that "All too often comparisons are made between features that are purely external, and the conclusion drawn that one was borrowed from the other."[20] Reinhardt's statement suggests the direction of this inquiry. The better questions to ask are whether Sophocles has so completely subverted the form of the suppliant drama that he has rendered it unrecognizable, and, if so, what ramifications this subversion has on our understanding of the play. In fact, the *Oedipus at Colonus* stands so far apart from the other suppliant plays in plot and action that it scarcely qualifies as such, save on precisely that purely external level that Reinhardt describes.

Let us consider the plays that Reinhardt and Burian have posited as models for Sophocles' portrayal of Oedipus as a suppliant.[21] The begin-

---

18. *Sophocles,* 196.

19. Hogan, *Commentary on the Plays of Sophocles,* 80–81.

20. *Sophocles,* 241.

21. The brief plot summaries that follow in the text are designed simply to elucidate key points for the discussion of suppliant drama, not to provide a thorough account of the plots.

ning of the works should be especially telling, for true suppliant drama, as practiced by Aeschylus and Euripides, invariably declares itself as such from the outset. In Aeschylus' *Suppliants,* the choristers, made up of the daughters of Danaus, have fled to Argos with their father to avoid marriage to their cousins, the sons of Danaus' brother, Aegyptus. Once they have arrived at Argos they seek the protection of Pelasgus, the Argive king. The play begins with the daughters' appeal to Zeus Aphiktor, a god of suppliants, and the daughters later repeat, in order, a supplication to Zeus Soter, the city, the earth, the waters, and the gods above and below the earth. They further expand on their identity as suppliants by referring to "the olive-wands wrapped with wool" *(toisd' hiketōn egcheiridiois eriosteptoisi kladoisin,* 21–22), the traditional sign of supplication, which they bear in their hands when they arrive. They also reveal the reason for their voluntary flight: their fear of an unlawful marriage. And they leave no doubt as to the consequences of their actions, for themselves or the city that receives them. The Egyptian youth will pursue them, and they will require military intervention on the part of their hosts to protect them from their unwelcome suitors. In short, the beginning of Aeschylus' *Suppliants* corresponds very closely to the model of suppliant drama offered by Burian: flight, the threat of pursuit, and the requirement of military intervention by the city and king whom they have approached.

To summarize the remainder of the plot insofar as it concerns the workings of suppliant drama, Pelasgus, the king of Argos, and his retinue arrive to question the women. He announces his identity and discusses briefly his family background, the degree and extent of his dominion, and the history of the immediate locale. After he learns the nature of the women's request for aid and their reason for flight, the king explains to them that their unexpected arrival in Argos and their request for asylum has placed him in an extraordinarily untenable position. It would be unthinkable to risk offending the gods to whose authority and protection, like his own, the women have appealed; but he is understandably reluctant to lead his people into a costly, destructive, and probably futile war with the Egyptians. He declines therefore to make an immediate disposition of the women's suit and indicates rather that he must refer the women's case to an assembly of the people. The women attempt to flatter, cajole, or extort a speedier resolution to their case, all in vain. Only when they threaten suicide at the altar of the gods does Pelasgus quickly agree to counsel the assembly to grant their appeal. Danaus then withdraws to supplicate further both the

gods and the citizens. After the Argive assembly has returned a positive verdict on the women's request, an Egyptian herald arrives and
threatens the women, but Pelasgus returns and informs the herald that
the city will fight, rather than yield the suppliants to the invaders. The
herald leaves, pledging war by the Egyptians against the Argives. The
play ends as it begins, with a choral lyric.

Aeschylus' *Suppliants* was the first play in a trilogy. The ensuing
arrival of the Egyptian forces and the consequent events formed the
plot of the remaining plays, now lost. Thus, we cannot be sure how
Aeschylus portrayed the consequences of receiving suppliants for the
city of Argos.[22] Still, on the basis of the surviving tragedy, which provides the first known example of suppliant drama, we may reach some
conclusions. The most notable features, for the purpose of this inquiry,
are the clear and frequent repetition of the daughters' identity as suppliants, the exact nature of that identity, and the role of the king and the
people of the city. These repeated features require more specific enumeration, for they make clear the real nature of the suppliant drama.

The daughters of Danaus assert their position as suppliants *(hiketai)*
from the very outset of the play, and in one fashion or another they
reassert that role throughout. Specifically, they refer to themselves as
hiketai of Zeus and the city at 21 and 27 and again of Zeus at 641 and
815; they carry the wands of suppliants *(leukostepheis hiktērias)* at
191–92;[23] they employ the alternative form *hiketin* in 350 (where it is
combined with the word *phugada*, "fugitive") and again in 428, in each
case while addressing Pelasgus; they warn the king of the potential
wrath of Zeus Hikesios at 347, a warning repeated by Danaus in 616;
and in 360 they appeal to Themis Hikesia.

In addition to the mere repetition of key words, frequent consideration and analysis of the consequences attendant on the request of the
maidens and on the decision of Pelasgus regarding their fate occupy
large portions of the text. The king boasts without hesitation the extent
of his power (249–73), but when confronted with the maidens' request
for asylum and possible military assistance, he defers.

---

22. The fragments of the remaining plays are too scanty to permit more than
a tenuous estimate of their contents; see Spatz, *Aeschylus*, 61–63; for a heroic
effort at reconstruction, see R.P. Winnington-Ingram, *Studies in Aeschylus*
(Cambridge, 1972) 57 ff.

23. This parallels the reading of 21–22, mentioned earlier.

You have not come [as suppliants] to the hearth of a private home. If the state becomes stained by a common pollution, let the people in common work out a cure. I will not make any promises before I have consulted with all the citizens on this matter. (365–69)

After the daughters press their claim, he reasserts his stand.

This is no easy matter for judgment, so do not make me the judge. I have already stated that I will do nothing without the people's consent, even though I am their ruler, lest the people should say (if something goes wrong), "By honoring strangers you destroyed the state." (397–401)

Only after the women threaten to hang themselves in the temples from the statues of the gods, an action that would entail far worse consequences than either their acceptance or rejection by the city, does Pelasgus relent, and even then he still hedges his bets. He promises only that he will call the assembly of the citizens, recommend that they treat the suppliants favorably, and advise Danaus on what to say in order to sway the Argives (516–19). Pelasgus' cautious behavior demonstrates clearly that the power to rule does not automatically grant the king the right to commit his people, without their consent, to a course that could lead to their own destruction.[24]

Euripides' *Suppliants* begins in a very similar manner. The choristers, a group of Argive mothers, have come to Attica as suppliants. At the outset, they make the familiar and requisite appeal to the divinity, in this case, Demeter at Eleusis, in whose temple the women have arrived. Euripides' treatment varies slightly from Aeschylus', in that the suppliant women do not initially speak for themselves. The first address comes from Aethra, on behalf of both the Argive women and Adrastus, the disgraced king of Argos. Aethra has been asked by Adrastus to intercede for him with her son, Theseus, in order to obtain proper burial for the Argive host slaughtered in the internecine insanity at Thebes.

In due course, Theseus arrives, and Adrastus explains the nature of

---

24. Winnington-Ingram makes the key point that "In *Supplices* Pelasgus insists upon the sovereignty of the people; the Danaids are obstinate at first and refuse to entertain the idea. Since it is important that the city as well as the king should be committed to the protection of the suppliants, we cannot say that the theme lacks relevance" (*Studies in Aeschylus*, 67).

his request. Theseus initially refuses, citing the evil purpose of the assault on Thebes, and only after an exchange with his mother does he agree, like Pelasgus in the Aeschylean drama, to consult with the city on the matter. When the Athenian king returns from the assembly of the citizens with an endorsement of Adrastus' plea, he readies his troops to move to the Theban frontier and to demand that the bodies of the dead be surrendered to him under threat of invasion. His preparations are forestalled when a Theban herald arrives and warns Theseus to dismiss Adrastus or risk a preemptive strike from Thebes. Theseus stands firm in the face of the herald's warning and attacks Thebes, successfully. He defeats the Theban army, recovers the Argive dead, and returns with them to Eleusis, where the dead are burned, Evadne commits her famous suicide on the pyre of her husband, Capanaeus, and Athena commands Theseus to extract an oath from Adrastus, swearing that Argos will never invade Attica.

Again, as in the *Suppliants* of Aeschylus, we see a strong insistence on the role of the women as *hiketai*, emphasized by the frequent repetition of suppliant language throughout the play. At the beginning of Euripides' *Suppliants*, Aethra notes that they have arrived at Eleusis with the suppliant's wand *(hiktēri thallō{i, io})*, and she restates the point at 102, in her conversation with Theseus. The women bear with them the necessity of suppliants *(anagkas hikesious, 39)*. The first word of the choristers is *hiketeuō*, "I beg," (42), thereby effectively setting the tone for their *parodos*, and emphasizing the force of the verb is the graphic detail of the choristers falling on their knees before Aethra *(pros gonu piptousa to son, 44; repeated again at 279, in this instance referring to Theseus).*[25] They are wandering suppliants *(hiketan alatan, 280)*. Reciting words familiar from Aeschylus' play, Adrastus in turn makes even clearer his own identical position, that he comes to Theseus as "your suppliant and a suppliant to your city" *(sos hiketetēs kai poleōs hēkō sethen,* 114). Like the Argive mothers, he too has fallen forward and embraced the knee of the one supplicated (165).

Equally familiar from Aeschylus' play is the hesitation of the king to accept the suppliants without first consulting the city. Theseus echoes the words of Pelasgus when he states at 246–47,

---

25. For an account of the significance of touching the knees or chin, see J. Gould, "*Hiketeia*," *JHS* 93 (1973): 75–78.

Shall I become your ally? What can I say that would make this
seem good to the state?

and later, at 349–53,

Yet I require all Athens to agree with me. My wish should win
their agreement; but if I give them good reason, they will be of
better mind about the affair. For I have made the land one city,
with equal vote for all.

Clearly, Theseus, on his own analysis of the situation, has the power to
compel the state to do his bidding, but power and authority are not the
same. In such a dangerous case, he feels that he needs the authority of
the whole people to accept the claim of the suppliants, for, as in
Aeschylus' *Suppliants,* the decision will effect the entire citizenry, as a
matter of peace and war.

In the two plays, then, we find an invocation of both deity and the
state, although we note early on that the traditional pattern of suppliant
drama that Burian had sketched does not quite hold. For the Theban
army has not pursued the Argive women to Eleusis, and though they
will threaten Adrastus, at the beginning of the play the Thebans have
simply denied the request to hand over the bodies of the Argive dead
for burial. Still, elements have repeated from Aeschylus to Euripides: in
each case, the suppliants have arrived intentionally at their destination,
seeking a specific favor from the god and the city; they repeatedly identify themselves as suppliants of both the gods and the city; they perform gestures appropriate to ritual supplication; and in both plays, the
supplicated kings insist that they cannot act without the authority of
the people.

The third of the suppliant plays, Euripides' *Children of Heracles,* better conforms to Burian's model: the drama begins with Iolaus com-
plaining that after Heracles' death, he and Heracles' children have
endured mistreatment at the hands of Eurystheus, the lifelong nemesis
of the late hero. Iolaus and the children have been driven from town to
town, in each case their requests for protection thwarted by the consequent threats of the Argive ruler against the natives of the place.
Finally, they turn to Athens and its king, Demophon, for refuge, arriv-
ing as suppliants and invoking the specific protection of Zeus in his
temple at Marathon.

Copreus, the herald of Eurystheus, arrives at Marathon and, after manhandling the aged Iolaus, demands that the chorus, made up of old men from the district of Marathon, dismiss the suppliants and turn them over to Eurystheus. Demophon, the Athenian king, arrives on the scene and learns of Copreus' attempts to intimidate the local denizens. Copreus asserts the rights of Argos over the suppliants and demands that they be handed over, under threat of war. Demophon rejects his plea, but while he makes a proclamation in the strongest possible terms to the effect that he will never yield the suppliants from fear, he does offer the possibility that Eurystheus could plead his rights in court, a telling echo of the hesitation that Aeschylus' Pelasgus and Euripides' Theseus had expressed about unilaterally committing their respective cities to almost certain war.

After an interval in which Iolaus praises Athens—while Copreus has returned to Argos and Demophon has readied his preparations for the approaching military campaign—the Athenian king returns with news of a horrible prophecy: a maiden of high birth will have to be sacrificed to Demeter's daughter (Persephone Kore) to guarantee the success of the Athenian forces marshaled against Eurystheus. Here Euripides returns, after an initial alteration, to the traditional form of the suppliant drama, for now Demophon's words to Iolaus recall the complaint of Pelasgus in Aeschylus' *Suppliants* (416–24).

> Some say it is right to render aid to suppliants but some of the people accuse me of folly. If I do this [sacrifice a maiden], civil war will erupt. Look to this, then! Help me find a way that I can save you and the city, and that I shall not be blamed by my own people. For I do not rule as a barbarian lord, but I receive just due by being just. (416–24)

Iolaus then offers to go voluntarily to Argos, in hopes that his death will satisfy their king. Demophon rightly observes that this action will scarcely satisfy Eurystheus' blood lust. Fortunately, Macaria, the daughter of Heracles, offers herself for the sacrifice. After a choral exchange, the extremely improbable appearance of Heracles' mother, Alcmena, a discussion between Iolaus and Alcmena's attendant that reveals that Iolaus intends to arm himself for one last battle, and still one more choral passage, a messenger arrives with news of the Athenian victory. After his account of the victory and the remarkable feats-at-arms performed by Iolaus, the army returns with Eurystheus in tow. Alcmena, enraged by the incessant torture that her son received at the Argive's hands, demands his death but agrees to return his body to Argos for burial. Eurystheus, somewhat surprisingly under the circumstances, acquiesces rather serenely to his own sacrifice but requests instead that he be buried in Athens, before the Pallenian, in accordance with an oracle of Apollo. His tomb will become a blessing for Athens.[26]

This work again exhibits many of the traits common to one or both of the other suppliant plays. Iolaus and the children are in flight from a much stronger enemy (15–22). There is persistent repetition of the identity of the suppliants qua suppliants, particularly at the beginning of the play; Iolaus identifies himself and/or the children as such four times in the first 101 lines (33, 70, 94, and 101). Lest anyone happen to forget this identity, the audience is subsequently reminded of it by the chorus (123, 364, 758, 764), Iolaus (196, 224, 345), Demophon (246, 254, 417), Macaria (508), and, for good measure, the late-appearing Alcmena (955). The suppliants make the familiar appeal to both the god and the state (94). The threat that the request for asylum carries with it is significant enough that the king feels the need to win approval of the city, although Euripides, as noted already, handles this detail a bit differently than it is handled in the other plays.

To summarize, in the three traditional suppliant plays, the suppliants identify themselves as such early and often and indicate clearly that they are suppliants of both the gods and the state to which they have come. In all three plays, the supplicated kings exhibit various degrees of reluctance before accepting the suppliants, a reluctance predicated on the possible consequences of their actions. The suppliants may carry ritual instruments of supplication or perform suitable gestures or both. At no time does any ambiguity attend on their position or the circumstances of their arrival. They arrive at the their host cities by plan, not by accident, in desperate need of assistance.

Investigation of the *Oedipus at Colonus* may now proceed in light of this account of the discreet components common to the traditional suppliant dramas. Let us compare the first scene of Sophocles' work with the beginnings of the suppliant dramas. Oedipus, aged, blind, exhausted, and attended only by his daughter Antigone, wanders into

---

26. If nothing else, this brief plot summary should make clear that Euripides' dramas seldom want for convolution.

Colonus, his only desire food sufficient to survive the day (3–4). In short, he arrives at the sacred grove as a beggar, not a suppliant. His presence in Athens, let alone Colonus, is not a matter of intention but rather an accident. In the three suppliant dramas, the suppliants had all arrived at a specific destination, and all had arrived with the specific intention of claiming from their hosts the rights of suppliants. Neither is Oedipus running away from anyone at the outset of the play, except, perhaps, himself. In his discussion of the opening of the play, Burian acknowledges this fact, but he then manipulates the discussion in advance: "The suppliant has reached his place of refuge, but he does not know where he is or that he is to remain."[27] The critic has prejudiced, or at least overstated, his case. A far more salient point to observe is that, in addition to being ignorant of his whereabouts or his immediate prospects, Oedipus does not even know that he is a suppliant. He carries no token of supplication and makes no mention of it. In the other three suppliant dramas, the characters are aware of their role from the outset and declare that role to the audience. Such awareness is a characteristic, too, of the protagonist in another drama in which supplication plays a major role, Euripides' *Andromache*.[28]

At first glance, this may seem a rather small point about which to cry, "Distinguo!", or it may even reinforce Burian's argument that Sophocles has in this play merely altered the traditional form of the suppliant drama. But the first impression does cast doubt on his claim and suggests that the inquiry, once begun, may reveal further inconsistencies between this play and the aforementioned works. In light of the standard elements of suppliant drama that were disclosed by the preceding analysis of the three archetypal works of the genre, closer examination of the *Oedipus at Colonus* demonstrates little beyond, at best, an occasional surface affinity between Sophocles' play and the supposed earlier models.

Antigone and Oedipus engage in a brief discussion of their situation, which serves primarily the function of exposition, and they reveal to the audience that they have arrived in Athens but that Antigone does not recognize the specific locale. Then a local resident, the *xenos* of the play, arrives. Only after they learn from him that they have wandered

---

27. "Suppliant and Savior," 410.
28. The play opens with Andromache seated at the altar of Thetis, seeking protection against the jealous and murderous Hermione.

unwittingly into the grove at Colonus sacred to the Eumenides does Oedipus first identify himself as a suppliant, at 44.[29] At this juncture, he states clearly that he offers his supplication only to the goddesses; he makes no mention of the state.

> Then may the gracious ones receive their suppliant. For I will never leave my place in this land.[30]

Critics duly note this moment yet uniformly fail to note the full significance of the revelation, which is not, to be sure, immediately apparent.[31] Line 44 suggests a great difficulty in the interpretation of the *Oedipus at Colonus*. The problem, although regularly ignored, is one that plagues so many details of this play: how does Oedipus' prior knowledge of his eventual destiny affect our reading of the work?[32] As he later tells Antigone, he has long known that this is his final resting place, promised to him by Apollo at the same time he learned that he would kill his father and marry his mother (84 ff.). Thus, he addresses the goddesses,

> O fierce-looking divinities, since I rest now in your holy sanctuary in this land, do not mistreat me or Phoebus, who, when he told me of all the evil things to come, told me also that I would reach at some distant time, a place of rest, the land where I would be destined to die *(chōran termian)*, where I would find a home as the guest of the revered goddesses. (84–90)

Sophocles has already referred to Apollo's promise and Oedipus' knowledge that Colonus will serve as his eventual resting place as the

---

29. Whitman writes, "Sophocles has symbolized [his polluted status] nicely in the first part of the play by making him once more stumble into defilement" (*Sophocles*, 200; noted by Burian in "Suppliant and Savior," 410).

30. For *an exelthoimi* as a statement of Oedipus' resolve, see Jebb, *Oedipus at Colonus*, 74.

31. Hogan launches forthwith into his discussion of the theme of supplication that he finds repeated throughout the play (*Commentary on the Plays of Sophocles*, 80–81).

32. In my estimation, only Rosenmeyer has been prepared to face this question squarely: see T.G. Rosenmeyer, "The Wrath of Oedipus," *Phoenix* 6, no. 3 (1952): 92–112.

xynthēma, translated by Jebb as "the watchword of my fate,"[33] *xynthēma*
being a military term to note a signal agreed on in advance (46). If anyone in the entire mythic tradition of the Greek world should be in a
position, given all his experiences, to verify the accuracy of Apollo's
oracles, it is Oedipus. Hence, he can, to some extent, take as a given the
accuracy of this *xynthēma*, this pledge. His foreknowledge gained by
prophecy, by which he has also discovered that wherever he finally
dwells, he will be a blessing to those who received him and a curse to
those who cast him out, has immediate ramifications for our understanding of his response to the *xenos* at 44–45 (quoted earlier). As soon
as he learns from the *xenos* that he is in the grove of the Furies, he
knows that he is now living out the last part of Apollo's prophecy;
Oedipus may not clarify the point to Antigone or the audience for
another forty lines, but there is no escaping the logical conclusion.[34]
Hence, his prayer that the Furies receive him suggests a certain disin-
genuousness. Sophocles and Oedipus make quite evident that they will
do so, for by this point in his life he has certainly endured the "many
evils" *(polla kaka),* which Apollo had promised (87); and the hero best
known for his cleverness, who acknowledges at the outset of the play
that "suffering and an attendant length of time" *(hai pathai me chō
chronos xunōn makros)* have been his principal teachers (7–8), should be
able to make the obvious connections. So should the audience. To
assume otherwise is to suggest that Sophocles insults their intelligence.
A sense of piety, then, or even convention, may constrain Oedipus to
identify himself as a suppliant, but that must, indeed, be pro forma, for

---

33. *Oedipus at Colonus,* 74.

34. Bushnell, in her discussion of this passage, refers to the oracles as
promises: "He [Oedipus] recognizes that his own promise is now bound up
with Apollo's promise, each depending on the other" (R. Bushnell, *Prophesying
Tragedy: Sign and Voice in Sophocles' Theban Plays* [Ithaca, 1988], 91). But to take
an oracle as a promise is to misrepresent the situation; for a promise can be broken, but as Oedipus' entire career demonstrates, an oracle remains fixed. Knox
does somewhat better when he states that Oedipus has blind faith in the
prophecy, although he does not know how, exactly, it will work (*Heroic Temper,*
150). Still this view ultimately falls short, for, unless Sophocles wishes us to
believe that Oedipus has lost his rational capacity, he has given the character
and the audience more than adequate information with which to reach his conclusion. I address the matter of oracular knowledge more thoroughly in chapter 5.

he knows that his prayer will be granted. In effect, by his mere accidental entrance into the sacred grove, it already has been. This interpretation becomes far less troubling in view of the fact that he has not come
to Athens or Colonus as a traditional suppliant at all. In the ordinary
suppliant plays, as we have seen, the suppliants have fled to, or at least
arrived at intentionally, a suitable temple, either fearing pursuit or
seeking a favor, with no certainty of success. Neither circumstance
applies to Oedipus, who has simply stumbled by accident into the district of the Eumenides (14–21).

Indeed, although during his initial conversation with the *xenos* Oedipus does identify himself as a suppliant of the goddesses (and not, in
violation of the pattern established in the other suppliant dramas, the
city), he subsequently begs the local man not to disregard his identity
as a wanderer (*alētēn*, 50) rather than a suppliant. Thus, he first claims
from the city not refuge but simply shelter. He reinforces this point
later, when he states that Apollo has promised him a place of *xenostasis*;
hence, not *hiketeia* but *xenia* forms the basis for his claim to remain in the
grove.

The distinction maintained here has no little significance for our
understanding of the play and is underscored by Oedipus' recurrent
insistence that, in return for the *xenostasis* he claims, he has something
to offer the state (72, 74). The manner in which Oedipus doles out suggestions of the benefit that he can bring to Athens yet declines to reveal
promptly the specific nature of the benefaction, thereby indicating yet
masking the extent of his own power while all the time keeping the
men of Colonus in line, recalls the cleverness of the hero who defeated
the Sphinx and the confidence that marked the provident and omni-
competent monarch of Thebes. As Norwood observes, "The king who
appears in the *Oedipus Tyrannus* can here still be recognized."[35] Anything less would of course prove disappointing, for suffering, even at
the level that Oedipus has experienced, does not break heroes in the
ancient world. Heracles provides the locus classicus.

The repeated offer of a potential benefit to the city predominates
throughout the first part of the play. Hence Oedipus announces that he
can offer the following: *onēsis*, "benefit" (288); *kerdos*, "advantage" (92,
578, 579); *ōphelēsis*, "service" (401); *arkesis*, "aid" (73); *dōron*, "gift" (577);

---

35. *Greek Tragedy*, 169.

prosphora, "profit" (581); and *dōrēma*, "present" (647).[36] No careful reader can ignore the point: Oedipus, reverent, perhaps, before the gods, but clever always among men, is now looking to make a deal, an element absolutely foreign to the suppliant dramas of Aeschylus and Euripides. Oedipus makes clear the reciprocal nature of his offer to Athens, when, having asked the chorus if Theseus will come, and having been assured that he will, he states:

> Well, then, may he come bearing blessings to his state and to me.
> For what generous man does not turn out to be a friend to himself.
> (308–9)

By contrast, in the true suppliant dramas, the daughters of Danaus, the women of Argos, and the children of Heracles offer their hosts and benefactors nothing in return for their help, except the satisfaction of having honored the gods, possibly at the cost of their own and their citizens' lives.[37]

While Oedipus states and restates, in different formulations throughout the first part of the play, the advantage that he can provide to his hosts, he all but drops the suggestion of his presence as a suppliant, except when the suppliant role may prove useful to him. For Oedipus, the suppliant's role is a mask, a disguise, to be trotted out only when necessary and discarded when it has served its purpose. After the *xenos* has learned that Oedipus, displaying his characteristic stubbornness, will not leave the sacred grove, he departs to fetch his fellow residents of the deme of Colonus, who will comprise the chorus of the play. Then follows the key passage, already discussed, in which Oedipus declares to Antigone the import of the oracle of Apollo and reveals to the audience the critical fact that he knows (as Creon and Polyneices

---

36. I have here employed the helpful list compiled by Slatkin in her article *"Oedipus at Colonus."*

37. To a great extent, the offer of the gift severely compromises the interpretation of the play offered by Slatkin, the compiler of the preceding list of things Oedipus offers. She argues that Oedipus' presence and his reception into Athens mark a challenge to the Athenians, a challenge to confirm the openness of their polis and their belief in their own values. Surely, the other suppliant plays, in which the suppliants can offer no reward to the city that receives them, provide better examples of that openness than the *Oedipus at Colonus,* in which the citizens never do exactly welcome Oedipus, though they do acknowledge the potential value of his role as savior of Athens (462–63).

will later discover) that he has arrived in the grove to stay.[38] This episode also contains the lone instance in which he asks Athens to take pity on him: *oiktirat' andros Oedipou tod' athlion eidōlon* (109–10). Athens itself, however, in the form of either the men of Colonus or the king, is nowhere to be found and hence cannot hear his request for pity; his appeal comes in the course of his prayer to the Eumenides (108–9), and the word *suppliant* is not used.

The choristers then make their entrance and begin their search for the mysterious sojourner (*planatas*, 123). After he reluctantly indicates his presence, a lengthy discussion ensues between the chorus and the "wanderer." Gradually, the local men coax him from the immediate precinct of the Eumenides and move him to more suitable ground, on their promise not to expel him from the land. They begin to inquire after the homeland and identity of the stranger, and only after the greatest hesitation does he disclose to them his name and family. The revelation leads to an automatic and predictable exchange between the chorus and Oedipus at 226–36.

> *Cho:* Both of you [Oedipus and Antigone], leave our land.
> *Oed:* Is this how you keep your promises?
> *Cho:* There is no punishment for a person who pays back one wrong with another. Deceit that answers a prior deceit gives pain, not pleasure, as a result. Leave this place immediately, before you bring to our city a heavier curse.[39]

Antigone then pleads her father's case in vain, as the chorus ignores her appeals, despite the evident moral force of her arguments. Her words move the choristers to pity, but not to action, for they are evicting Oedipus out of respect for the actions of the gods (*ta d' ek theōn tremontes*, 256). Then Oedipus lashes out in his own defense. The tone of the speech rings a dissonant chord with other suppliant appeals, for to a great extent, Oedipus offers to his hearers less an appeal than a lecture.

---

38. Whitman notes, "From the first moment of his arrival, Oedipus has put down roots in Attica" (*Sophocles*, 196). It is not, then, coincidental, that when the chorus first seeks Oedipus, they ask, "Where does he dwell?" They here employ the verb *naiei*, most commonly used in Greek in the context of a permanent dwelling.

39. The Greek here is rather confusing. For a discussion, see Jebb, *Oedipus at Colonus*, 96–97.

He suggests to the chorus that the reputation of Athens for piety is a sham. He alleges that the city should receive the "harried stranger" (*kakoumenon xenon*, 261). He asserts his essential innocence, proclaiming his moral purity in that he killed Laius in self-defense (and conveniently ignoring the more difficult question of incest with his mother). Then he alleges that they had received him as a suppliant and have now betrayed his trust.

> Just as I approached you, you received me as a suppliant, and you promised to protect me. (284)

This sentence would seem to render unassailable the claims of those critics who have argued for Oedipus' suppliant status. A difficulty arises, however, for as convincing and dramatic as this denouncement of betrayal is, it is simply untrue. In his first encounter with the *xenos*, Oedipus had declared himself a suppliant to the gods, but not a suppliant to the city—an important distinction, since, as we have seen, this identity as a suppliant to both the gods and the city is a fundamental element in the other suppliant plays. To the *xenos*, the exile merely claimed to be a wanderer who has brought with him a potential favor for the city. Moreover, the *xenos* made no promise to Oedipus at all; he simply admitted that he lacked the authority to do anything definitive with Oedipus, one way or the other, and went to seek the help and counsel of his fellow townspeople. When the chorus arrives, Oedipus chooses to restate his identity as a traveler and a potential benefactor. He does not in their initial conversation declare himself to be a suppliant. When the choristers, for their own part, announce that they will not drive him off against his will (177–78), they are honoring *xenia*, not *hiketeia*. As he had never referred to himself as *hiketēs*, there could be no question of their receiving his supplication. The matter had not been raised. When Oedipus makes his identity and position clear, they in turn defer the matter to the ruler. We should not be surprised at this, even if we allow Oedipus his subterfuge in claiming rights as a suppliant. For as Aeschylus and Euripides had made clear in their dramas, *hiketeia*, were it applicable, is a state matter, and collectively the locals are no better equipped to render judgment than the first citizen of Colonus whom Oedipus had encountered. An issue of such importance must await the decision of Theseus. Hospitality, however, any individual could grant; but as the Greeks had maintained since the *Odyssey*, hospitality could be withheld if it were being abused. So, precisely, the choristers understand the situation when they attempt to force him to leave the area (229–35). On these grounds, the choristers could attribute their change of heart and their attempt to remove the exiles to their reverence for the gods (256–57).

Hence, when Oedipus demands his rights as a suppliant, he claims them falsely, as though they had already been guaranteed. In fact, he knew better. So too would any observant soul in the audience. We should ask ourselves why, then, Sophocles chooses to portray his hero making a claim that was blatantly untrue. One answer suggests itself. Rather than making a real argument, which under the circumstances would have been wasted, Oedipus relies on emotional manipulation. He is interested in results, not niceties and banalities of logic.[40] A cynical person might suspect that he does so simply to buy himself some time, until Theseus arrives, and a cynical person would be right. Time, at least, he gains; the choristers do take pity on him and permit him to stay until Theseus can make a final dispensation of the matter. They even explain how he might expiate the sacrilege he has committed by his trespass into the grove, through the appropriate sacrifices to the local divinities.

In this context, we should note that in addition to pity, another consideration prompts the choristers to show the visitor as much courtesy as possible: Oedipus' frequently self-proclaimed status as a potential savior of Athens (461–64). On the one occasion that they do appear to call him *hiketēs*, they are suggesting a prayer that Oedipus or his representative should offer to the Eumenides as a request that the goddesses receive the suppliant.

> As we call them the kindly ones [Eumenides], [pray] that they would offer their suppliant their saving grace. (486–87)

The section of the play in which Ismene arrives with news from Thebes and Oedipus learns of the Theban plan to return him not to

---

40. Here and in many other instances we see the reversal of the rule posited by R.C.T. Parker that "good arguments are not reserved for good men," which Parker advances (rightly) to explain the superficially sound and justifiable arguments of Creon when he attempts to seize Oedipus and his daughters (R.C.T. Parker, *Miasma* [Oxford, 1982], 311). Neither are bad arguments, in this formulation, reserved for bad men.

Thebes but to a place outside the city yet under its control adds nothing to this particular discussion of the role that supplication plays in the drama and is best discussed elsewhere. Theseus' arrival at line 551 marks the beginning of the end of the first part of the work in Bowra's division, and his reception of Oedipus into the city at line 637 effectively makes unimportant any further inquiry into the suppliant nature of the play.

In fact, it is only after the entire matter has been rendered moot that the only other instance at which Oedipus refers to himself as a suppliant of the city occurs. At 1008, he upbraids the Theban representative, Creon, for trying to seize him, "an old man and a suppliant of this land." However, it is worth noting that he addresses the remark to Creon only to chastise him for his violation of traditional norms of the good behavior expected by visitors in any land, and thus this passage cannot be considered part of his argument for reception into Athens, which, at any event, had been accomplished long since.

Theseus does finally appear and straightaway declares that he has heard of Oedipus (a little surprisingly, for Oedipus had not heard of him; he has to learn the identity of the king from the *xenos* at line 68) and that he stands ready to help the Theban outcast and his daughter. For Theseus himself has been an exile.

> Like you, I too was raised in exile, and in foreign lands *(epi xenēs)*
> I encountered many dangers. So no stranger *(xenon)* will I turn
> away or fail to help, especially not you. (564–67)

Oedipus, in turn, responds by stating that he has come to offer the city a gift. He advances no claim on the king's pity, makes no mention of supplication per se. In fact, Oedipus never demands the rights of a suppliant from the king, the one person who could, on the basis of the models provided by the earlier suppliant dramas, actually grant those rights to him. He instead tells the king of the oft-mentioned benefit that he brings to Athens (although he remains almost intolerably vague on the specifics), requests the favor of burial, and explains that he is afraid that Thebes will try to force his return, as Ismene has reported. Theseus, at first, does not understand Oedipus' refusal to go back and chides him for petulance, until Oedipus explains that Ismene has indicated that the Thebans cannot return him to the city but can only place him on the frontier. At this point, Theseus becomes more receptive to the wanderer's arguments.

During his famous monologue on the nature of time (607–28), Oedipus declares that, at some future point, Theseus will consider that Oedipus has not proved to be a useless resident *(achreion oiketera)*: this is hardly a description appropriate to suppliant drama, in that the suppliants from the earlier plays seem not to have become *oiketeres* at all, except, perhaps, the daughters of Danaus. Indeed, in this passage Theseus observes the distinction that Oedipus had initially maintained, that Oedipus is a suppliant of the gods, while, to the city and to the king himself, he has paid "no little tribute" *(dasmon ou smikron, 635)*[41]—again, a detail completely without precedent in the other suppliant dramas. For the purposes of the city and the king, the tangible offer of the benefit that Oedipus can bestow proves decisive, for Theseus meets the generosity of Oedipus with his own offer: *hagō sebistheis oupot' ekbalō charin tēn toud', xōra{i} d' empolin* [or *empalin*: see chap. 3] *katoikiō* (636–37). I offer a translation of the version printed in most editions.

> I will respect his claims, and I will never reject his favor; no, I will settle him in our land as a fellow citizen.

Reading *empalin* instead of the emendation *empolin* changes the translation of the last line to "I will in turn settle him in this land." This passage, along with the following choral ode, marks the conclusion of the first part of the play.

For all of the buildup—there are over five hundred lines between the first suggestion that Theseus will appear and his eventual arrival at the grove—this scene carries little dramatic weight. Burian alleged that the scenes between the chorus and Oedipus and the subsequent encounter of Theseus and Oedipus provide examples of the skillful manner in which Sophocles has transformed the traditional material of the suppliant drama.

---

41. *Dasmos* is a compelling word, with a Homeric, and therefore heroic, association; in the *Iliad*, it refers to the sharing of spoils (see *Il.* 1.166). The word appears one other time in Sophocles, at *Oedipus Tyrannus* 36, where it refers to the tribute laid on Thebes by the Sphinx. One can never move too far through this play without being reminded of the rather common view that *Oedipus at Colonus* is a sequel to the *Oedipus Tyrannus*.

The difficulties that beset the suppliant in winning asylum and protection have not been eliminated from *Oedipus at Colonus*, but rather transferred from his encounter with the King to the earlier confrontations with the stranger and the chorus.[42]

Burian was correct that much of the exposition that takes place between suppliant and king in the suppliant dramas has here been replaced by an extended dialogue with the chorus. However, the plain facts of the text demand a somewhat different interpretation. For Oedipus' negotiations with the local citizens have remarkably little to do with the traditional suppliant form, since, as we have already observed, Oedipus approaches the city not as a suppliant but rather as a benefactor. Suppliants plead; they do not bargain. As my examination of the earlier suppliant dramas showed, those seeking protection from another city asseverate both their identity and their rights as suppliants. Oedipus, in fact, does neither. Moreover, suppliants do not insist on the nobility of their own nature, as Oedipus does even before his first meeting with the locals (8). Hence, Oedipus does not perform the typical suppliant gesture of throwing himself at the knees of the king, as do Adrastus and Iolaus. Knox has stated that the different trials that Oedipus encounters demonstrate his growing awareness of his own heroism.[43] I argue quite the opposite. For Oedipus, there is no "growing awareness" but simply a demand for the recognition of his heroic stature, undiminished by his suffering or his crimes. To arrive at the city as a suppliant would in fact be a recognition that his own nobility had suffered, a concession Oedipus never makes and never could make. The real dramatic situation differs considerably.

To demonstrate further the minimal influence of suppliant drama on the work, let us examine those specific passages in the first part of the drama, during Oedipus' exchanges with the *xenos* and the chorus, that Hogan argued "keep the suppliant theme before us." He cites, specifically, 49–50, 90, 142, 237–53, 275–77, and 284. Closer investigation

42. Burian, "Suppliant and Savior," 415.

43. Knox argues that Oedipus' remarks at the beginning of the play constitute a "speech which is a total renunciation of the heroic temper" (*Heroic Temper*, 146), and he stresses the gradual awakening of Oedipus' own sense of his heroic power (148 ff.). Whitman, on the contrary, seems to grant that Oedipus is fully aware of his heroic status at the outset (*Sophocles*, 198). See also Winnington-Ingram, *Sophocles*, 256–58.

reveals that, for the most part, those passages do no such thing. In the first example (49–50), Oedipus says,

> By the gods, do not dishonor me, a wayfarer *[alētēn]*, but tell me what I ask.

As far back as Homer, the word *alētēs* indicates a traveler, and nothing at all in this passage automatically suggests that Oedipus is a suppliant. Travelers, as well as suppliants, may fairly expect the protection of the gods. Such is the nature of *xenia*.

Neither does the second example (90) genuinely assay a suppliant theme. While relating to Antigone his account of the oracle of Apollo, the one in which the god promised him an eventual dwelling at Colonus, Oedipus states,

> He [Apollo] spoke of this rest to come after many long years, . . . a place of rest for strangers, guaranteed by dread divinities. (88–90)

The seat of the gods *(semnōn hedran)* does fit the suppliant mode: Aeschylus' suppliants arrive at a common temple to the Argive gods; Euripides' suppliant women appear in the temple of Demeter at Eleusis; and the children of Heracles take shelter in the temple of Zeus at Marathon. However, this coincidence of locale hardly negates Oedipus' far more important role as *xenos*. Moreover, balanced against the suggestion of a suppliant role is the grant of *xenostasin* that Apollo had pledged. The word *xenostasin* is found only here and in Sophocles' *Inachus*, and in the latter it is glossed by Pollux simply as "quarters for strangers" (9.50).[44] Hence, on any interpretation, Sophocles lays his primary emphasis on Oedipus' role as a *xenos* in Athens.

Line 142 proves even more indifferent for the argument that the play is structured around the suppliant theme. Oedipus addresses the chorus,

> Do not, I beg *(hiketeuō)*, treat me as an outlaw.

Obviously, this has nothing to do with supplication but is simply a way of expressing a request. In fact, Ellendt long ago remarked on this use

---

44. Jebb, *Oedipus at Colonus*, 80–81.

of the verb, "Saepe *hiketeuō* et *hiketeuomen* medio sermoni sine ratione inseritur."[45] For parallels, he also cites 518, where the choristers use the same word as part of their incessant badgering of Oedipus to recount for them the specifics of his past actions (an interest that Knox correctly described as "almost prurient").[46] There can, of course, be no thought of the choristers viewing themselves as suppliants to Oedipus. Again, the same is true for Antigone's use of the word at 241, where she begs the choristers to reconsider their decision to try to expel Oedipus, once they have learned his identity. In all these instances, the obvious parallel word from archaic English would be *prithee*.[47]

The use of *hiketēs* at 284 has been discussed. Oedipus claims the identity and attendant rights of the suppliant only when he senses it is to his advantage, and in fact he attempts to mislead the chorus (and the audience?) about the nature of their relationship; he has, in fact, consistently represented himself as a *xenos* to the city before this, and so the citizens in turn have repeatedly identified him as such. As to line 634, when Theseus refers to Oedipus as a suppliant, he states very clearly that Oedipus is a suppliant of the gods *(hiketēs daimonōn)*; he draws no inference from this that Oedipus is also a suppliant of the city, and, in point of fact, Oedipus has mentioned no such thing.

If, in the first part of the play, the suppliant theme survives only in a form so attenuated as to render it virtually invisible, where does the controlling idea for this part of the drama lie? Clearly, *xenia* provides the basic theme on which the playwright has fashioned his story. A fuller inquiry into the nature of that institution should offer far greater insight into the workings of the play, the motivation of its protagonist, and the nature of the hero than can any superficial coincidence between this play and the earlier suppliant dramas. For *xenia* is an old institution, an institution that fostered and maintained the personal relationships that existed between heroes, and one that, in Sophocles' own time, both recalled the heroic past and existed to the present—a perfect milieu for Oedipus.

At the simplest, most essential level, *xenia* was merely hospitality, an institution that supplied some ground rules for the relationship

45. F. Ellendt, *Lexikon Sophocleum* (1872; reprint, Hildesheim, 1958), 334.

46. *Heroic Temper*, 152. Burian makes a very good point in contrasting the chorus' interests to Theseus humane reception of Oedipus: Burian, 414.

47. Were supplication a common theme running through the drama, of course, one would then have to concede Hogan his point.

between guest and host. That the same word, *xenos*, referred to both parties, testifies to the sense of mutual interdependence that the relationship created. This identity of terminology fits perfectly the reality of the situation in that, in a very real sense, guest and host undertook an identical risk in the relationship. Moreover, like *hiketeia*, *xenia* even had its own god, a particular manifestation of Zeus, Zeus Xenios.

Homer, in the first demonstration of *xenia* in Greek literature, shows decisively that the demands of the institution overrode all other considerations in interpersonal relationships. Thus, when Diomedes, the Greek chieftain, during the course of his lengthy *aristeia* in the early books of the *Iliad*, faces Glaukos, a Lykian captain, the two discover, during the course of a somewhat improbable battlefield discussion, that their families are bound by *xenia* through the travels of the mythological hero Bellerophon, even though they themselves had never met (6.119–236). The power of the institution becomes apparent when the two warriors immediately suspend hostilities and exchange gifts on the battlefield.[48] This scene has been more than adequately discussed by other scholars,[49] and it would be laborious and well off the topic to consider it in too much detail. Still, a general point, on the necessity of such an institution in a violent world, can be made with profit. Thus, M.I. Finley has noted:

> In primitive times [the poet seems to be suggesting] man lived in a state of permanent struggle and war to the death against the outsider. Then the gods intervened, and through their precepts, their *themis*, a new ideal was set before man, an obligation of hospitality. . . . Henceforth, men had to pick a difficult path between the two, between the reality of a society in which the stranger was still a problem and a threat, and the new morality, according to which he was somehow covered by the aegis of Zeus. . . . Institutionally it was guest-friendship above all that weakened the tension between the two poles.[50]

Proceeding from the *Iliad* to the *Odyssey*, we find that the later work supplies better information on the workings of *xenia*, both of its proper

---

48. To Glaukos' great disadvantage, as Homer points out.

49. For a thorough overview, with references, see G.S. Kirk, *The Iliad: A Commentary*, vol. 2, bks. 5–8 (Oxford, 1990), 170–91.

50. M.I. Finley, *The World of Odysseus* (New York, 1954), 106–7.

use and of the obvious potential for abuse.[51] In book 7, Homer gives a
sense of the seriousness with which the institution is taken. Echeneus,
an old nobleman, reminds Alcinous of his duties.

> Alcinous, it is neither right nor proper for the stranger *(xeinon)*[52]
> to sit on the ground in the ashes at the hearth, while your atten-
> dants hold back, waiting for your orders. But tell the stranger to
> rise and sit on the silver-inlaid chair, and order your servants to
> mix wine. (7.159–64)

The Phaiacaeans confirm this initial act of hospitality with a great feast
and parting gifts for their guest (bks. 8 and 13). And hospitality was not
limited to the upper classes. As Eumaeus remarks to Odysseus:

> Stranger *(xein')*, I have no right to reject a stranger, not even if one
> came who was worse off than you. All strangers and paupers are
> under the care of Zeus. (14.56–58)

Later, the suitors remind Antinous that the mistreatment of beggars
may entail consequences far more severe than at first apparent.

> Antinous, you were wrong to hit the unhappy wanderer: a curse
> on you, if he turns out to be one of the gods from heaven.
> (17.483–84)

The suitors, of course, occupy a perilous role in the relationship of
xenia. As they abuse the institution in neglecting their duties as hosts
by refusing hospitality to the beggar Odysseus, so too have they
abused their position as guests, by their consumption of Penelope's
resources.[53]

The importance of *xenia* cannot be overstated. As Murnaghan points
out,

---

51. I am indebted to Hogan, *Commentary on the Plays of Sophocles*, 81, for the
passages from the *Odyssey* that follow in the text.

52. In this passage, the "stranger," Odysseus, is also acting the part of a suppliant, but we should note that the identities are in fact separate, as he is genuinely a *xeinos* but only a suppliant on the advice of Nausicaa (6.310–11).

53. For an excellent discussion of *xenia* and the suitors, see S. Murnaghan,
Disguise and Recognition in the Odyssey (Princeton, 1985), especially 56–90.

In the Homeric world, hospitality is a social institution that provides outsiders, who are by nature without status, with that place in society that constitutes an identity.[54]

So pervasive is the importance of hospitality that *xenia* survives as an institution well into the fourth century.[55] In Plato's final work, the *Laws*, the Athenian stranger not only argues that the lawgiver should observe the rites of hospitality but divides *xenia* into four distinct levels (952d–953e).

A temptation arises to conflate artificially the stranger and the suppliant. But the two identities differ considerably, in provenience, cult, and, most importantly for this discussion, rights. The *xenos* may appear by happenstance or, according to the tradition recognized by the suitors in their reproach of Antinous, may even be an epiphany of a god. The suppliant, on the contrary, arrives by plan at a designated spot. This was precisely the case in the suppliant plays discussed earlier. Moreover, to leave the realm of tragedy for a moment, even Odysseus, who is called a suppliant by Arete, only chooses to present himself to her as such on the advice of Nausicaa. Had he simply wandered into the court of the Phaiacaeans, his status might have been quite different. Supplication, in brief, can never be accidental, since it usually involves serious consequences for those receiving the suppliant. Furthermore, while Zeus guarantees the rights of both *xenos* and *hiketes*—in his dual manifestations as Zeus Xenios and Zeus Hikesios (or, as in Aeschylus, Zeus Aphiktor)—the two identities, although close, remain separate.[56]

Finally, as to the matter of the rights of suppliants and strangers, we find a considerable divergence of practice. *Xenia*, as the case of Diomedes and Glaukos demonstrates, overrides all other considerations, even the violence of battle. The only way in which *xenia* could be abrogated is if, as in the case of the suitors of Penelope, the privileges

---

54. *Disguise and Recognition*, 76.

55. For a thorough discussion, see G. Herman, *Ritualised Friendship in the Greek City* (Cambridge, 1987), which is considered in more detail in chapter 3.

56. Farnell calls Zeus Xenios "a narrower but cognate conception" of Zeus Hikesios; see the discussion of the distinctions between the two in L. Farnell, *The Cults of the Greek States* (Oxford, 1896), 1:64–74. Among other distinctions, Zeus Hikesios was worshiped with a sacrifice of swine. Farnell's view is preferable to Lloyd-Jones' assertion that the two "are in their origins practically identical;" see H. Lloyd-Jones, *The Justice of Zeus* (Berkeley, 1971), 5.

accorded by the relationship were abused. The reason is obvious: the relationship between *xenoi* is ultimately personal, and in the heroic era, the personal tended to outweigh the public in Greek life. Supplication, on the contrary, of necessity involved the state. Homer drives home this very lesson in the *Odyssey*, since he relates that the Phaiacaeans were punished for assisting Odysseus' return to Ithaca.[57] As a result, suppliants could be and were turned away in historical times. For example, Thucydides, in his account of the events in and around Epidamnos that helped speed the onset of the Peloponnesian War, states that ambassadors from Epidamnos, who had come to their mother city, Corcyra, and were seated at the temple of Hera as suppliants, were turned away by the Corcyrans.[58]

Art often follows life. So, the kings in Aeschylus' *Suppliants* and Euripides' play by the same name argue that the rights of suppliants do not, automatically, take precedent over all other considerations. Each king fears to go to war to protect the suppliants or enforce their rights, lest his own state be harmed. At first glance, this seems merely sensible caution. However, the complications arising from the presence of the suppliants are greater than first appears. For example, Pelasgus, after all their pleas had been voiced, remains insufficiently moved by the claims of the daughters of Danaus and still declines to take action on his own initiative, without the advice of the state. The argument that proves decisive is simply blackmail: the women threaten suicide in the very temples of the gods.[59] That pollution, certainly, would cause more harm than Argos could withstand, and thus the women were able to force the king's hand.

Theseus does no better. Despite his role of "ideal patriot" in Euripides,[60] his first instinct in the *Suppliants* is to reject the claims of Adrastus and the Argive women out of hand, preferring not to align himself and the state with the perpetrators of the mindless slaughter resultant from the expedition against Thebes. Only his mother, Aethra, through

---

57. *Odyssey* 13.159–64; Poseidon turns to stone the ship that carried Odysseus back to Ithaca.

58. Thucydides 1.24. For other examples of the denial of supplication, by fair means or foul, in historical times, see Gould, "*Hiketeia*," 82–85.

59. For the strong element of coercion involved, see Spatz, *Aeschylus*, 83; for the violent nature of Aeschylus' suppliants, see Winnington-Ingram, *Studies in Aeschylus*, 57.

60. On this role, see Reinhardt, *Sophocles*, 213; Whitman, *Sophocles*, 223.

her tears and reproaches, manages to persuade the king to change his mind, and even then Theseus agrees only to confer with the citizens on the subject. The essential point remains intact: the state could send the suppliant away. Honor may demand better, as Aethra convinces her son, but the institution of *hiketeia* cannot make sweeping claims that prefer the individual to the state.

Demophon, admittedly, appropriates the role of the protector of suppliants far more readily in the *Children of Heracles*. Only in this work, of the three earlier suppliant dramas, does the author portray as unequivocal the rights of the suppliants. Still, although Demophon states in no uncertain terms that he will protect the children at all costs, when he actually discovers what the true cost will be (i.e., the sacrifice of a noble maiden to Persephone), he too recognizes the untenable position in which his admirable generosity has placed both himself and Athens. And he cannot resist wishing, at least, that some other way out of his difficulty would present itself.

These distinctions between *xenia* and *hiketeia* having been made, Oedipus' true position in the *Oedipus at Colonus* becomes much clearer. Against the reading of Oedipus as a suppliant, or an interpretation of the work as a suppliant drama, stand the facts of the play, as understood against the background of the previous tragedies that served as supposed models. Contrary to the other three works, Oedipus has not arrived in Athens seeking refuge from a powerful assailant or asking any favor beyond his daily bread. He never claims that he is a suppliant of the city, and when he alleges that the men of Colonus have received him as a suppliant, he lies or, to put it more gently, errs. He never throws himself at the knees of the king. Unlike the suppliants in the other dramas, he brings with him a benefit. Far from adapting or reshaping the suppliant drama, Sophocles has to the greatest extent possible avoided it. Two questions remain: why did the poet do so, and what he did he wish to achieve in emphasizing Oedipus' position as *xenos*?

The short answer to the first question has already been suggested: suppliants are not heroes, particularly not tragic heroes of the stature of Oedipus. No matter how one interprets the *Oedipus Tyrannus* or solves the underlying problem of fate versus free will, on the dramatic level the commanding force of Oedipus' own personality sweeps the play along, from his relentless pursuit of the truth about himself to his fierce, destructive, and irrevocable act of self-mutilation. He is brilliant, uncompromising, and consequent. Those characteristics survive undiminished and operate just as strongly in the later play. His relentless will, the determination in the face of adversity that he demonstrates to Creon, and the decisive manner in which he rejects the appeal of Polyneices command respect even over time and distance and demand that the playwright render a more heroic portrayal for the character from the outset than suppliant drama permits.

Much has been made, and rightly, of the self-destructive nature of Oedipus' self-blinding in the *Oedipus Tyrannus*. Yet the mere fact of his continued existence, in light of the horrific revelations of incest and patricide, testifies eloquently to his determination to survive. Suppliants betray dissimilar tendencies. The suppliant women of Aeschylus threaten suicide; in the *Children of Heracles*, Iolaus offers to surrender himself to Eurystheus, and Macaria does kill herself. Euripides' *Suppliants* also capitalizes on the suicidal aspects inherent in *hiketeia*, when Evadne kills herself on the pyre of Capaneus. Such action is not for Oedipus. Although he knows that he has reached the place of his final rest, and though he thus should know that the hour of his own death is at hand, he demonstrates power, not resignation. When a hero, such as Ajax or Heracles, does kill himself, his motives are not surrender but arrogance.

The *xenos* manifests none of the hysteria of the *hiketēs*. The rights and obligations of *xenia* imply, in theory if seldom in practice, a calm, ordered system that differed considerably from the generally chaotic situations that obtained in the heroic period during which *xenia* came into existence, the circumstances of which Finley wrote in the passage quoted earlier. Hence, *xenia* could be abridged only by the misbehavior of the parties involved. Moreover, as Murnaghan observed, the *xenos* maintained a strong and distinct identity, which other relationships might in turn compromise. Thus, in her discussion of the Nausicaa episode in the *Odyssey*, at the points in which Nausicaa and Antinous moot briefly the suggestion that Odysseus would make a more than suitable spouse and son-in-law, respectively, Murnaghan wrote:

> To enter into such a marriage is to take on a role that is prestigious but also subordinate. Someone in such a position is subsumed into his wife's family and derives his identity not primarily from his own qualities and accomplishments but from his membership in that family.

Later Murnaghan wrote,

> Nor does a guest-friend have an established place within a stable
> structure, as a family member does; rather the guest-friend main-
> tains an autonomous and equal status that can easily be turned
> into a competition.[61]

The "autonomous and equal status" noted by Murnaghan suggests
the relationship between Oedipus and Theseus that Whitman observed
when he remarked that "Hero recognizes hero as a fellow stranger in
this world."[62] The Thebans, according to Ismene, wish to deny Oedipus
that power by burying him in an area under Theban control.

> For this reason they want to keep you close at hand, for the sake
> of the power [of your tomb], rather than leave you as your own
> master. (404–5)

Later, Oedipus will ask from Theseus that his autonomy be preserved
in the face of a perceived threat from Polyneices.

> One thing, sir (tellingly, *xen'*): if that man is coming here, let no
> one take possession of me. (1206–7)

Thus, *xenia* serves to provide what Oedipus desires: recognition of his
own heroism, an identity that will resist submersion into any collective,
and genuine autonomy. *Hiketeia* appears to be a negligible element in
the *Oedipus at Colonus*, whereas *xenia*, by comparison, proves essential
to our understanding of the play. Only *xenia* can offer a solution to the
difficult interpretation of line 637 and provide grounds for choosing
between the manuscript reading of *empalin* or Musgrave's emendation,
empolin, in Theseus' offer to receive Oedipus. That discussion is undertaken in the next chapter.

---

61. *Disguise and Recognition*, 95, 96.
62. *Sophocles*, 205.

3

Empalin or *Empolin*

Necessary background dispensed, we come to the crucial moment in the first third of the *Oedipus at Colonus,* the passage that commentators so frequently cite in the course of their interpretations of the play. Less neutral ground than one would suppose is allowed here, given that the discussion hinges on a single word: critics since Musgrave invariably feel compelled to discuss 637 at some point. That the line has generated such discussion is unsurprising, for however one reads the line and the problematic *empolin* or *empalin,* the scene of Theseus' welcoming of Oedipus provides the resolution of the conflict that dominated the first part of the work. From Oedipus' first stumbling, inadvertent entrance into the grove, we have witnessed an extended conflict of will and intellect between the chorus and the protagonist that only Theseus, ultimately, has the competence to decide. Will the ignorance, fear, and superstition of the chorus lead to yet another banishment for Oedipus, or will his evident humanity and his concomitant insistence on his heroic character avail to permit him to remain in the grove? Until the advent of the Athenian king, Sophocles leaves the issue in doubt, and the obstinate, prurient behavior of the chorus inspires no automatic confidence in the observer that the correct or desired outcome will be reached. In the event, Theseus, recognizing a fellow hero regardless of the unpromising external circumstances of the Theban, decrees that Oedipus will stay. But in what specific capacity he will abide in Athens remains unclear. How does the status granted to Oedipus, determined as precisely as possible, affect our understanding of the remainder of the *Oedipus at Colonus*? To answer that question, the text of 637 must be established beyond doubt.

The verse has been much disputed since the beginning of the last century. Lines 636 and 637 must be taken together in order to discover the sense of the passage. The manuscripts read *hagō sebistheis oupot' ekbalō xarin tēn toude, chōra{i} d' empalin katoikiō.* In his posthumous 1800 edition, Musgrave emended *empalin* to *empolin* and began an argument that has continued to the present.[1] If we read the manuscripts' *empalin*, we must take it, as the scholiast does, as *ek tou enantiou*, that is, "on the contrary."[2] If we prefer Musgrave's *empolin*, we should likely read it as "citizen, man of the polis." In the first reading, Theseus merely acknowledges that he will never cast Oedipus out but rather will permit him to stay at Athens under the protection of the king. In Musgrave's version, however, Oedipus becomes an Athenian citizen. Or so the vast majority of critics have maintained.

A brief review of the history of the argument that ensued over Musgrave's emendation may be helpful. Nineteenth-century editors were about evenly divided. Brunck, Schneider, Hermann, and Linwood rejected *empolin* outright, and Blaydes acknowledged the reading without enthusiasm, offering as an alternative possibility the rather improbable *empedon*.[3] Dindorf and Campbell both initially retained the manuscript reading, although both later changed their minds.[4] Ellendt rejects unequivocally Musgrave's suggestion, referring to *empolin* as an "inanis coniectatio."[5] In contrast, Bothe, Reisig Thuringus, Schnedwin-Nauck, and Wunder accepted *empolin*, and the authority of Jebb seems to have persuaded most, but not all, later editors.[6] Kamerbeek has

---

1. S. Musgrave, *Sophocles*, 2 vols. (Oxford, 1800).

2. See J. Kamerbeek, *The Plays of Sophocles, Part VII: The Oedipus Coloneus* (Leiden, 1984), 101.

3. R.F.P. Brunck, *Sophocles*, vol. 1 (Oxford, 1826); T.H.G. Schneider, *Sophocles* (Weimar, 1825); G. Hermann, *Sophocles*, vol. 2 (London, 1827). W. Linwood, *Sophocles* (London, 1846), 107, express amazement that anyone could accept Musgrave's emendation. Blaydes (in addition to disclosing the fact that Brunck was an inveterate plagiarist) cannot accept the emendation, although he acknowledges the wide acceptance it received. However, he misrepresents Reisig Thuringus (cited in my note 6 in this chapter) on the question. See F.H.M. Blaydes, *Sophocles* (London, 1859), especially xlvi.

4. Dindorf printed the manuscript reading in his 1832 edition but changed his mind four years later; cf. W. Dindorf, *Sophocles* (Oxford, 1832), and Dindorf, *Annotationes* (Oxford, 1836). Campbell rejected the reading on grammatical grounds but later recanted as well; cf. L. Campbell, *Sophocles* (Oxford, 1879), and Campbell, *Paralipomena Sophocles* (Oxford, 1907).

5. *Lexikon Sophocleum*, 235.

6. F. Bothe, *Sophocles*, vol. 1 (Leipzig, 1806). C. Reisig Thuringus, *Oedipus Coloneus* (Jena, 1820), seems indecisive. He initially characterizes Musgrave's emendation as "minime inepta," but in almost the same breath he congratulates Musgrave and Bothe for printing *empolin* (283). See also F.W. Schnedwin and A. Nauck, *Oedipus auf Kolonos* (Berlin, 1878); E. Wunder, *Sophocles* (London, 1855); R.C. Jebb, *Sophocles* (Cambridge, 1900).

expressed considerable, well-founded doubts about Musgrave's reading, and in their 1960 edition Dain and Mazon originally printed the
manuscripts' *empalin,* although the reading was later changed to
empolin.[7] Colonna has recently printed the original text.[8] Vidal-Naquet
has since demonstrated the substantial difficulties entailed in reading
empolin as "fellow citizen," and although he expends considerable
effort to find some justification for retaining Musgrave's emendation,
he also concedes that *empalin* is a far simpler suggestion.[9] However,
Musgrave's *empolin* is so firmly entrenched that Lloyd-Jones and Wilson, in their magisterial *Sophoclea,* pass over the line without discussion.[10]

As modern text editors have, on the whole, been won over by Musgrave's *empolin,* so too have the literary critics. To cite all of the critics
verbatim would quickly prove tiresome, but a look at the remarks of a
few major scholars will be instructive. To begin with the greatest, Whitman says,

> Theseus is impressed at once by the authority of the old man's
> manner and promises him not only burial in Attica, but also full
> protection and citizenship.[11]

For Burian, who connects this verse with his reading of the *Oedipus at
Colonus* as a suppliant play,

> Theseus, however, goes beyond the promise of protection
> required by the [suppliant] pattern, and indeed beyond what
> Oedipus has requested, by making him an Athenian citizen.

In this context, Burian also notes the elegant shift by which the hero,
described as *apoptolis* at 208, becomes *empolin* at 637.[12]

---

7. Kammerbeek, *Plays of Sophocles,* 101; A. Dain and P. Mazon, *Sophocles,*
vol. 3 (Paris, 1960). Dain and Mazon change their reading in their 1963 edition.

8. A. Colonna, *Sophoclis Fabulae,* vol. 3 (Turin, 1983). I owe this reference to
Vidal-Naquet; see Vernant and Vidal-Naquet, *Myth and Tragedy,* 488 n. 44.

9. See his essay "Oedipus between Two Cities," in Vernant and Vidal-
Naquet, *Myth and Tragedy,* 329–59.

10. H. Lloyd-Jones and N. Wilson, *Sophoclea* (Oxford, 1990).

11. *Sophocles,* 195–96.

12. "Suppliant and Savior," 416–17.

For Knox, especially, the prospect of a grant of Athenian citizenship
to Oedipus, the supposition of which underlies the acceptance of Musgrave's emendation, seems most crucial. In a passage much criticized
by Vidal-Naquet, Knox states,

> Oedipus is a citizen of Athens now and when, under Creon's
> assault he calls for help (*io polis* 833), it is Athens he is calling on
> for help against Thebes.[13]

Knox predicates his view, as Vidal-Naquet observed,[14] on the belief
that Oedipus expects the city's protection precisely because of his
rights as a freshly minted citizen of Athens.

Segal likes Musgraves' reading so much he refers to the word or the
line eight times in a forty-page chapter on the play.[15] Hogan, in his
commentary on the line, refers in good American legalese to the "naturalization" of Oedipus.[16] For Bernidaki-Aldous, Theseus' grant of citizenship is a proclamation of Oedipus' right to stay in the place to which
he is fitted by nature.[17] Slatkin claims that, by accepting Oedipus as a
citizen, the Athenians are confirming their own democratic values of
inclusion and openness, as opposed to Thebes, which can only exclude
the parricide.[18] Winnington-Ingram seems neutral on the subject of citizenship in his primary essay on the play, but in an appendix he cites
the line and claims explicitly that Oedipus is made a citizen.[19] More
cautious positions are maintained by others, for example, Zeitlin and
Blundell.[20] To consider one in greater detail, Blundell, expressly following Burian, accepts Musgrave's *empolin* and states that Oedipus
becomes an Athenian citizen, but she does confess to some doubt in a
footnote. She also claims that the reading would make little difference

---

13. B.M.W. Knox, "Sophocles and the *Polis*," in *Sophocle: Entretiens sur l'An-
tique Classique*, ed. M. Bernard Grange (Geneva, 1983), 21. He stated a similar
position in *Heroic Temper*, 154.
14. Vernant and Vidal-Naquet, *Myth and Tragedy*, 347.
15. *Tragedy and Civilization*, 364, 373, 379, 380, 381 (twice), 382, and 388.
16. *Commentary on the Plays of Sophocles*, 97.
17. E. Bernidaki-Aldous, *Blindness in a Culture of Light* (New York, 1990), 159.
18. Slatkin, *"Oedipus at Colonus,"* particularly 219–21.
19. *Sophocles*, appendix E, 339.
20. Zeitlin refers to Oedipus' acceptance into Athens but makes no mention
of citizenship; instead, she refers to him as an "adopted stranger," which is a far
better reading of the line and the play. See Zeitlin, "Theater of Self," particularly 135.

to criticism of the *Oedipus at Colonus*.[21] In so doing, she espouses a deceptively moderate view, for the reading ultimately makes a great deal of difference to our understanding of the play. Moreover, on a purely practical level, the reading of the passage must make some difference, or scholars would not have been so ready to make use of it. Critics seize eagerly only onto those conjectures that prove useful for their own arguments. Should the conjecture be lost, the critical stance must be reevaluated. Such must be the case for this passage in the *Oedipus at Colonus*. In reality, little beyond the persistence of its adherents commends Musgrave's emendation. Sound arguments have often been adduced against the reading, only to be ignored by critics exhibiting the parasitic orthodoxy that engulfs so much of the literature on this work.

In the first place, one really should not start altering manuscript readings without solid reasons, and this line presents none.[22] The *empalin* that Musgrave and his successors have found so offensive requires no correction. The primary objection to reading *empalin* as "on the contrary" has been that, more commonly, one would expect *to empalin* (or, better, *toumpalin*) in this context. Yet *empalin* is not thereby rendered automatically suspect, for a perfectly valid parallel exists in Sophocles. At *Trachiniae* 351–58, the messenger reports to Deianeira:

> I myself heard this man [Lichas] say—in the presence of witnesses—that for the sake of this girl, Heracles destroyed Eurytus and his lofty-towered city of Oechalia, and that it was Eros alone, of the gods, who charmed him into this violent deed—not his service in Lydia for Omphale, nor rather because Iphitus was hurled to his death. Having forgotten all this, he now tells a different story.

In the Greek the last sentence reads, *hon nun parōsas houtos empalin legei*, which may be translated, "now this man, having brushed this [version] aside, speaks in a contrary fashion. The force of *empalin* here is clearly adverbial, no *to* is in sight, and the passage without question indicates that Lichas is speaking in a manner contradictory to his previous speech.

---

21. M.W. Blundell, *Helping Friends and Harming Enemies* (Cambridge, 1982), 231 and n. 19.

22. A point soundly reiterated by Vidal-Naquet, in Vernant and Vidal-Naquet, *Myth and Tragedy*, 343.

Now let us consider in its full sense the passage in which the controversial *empalin* appears: *hagō sebistheis oupot' ekbalō xarin tēn toude,
chōra{i} d'empalin katoikiō.* As the manuscript reading stands, Theseus
vows, "Never will I, being a reverent man, cast the favor of this man
[Oedipus] out, but on the contrary I will establish it [metonymically,
him] in the land." Lloyd-Jones and Wilson have printed *sebas theis*
for *sebistheis,* but that alteration makes no difference to the reading
of the disputed clause.[23] Is there any call to change the manuscript
reading?

Certainly not. The first part of the sentence suggests (implicitly) and
rejects (explicitly) a proposed action, that of returning Oedipus once
more into exile. In the second clause, Theseus announces that he will
act contrary to the possibility mooted in the first clause. The parallel in
the *Trachiniae* clearly demonstrates that *empalin* can be used to indicate
that something stated at the moment is contrary to something stated
previously, and that same kind of use is evidenced here: surely, if one
can speak "opposite" of what has been spoken before, one can act
"opposite" of an action proposed before. Indeed, the best translation of
the offending word can be found in the French version by P. Masqueray, who simply renders it "Au contraire."[24] In fact, there are anal-
ogous uses of *empalin* found in Aeschylus and Euripides that confirm
that the manuscript reading of *Oedipus at Colonus* is certainly viable and
therefore should not be the object of frivolous emendation.[25]

So, in the first place, minimal investigation reveals Musgrave's
empolin as an unnecessary change. Recall, moreover, that a good many
scholars have felt the same. Is *empolin,* then, defensible or desirable? For
conservatives in such matters, desirability alone offers scant justification to change the manuscript reading, but editors do such things.[26] To

---

23. For their rationale, see *Sophoclea*, 236–37.

24. P. Masqueray, *Sophocles* (Paris, 1924), 180.

25. J. Kamerbeek has listed them in his commentary on the line (*Plays of
Sophocles*, 101).

26. See the introduction to the Lloyd-Jones and Wilson edition of Sophocles:
"If this edition were designed principally for the use of other professional
scholars, we might have made it our policy to obelize more of the unsolved difficulties. But the Oxford series is aimed at a wider circle of readers, and in order
to give them a text which can be read with few interruptions we have sometimes chosen to adopt a reading which is far from certain but seems to us to be
the nearest approximation to the truth" (H. Lloyd-Jones and N.G. Wilson,
Sophoclis Fabulae [Oxford, 1990], vi).

consider the question of desirability or even possibility, then, we must examine more carefully the word *empolis,* in order to be sure of our terms. This is a rare word, appearing in the playwrights only twice (ignoring Musgrave's proposal), and in both cases the commentators have invariably taken the word to mean "fellow citizen."

First, a parallel use appears in the *Oedipus at Colonus* itself. At 1149–59, Oedipus and Theseus have the following exchange, after the Athenian king returns to Oedipus his daughters.

> *Thes:* Word has just reached me, while I was on my way here. It is a small matter, but worth a thought. I would like your advice. No man should ever underestimate the importance of even trivial things.
>
> *Oed:* What is it, son of Aegeus: Tell me, as I know nothing of what you ask.
>
> *Thes:* They say a man, no countryman of yours, But a kinsman, has taken sanctuary at the altar of Poseidon, where I had been sacrificing when I was called away.

In this manner Sophocles introduces Polyneices, the elder son of Oedipus, who has come to beg for his father's aid in the assault on Thebes. Polyneices has of course been cast out of Thebes by his brother, Eteocles, and has in consequence formed an alliance with Argos to have himself restored to the throne. In fact, we discover later from Theseus that Polyneices appears to be an Argive.[27]

The word translated as "countryman" is *empolin,* the accusative of *empolis.* The word appears only here in Sophocles, aside from Musgrave's emendation, and it clearly must mean, at the least, "person from the same city." Fellow citizen, then, seems a certain rendering. Theseus would not, presumably, have attempted in this context a carefully refined discussion of the appearance of citizens versus that of metics or that of slaves.

The word *empolis* also occurs in a fragment of Eupolis' *Diade,* where the grammarian Pollux has glossed it with the terms *astos, enchōrios,* and *entopios.*[28] *Astos,* "man of the *astu,*" the grammarian's first offering,

---

27. Jebb assumes that Theseus has inferred this from some clue in Polyneices' attire (*Oedipus at Colonus,* 205).

28. Pollux *Onomasticon* 9.27.

certainly indicates, on the basis of overwhelming use in the Attic authors, a citizen. For the purpose of this play, we note that *astu* and *polis* often are coextensive and employed interchangeably. Thus, in response to her father's query, "whose city?" (*tinōn andrōn polin?*, 2 and 24), Antigone refers to the area in which she and Oedipus have arrived as Athens, even though the *astu* is separate from Colonus. And unless one would attempt to deny that the chorus of men from Colonus hold citizenship in Athens, no other definition can be offered. Thus, the choristers, who make a point of identifying themselves with the *astu*, Athens, even though they dwell in Colonus, are referred to as *astoi* twice in the play, while Sophocles employs the word in the clear sense of citizen a total of six times.[29] In two of the most striking formulations, the *astoi* are opposed to *xenoi*, thus establishing the dichotomy that appears throughout this work.[30] To continue along the lines suggested by Pollux, Creon also refers to the choristers as *enchōrioi* at 871; this reference confirms that Sophocles used the word to refer to citizens.

So *empolis* denotes a citizen, at least as the dramatic playwrights use the word and as Pollux has glossed it. Now we come to the first major objection to *empolin*. If we understand the word to mean "fellow citizen," in the sense that critics have routinely taken it, we find no confirming evidence for the emendation in the play. Nothing at any other place in the text—no word, no term, no plot point—suggests that Oedipus has been made a citizen of Athens.

At the most obvious level, after 637 no character ever refers to Oedipus by a term that commonly designates a citizen—we look in vain throughout the remainder of the work for *politēs, sumpolitēs, astos,* or any similar word. Arguments from silence often prove hazardous, but in this case, the silence renders a decisive verdict. Quite simply, no verbal evidence in support of *empolin* exists. On the contrary, before Theseus' offer, whatever it may be, Oedipus refers to himself and is addressed by the chorus and, in one instance, by Theseus as a *xenos*—twelve times prior to line 637.[31] In turn, he and Antigone refer to the

---

29. See lines 13, 171, 288, 928, 1501, 1528. The references at 171 and 1501 are clearly to the chorus.

30. See line 928, where Theseus lectures Creon on the proper behavior of the *xenos* among *astoi,* and line 1501, where Theseus clearly refers to Oedipus as a *xenos.*

31. See lines 13, 62, 75, 161, 184, 215, 261 492, 505, 510, 518, 565.

choristers and the choral leader as *xenoi* and *xenos* fourteen times.[32] After 637, where we should expect some acknowledgment of Oedipus' change in status, Oedipus is referred to as a *xenos* nine more times: once by Creon, who, not having been present for the hypothesized naturalization, could perhaps be forgiven the blunder; six more times by the choristers, who were, after all, present when Theseus accepts Oedipus; and twice by Theseus himself, who, if he had intended to grant citizenship to Oedipus at 637, should really be expected to know better.[33] In turn, Oedipus addresses Theseus twice more as *xenos* and the choristers three times more as *xenoi*.[34] We must, then, severely fault Sophocles for missing the attendant dramatic opportunities if he in fact intended that we should consider Oedipus as a citizen of Athens.

Three of those opportunities are worth discussing, if only to drive home the point and banish *empolin* forever. One painfully obvious instance occurs immediately after the grant of citizenship has allegedly been made. If we look at the next verse, we find something strikingly amiss. For at 638, Theseus offers Oedipus a choice between staying at Colonus and accompanying him. The king states,

And if the stranger prefers to remain here, I place him in your charge; if he would rather come with me—he may choose . . .

Quite literally, the king says, "sweet [or pleasurable] to the *xenos*" (*hēdu tō{i} xenō{i}*). One cannot reconcile such diction with an offer of citizenship supposedly tendered in the preceding verse.

Another missed opportunity appears during Creon's unsuccessful attempt to induce Oedipus to return with him to Thebes. After Creon has made his pitch, Oedipus responds, with justifiable contempt, that Creon and Thebes had cared nothing for his wishes when he desired exile (just after the suicide of Jocasta and his own self-blinding) and still less when he no longer felt compelled to leave the city and they nevertheless drove him out. Now, however, when he has found haven in Colonus, Creon and Thebes want him back. In this context, in an extremely damaging passage for those who would read Musgrave's

---

32. See lines 33, 49, 81, 174, 207, 237, 242, 275, 296, 457, 468, 493, 521, 530.

33. See lines 745 (Creon); 668, 824, 1014, 1096, 1449, 1562 (chorus); 638, 1501 (Theseus).

34. See lines 1119, 1206 (Theseus); 822, 844, 1552 (chorus).

empolin, the best claim that Oedipus can manage with reference to his newfound allies—"Now when you see this city and all the people have come together favorably disposed toward us . . ." (*nun t' authis henik eisora{i}s polin te moi xunousan eunoun tēnde kai genos to pan . . .,* 772–73)—seems a bit weak. He does not mention an offer of citizenship. At this moment of considerable potential danger (Oedipus has been forewarned by Ismene of Thebes' intentions), we should expect Oedipus to make his newfound position, and the assistance he could expect as a result, clear to Creon in the strongest language possible. "Favorably disposed toward us" conveys too little force to the Theban, given the circumstances. This response, in fact, negates any possibility of such an offer of citizenship. The language is simply too mild to describe the circumstances that Musgrave's proposed *empolin* would cause us to expect.

Vidal-Naquet points out an additional instance, in the same vein, in which the action and language of the play deny plausibility to the claim that Oedipus has been made a citizen.[35] At 1083 ff., the choristers ask for the help of the gods Zeus, Athena, Apollo, and Artemis, begging them to lend their twofold power to the land and the citizens. Then, in an obvious disjunction, they turn to Oedipus and address him as "wandering stranger" (*xein' alēta,* 1095). Once more, Sophocles has passed over a clear opportunity to allude to Oedipus' citizen status, if it existed. Certainly, then, he never wished to suggest that Oedipus was made *empolis,* at least as the critics have regularly understood the word.

One aspect of the underlying logic of the play also demands that we rethink the supposed grant of citizenship. Citizenship mandatorily entails consequences and responsibilities, duties that are antithetical to the heroic identity. What Oedipus seeks, rather, and ultimately obtains, is personal autonomy. The work makes clear the protagonist's essential desire for that autonomy in a number of different ways throughout. Recall the hero's initial remarks, as he appears on the stage.

Who will provide the beggar Oedipus with some handout today? He asks little, and gets still less—but that less is enough For suffering and the long years proceeding apace, and last my inbred nobility, have taught me to endure. (2–8)

---

35. Vernant and Vidal-Naquet, *Myth and Tragedy,* 348.

Obviously, on his own testimony, Oedipus' hardy endurance of his misfortunes is a function of his inbred nobility of character, his *to gennaion*. This nobility has, in fact, made it possible for him to endure so much with so little, and that capacity, in some improbable and no doubt idiosyncratic fashion, has become desire. For in Oedipus' powerlessness he has found power, if only the negative power that derives from knowing that nothing worse can happen to him. His resigned contentment with his fate is in fact unremarkable, since at the moment of his greatest power, fame, and wealth he was struck down. At least, when he has nothing, nothing more can be taken from him. Therefore, he stands intuitively on guard against any excess, or even semblance, of good fortune.

After Oedipus learns that he has entered the grove sacred to the Eumenides, in which Apollo has prophesied that he will die, we discover very clearly the limitations of his own desire. He who once created his destiny by fleeing it has learned to conform his wishes to Apollo's prophecies.

> Do not mistreat me or Phoebus, who, when he told me of all the evil things to come, told me also that I would reach at some distant time a place of rest, the land where I would be destined to die, where I would find a home as the guest of the revered goddesses. (86–91)

Thus Apollo spoke: he made no mention of citizenship, of even being welcomed into a polis. In fact, he gave only a concrete promise of *xenostasis*, glossed by Pollux as "quarters for strangers."[36] Oedipus knows better than anyone the authority of oracles. To attain his promised *xenostasis* is to achieve quite literally a sort of permanent *xenia*, the condition in which his heroic status could be maintained. Theseus would not, as Burian claimed, "go beyond the promise of protection required by the [suppliant] pattern" and make Oedipus a citizen. To do so would exceed not merely the norms of a tragic model largely inapplicable to this play but also the requirements of Apollo's prophecy. And the prophecy of Apollo promised autonomy, a condition that suited Oedipus much better than would any grant of citizenship, which he could never live long enough to enjoy.

---

36. Pollux *Onomasticon* 9.50; cf. Jebb, *Oedipus at Colonus*, 80.

The arrival of Ismene, with her information regarding the political intrigue at Thebes and the desire of the Thebans to attain Oedipus' body, confirms the importance of autonomy to the exile. In the course of an extended discussion, as she explains Thebes' intentions, Oedipus articulate his own views on the questions of status and power.

Ism: [The oracle states that] for the sake of their own prosperity, the men at Thebes must find you, living or dead.
Oed: And who would benefit from someone like me?
Ism: They say that their sovereignty depends on you.
Oed: So, when I no longer exist, then I am a man again?
Ism: The gods who once laid you low now lift you up again.
Oed: A trivial matter, to raise an old man who fell when he was young.
Ism: Be that as it may, for this reason alone Creon is coming—and he is coming soon.
Oed: Why, my daughter? Explain it to me.
Ism: To place you near the territory of Thebes, so that they may have power over you but not allow to enter their territory.
Oed: What do they gain, if I lie at the gates.
Ism: Your tomb, if not properly tended, will lay a curse on them.
Oed: A person should be able to figure that out without help from the gods.
Ism: They want to have you nearby, not someplace where you would be your own master.
Oed: Will they bury me in Thebes?
Ism: No, father, the crime of Laius' murder does not allow that.
Oed: Then they shall never have power over me. (389–408)

The question of power dominates this exchange, a concern manifested particularly in the frequent repetition of the verb *krateō*. Who will have power over the hero's body? At 400, Ismene says that Thebes will bury Oedipus near their border "in order that they may have power over you" (*hopōs kratōsi men sou*). Later she confirms their intention in similar language, claiming that they would prefer to keep Oedipus near at hand "so that you might not have power over yourself" (*mēd' hin' an sautou kratois*, 404–5). Finally, Oedipus—having discovered that the Thebans will not, in any case, restore him to the city but will station him outside the borders—responds, "they will never have power over me" (*ouk ar' emou ge mē kratēsōsin pote*, 408).[37]

Indeed, Oedipus' plans run in quite the opposite direction. Far from permitting himself to fall under the sway of his former city, he instead asserts that he will attain power over them, if only he can stay in the grove at Colonus. When Theseus, having permitted Oedipus to remain, offers him the choice between abiding in the grove or accompanying the king, Oedipus answers that he would prefer to stay, for "here [*en hō{i}]* I shall vanquish *(kratēsō)* those who cast me forth" (646). At this stage of his life he seeks personal power, and only burial at Colonus can guarantee it. Citizenship in Athens can do nothing to advance his aims and may even prove a hindrance, for it entails a risk of compromise, which is alien to the hero's character.

The verb *krateō* appears early in the play, in a passage the import of which has been overlooked. When Oedipus meets the *xenos* from Colonus, he inquires about the political structure of the place.

Oed: [Are they] ruled by a king or by the will of the people?
Xen: The king of Athens also rules us.
Oed: Who holds the power *(kratei)*, great in word and might?
Xen: He is named Theseus, the son of Aegeus. (66–69)

The first verse has greater ramifications for the play, which will be discussed in their proper place.[38] For now, it is sufficient to observe that, if Oedipus becomes an Athenian citizen, he would lose, or at least limit, that control over himself that he desires. He must, perforce, become one of those whom Theseus rules *(kratei)*, just like any other Athenian citizen.[39] Hence, his own right to wield power against the Thebans becomes subordinate to the king's power over his subjects, a diminution of power to which Oedipus, doubtless, would not willingly accede.

For Theseus' rule, as portrayed in the *Oedipus at Colonus*, is in fact absolute. He receives Oedipus without soliciting input from his subjects, in contrast to the rulers in the suppliant plays, even though he has

37. Segal makes roughly the same point when he observes that *kratos* is primarily a Theban obsession (*Tragedy and Civilization*, 371, 378, and 386).

38. See chap. 6.

39. Jebb notes that Oedipus' inquiry is scarcely appropriate to the heroic age (*Oedipus at Colonus*, 77).

been explicitly advised by Oedipus that such an act may require military, and therefore civic, intervention; he resorts to military action on his own authority, again without consultation, in order to protect Oedipus and his daughters; and he is content that the knowledge of the location of Oedipus' grave should be a royal perquisite. Yet Oedipus has never approached the Athenian ruler as a subject, any more than he did as a suppliant. Rather, like an equal, he offers favors and seeks return for them. His behavior is a far cry from that of the denizens of Colonus, who provide the only referent we have for the behavior of Athenian citizens. These men, as we have seen, must refer any matter of importance to others. There is little autonomy, no exercise of *kratein*, to be found among them. Again, upon examination, no sign in the *Oedipus at Colonus* intimates that Oedipus received an offer of Athenian citizenship.

A brief look at the verb of 637, *katoikizō*, which appears in its future active form, *katoikiō*, provides a small but useful supplement to this argument. The verb, neglected in other discussions of *empolin* versus *empalin*, appears in only one other instance in Sophocles. At 1069 in the *Antigone*, Teiresias, in the course of his lengthy exposition of Creon's mistakes both in denying burial to the fallen Polyneices and ordering the burial of the living Antigone, berates the king with the claim that "you have, wrongly, buried a living soul, placing it in a tomb" *(psuchēn t' atimos en taphō{i} katō{i}kisas)*. Clearly, in the lone other certain use we have of the verb in Sophocles, *katoikizō* refers to matters of geographical location, rather than political disposition. No evidence allows us to believe that the author has something different in mind here.

Another objection to the line of thought that makes Oedipus become a citizen has been voiced by Vidal-Naquet. In his criticism of Knox's position on *empolin*, he notes the absence of any subsequent evidence in the text to support the commonly held assumption that Theseus grants citizenship to Oedipus, and he points out an attendant legal question: if Oedipus does become a citizen, then of what deme?[40] Accepting Musgrave's *empolin* simply leaves too many unanswered questions.

So, then, Oedipus was never made a citizen of Athens. Not a shred of evidence can be adduced to support the notion. Two questions remain. First, is there a possibility of saving Musgrave's emendation by

---

40. Vernant and Vidal-Naquet, *Myth and Tragedy*, 347.

reading *empolin* in some other way, and second, what are the ramifications for our understanding of the *Oedipus at Colonus* if we take away the offer of citizenship?

The first question admits of an easier answer. Can *empolin* be retained? Vidal-Naquet has made a heroic attempt to do so, despite his own observation that *empalin* needs no correction. Ultimately, his effort fails. Essentially, he attempts to read *empolin* as something like "resident" or "in the city," while ignoring the possible juridical issue of citizenship. He rests his efforts on supposed ambiguities in the word *empolis* itself and the cognate verb *empoliteuō*.[41]

As noted earlier, *empolis* appears in a fragment of Eupolis, where Pollux glosses it with the words *astos*, *enchorios*, or possibly *entopios*. The first two words do appear in the *Oedipus at Colonus* and in each appearance clearly designate individuals who hold citizen rights. Before Oedipus and his daughter meet the *xenos*, Oedipus assures her that they must, as strangers, learn from the *astōn*. Later, at 171, Antigone urges her father to obey the *astois*, the chorus, which is made up of men from Colonus. These men have already asserted, in the presence of Antigone, their coequal status with the men of Athens, and hence they must be citizens. Theseus, too, exploits the distinction between *xenos* and *astos*, when he reprimands Creon for his behavior, saying that, if their roles were reversed, Theseus as a *xenon* would learn how to behave from the citizens *(par' astois)* of the state he was visiting (927–28). Clearly, he would not be receiving his instruction from the metics and slaves, who would not necessarily be any better informed as to local usages. As to the use of *engchōrioi* in the play, Creon addresses the choristers as such long after they have established their credentials as Athenians (871). The terms then, may not automatically be juridical in nature, but certainly Sophocles uses them to designate only citizens. Vidal-Naquet admits this when he acknowledges that *astu* and *polis* are largely coextensive.[42]

As *empolis* is extremely rare, Vidal-Naquet attempts to adduce no further evidence from it. He does, however, discuss the word *empoliteuō* in Thucydides, Isocrates, and Polybius in order to find evidence for his

---

41. The discussion runs from ibid., 344–47, yet even Vidal-Naquet admits in advance, "Strictly speaking, I could rest my case there [i.e., on *empalin*] and declare the problem raised by Bernard Knox to be resolved, given the lack of any text to support his thesis" (344).

42. Vernant and Vidal-Naquet, *Myth and Tragedy*, 344 and n. 49.

claim that *empoliteuō,* and therefore, by extension, *empolis,* deals more with residency than citizenship.

Evidence from Polybius and Isocrates is too late to inform accurately a discussion of Sophoclean usage. Thucydides offers the only acceptable referent. *Empoliteuō* appears twice in Thucydides, both times in the historian's account of Brasidas' campaign against Amphipolis in 424 B.C. The historian relates that the Argilian population of *oikētores* are referred to as *empoliteuontes* (4.103.4): Vidal-Naquet would have us take the term simply as "residents." But Asheri argues, convincingly, that all the *empoliteuontes* at Amphipolis were citizens, as Vidal-Naquet duly notes.[43] And the text supports only that conclusion. For a bit later on (4.106.1), Thucydides refers to the Athenians resident in the town, saying that "few Athenians lived in the city, the greater number being a mixed multitude" *(brachu men Athenaion empoliteuon, to de pleon xummeikton).* There is little choice, given the ellipse of the verb. The Athenians in Amphipolis were certainly citizens. Thus, either all or none of the residents were citizens; and a city with no one exercising the rights of citizens is no city at all.

Let us, though, grant to Vidal-Naquet the ambiguity he seeks in the word *empolin.* Does that, finally, offer an interpretation that allows Musgrave's suggestion to remain? No, in fact, for there is another difficulty that Vidal-Naquet overlooks. *Empolin* in 637 of the *Oedipus at Colonus* cannot, certainly, mean "fellow citizen." Nor, however, can it mean something more neutral like "in the city." For we are left with the bizarre possibility that one of the greatest poets who ever lived wrote, in effect, "I will establish you in this city in this land." This will not work, for as Ellendt demonstrated, *xōra* and *polis* are largely coextensive in this play.[44] Ergo, it would be, at best, a meaningless redundancy. The last remaining hope for those who would retain *empolin* is to take the word as "resident," and that option simply conflicts with all other fifth-century evidence and with the testimony of Pollux, who gave pride of place to *astos* when he glossed the word in Eupolis. So, too,

---

43. D. Asheri, "Studio sulla storia della colonizzazione di Anfipoli sino alla conquista macedone," *RFIC,* 3d ser., 95 (1967): 5–30; cf. Vernant and Vidal-Naquet, *Myth and Tragedy,* 345 and n. 53.

44. Ellendt, *Lexikon Sophocleum,* 638, 791. This is also H. Lloyd-Jones' reading of the verse in the new Loeb edition, and the translation to which he must resort is, predictably, a bit awkward. See *Sophocles,* vol. 2 (Cambridge, Mass., 1994) 487.

Hesychius read *empolin* as "one having a fatherland" (*ho echōn patrida, Lexicon* v. empolis). If one is not a citizen of one's native land (omitting slaves and the like), what else is one?[45]

So, no real evidence supports Musgrave's emendation. Good scholars have often doubted *empolin* in 637, and a great scholar has had to resort to an extreme display of virtuousity to find some salvation for it. Why, then, have so many critics been so quick to accept it? In part, one no doubt sees the "herd of independent minds" at work. Scholars, after all, read other scholars: such is the nature of research. The emendation has been around almost two centuries and has been printed almost exclusively for the last hundred years, so one can scarcely fault critics for making use of it. But something more is at work here, something that has a great deal to do with our reading of the play. We must conclude, on the basis of the evidence, that scholars simply like the emendation. More specifically, they like the conclusions that the emendation permits them to reach. Ample reason has existed to dismiss *empolin*, but few have done so. At some level, the notion that Oedipus becomes a citizen of Athens appeals to our sense of justice. As Burian notes:

> Oedipus the *apoptolis* (208) is now *empolis* (637), fully associated with the city that protects him, as he will one day protect it. This complete acceptance of Oedipus is not only token of Theseus' generous nature. It is also a further indication of the way in which the King's decision in this play is unencumbered by the weighing of risk against risk.[46]

Without question, Theseus exhibits a generous nature in his acceptance of Oedipus and a profound sense of honor and duty when he protects the exile and his daughters from Creon and his minions. But there may be other elements involved in the king's decision, elements suggested by Burian's observation that Theseus' judgment "is unencumbered by the weighing of risk against risk."

At the root of the tendency to accept *empolin* and its ramifications is

---

45. We might also consider in this regard two other compounds of *polis, apolis* and *upsipolis,* the former referring to an exile from the city, the latter to a dominant person in the city. That either refers to anyone but a citizen, particularly in Sophocles (*apolis* at *Oedipus at Colonus* 1357; *upsipolis* at *Antigone* 370), strains credulity.

46. "Suppliant and Savior," 417.

the belief that somehow a grant of Athenian citizenship provides a fitting reward for Oedipus, a suitable—in fact, more than suitable—compensation for a lifetime of suffering at the hands of the gods. Yet that presumes too much, on two counts. First, it is problematic to what extent the gods, as opposed to Oedipus himself, are responsible for his fate.[47] Second, even if the gods could with certainty be established as the source of Oedipus' sufferings, would compensation be appropriate, desirable, or even possible? Oedipus himself dismisses without comment the possibility that he can be compensated or that such compensation is of any real value.[48] And an examination of Oedipus' own wishes has suggested that a grant of citizenship would be out of place. As to Oedipus' responsibility for his own fate, I shall take that up in its proper place.[49]

The precise nature of Oedipus' reception into Athens, his relationship to Theseus, and the manner in which the absence of a grant of citizenship impacts on the usual view of the play needs still to be settled. In the previous chapter, I argued that the suppliant dramas that critics have alleged were models for this play in fact provided very little beyond, perhaps, a bare framework for the action in the *Oedipus at Colonus.* The differences noted, however, were instructive. First, in each of the suppliant dramas, the suppliants arrive at their destination intentionally, and the characters refer to themselves specifically as suppliants of both the gods and the state. They repeat their identification as suppliants frequently during the course of the play and confirm their status by performing suitable gestures or carrying appropriate identifying tokens. Finally, each king who receives suppliants invariably seeks some approval of his actions from the people, since they must logically bear the military burden of defending the suppliants should their pursuers make good the threat of attack. In this play, virtually none of these norms are met. Oedipus does not arrive as a suppliant and never identifies himself as a suppliant of the city. He carries no tokens, no boughs, and no wreaths, and he makes no suppliant ges-

---

47. The ongoing debate in Western philosophy between fate and free will is far beyond my competence, but an observation suffices: prediction is not predestination. Oedipus ran squarely into the path of his own destiny, by his own volition.

48. As observed earlier, he reminds Ismene it is "A trivial matter to raise up an old man who fell when he was young" (395).

49. See chap. 5.

tures. Rather, he comes bearing a gift, which he offers in return for the favor of burial. He is persistently identified throughout the work as a *xenos*, not a suppliant. And, as we see in the exchange between Oedipus and Theseus leading up to line 637, the Athenian extends hospitality and protection to Oedipus without any consultation of his own people, even though he is specifically warned by Oedipus that such an action may entail war with Thebes.

So Theseus has welcomed Oedipus into Attica—not as a citizen, certainly, but as what? Vidal-Naquet offers a superficially attractive answer that, on examination, needs substantial correction. In his view, Oedipus becomes a privileged metic, a resident stranger who has earned that distinction through his status as an *euergetēs*. Oedipus' early interactions with Athens are, in effect, an *aitēsis*, a "request accompanied by a detailed memorandum on the candidate's qualifications, presented either in his own name or by a third party." Those "qualifications" are his ability to provide a *kerdos* to those who would receive him. The *aitēsis* is, of course, a procedure by which one is considered for citizenship. Oedipus' pollution disqualifies him from that position, yet the status of metic remains available.[50]

This argument seems, in many respects, just as vexatious as those adduced to defend the notion that Oedipus has been made a citizen. For Oedipus never exactly presents his credentials; even when dealing with Theseus, he withholds the specific nature of the favor that he brings to the city, until his own terms are met. Moreover, he makes it clear when he first arrives in Colonus that he asks for nothing appropriate to a living man, beyond his daily bread. Theseus correctly observes that the burial for which Oedipus asks is nothing more than life's last service. Indeed, given the Greek attitude toward the necessity of proper burial, Oedipus could just as well have asked anyone he had met to provide the duty. In addition, metics are assigned demes, just as are citizens; if Vidal-Naquet would note that the absence of such an assignment is a bar to considering Oedipus a citizen, in fairness he must grant the same obstacle to metic status. Finally, we hear of no duties or relief from duty, which metic status would suggest, and Vidal-Naquet's identification of the coryphaeus as a potential *prostates* seems to stretch the point.

Since scholars wish to assign a status to Oedipus in Athens, we

---

50. Vernant and Vidal-Naquet, *Myth and Tragedy*, 352.

should examine the most likely possibility. One status remains that is
so obvious that scholars have seemed amazingly reluctant to recognize
it. Oedipus is a *xenos* in Athens. Before and after 637, that is the one consistent identity that Sophocles grants his hero while in Athens. The
Oedipus at Colonus, the last play of the classical Athenian democracy,
discusses, describes, and examines *xenia,* the oldest Greek social institution. And the play's author finds it worthy.

For the Athenians, *xenia* was an ancient institution that still existed
into their own era. It operated off of an exchange of benefactions, and it
recognized the autonomy of the participants. To recall Murnaghan's
discussion, *xenos* itself was a status, a way of fixing the stranger within
a nexus of cultural and behavioral norms that guaranteed hospitality
and protection. As she observes in her discussion of the Phaiacaeans in
the *Odyssey,* to take on another status is to compromise *xenia,* an action
that may prove to be a poor bargain over time.[51]

Yet even to state that Oedipus is a *xenos* requires further investigation and has further implications for the play. For *xenia* undergoes
some changes in its long history, from the encounter of Diomedes and
Glaukos in the *Iliad* to the rather formalized rituals that we find in classical and Hellenistic Greece. We should, then, refine our discussion, in
order to see what stage of *xenia* our author has described in the *Oedipus
at Colonus* and, if we can locate Oedipus somewhat firmly in the development of *xenia,* how the particular status of the hero effects our reading of the work.

There are some givens. As Herman notes, *xenia* is a relationship that
exists between individuals who originate from different political
groups. One cannot be a *xenos* to a member of one's own city or tribe.[52]
As we see from the *Odyssey, xenia* is presumptive, assumed to exist and
to be appropriate whenever the stranger arrives in a group. To fail in
one's obligations of *xenia* incurs justifiable criticism, such as Echeneus
leveled against Alcinous in book 7 of the *Odyssey.* To recall Finley,
quoted earlier, the basic assumption that "all strangers are from Zeus"
made real social advance possible.

Moreover, in the heroic age, *xenia* tended to be absolute: only egre-
gious violations of hospitality, such as those committed by the suitors
against Odysseus' household and, eventually, against Odysseus him-

51. *Disguise and Recognition,* 95–96.
52. Herman, *Ritualised Friendship,* 11–13.

self, could terminate it. Ultimately, it was a heroic prerogative. As Herman puts it:

> For the poet, adherence to the code of guest-friendship was a supreme manifestation of the hero's free exercise of prowess. There was, in his world, neither overlord to demand feudal allegiance, nor communal group to claim social responsibility. The hero, the supreme pinnacle of a small social pyramid, was under no involuntary obligation to anyone. The guest-friendships he contracted were his own private affair.[53]

By contrast, in the historical age, *xenia* became less absolute, by necessity.

> But the community tamed the hero, and transformed him into a citizen. The citizen was an entirely new creation— a social type subjected to compulsory regulations.[54]

Hence, *xenia* could now be overridden by other considerations. The duties that the citizen incurred toward the polis could conflict with the obligations imposed by guest-friendship, to the disability of the latter. Thus, *xenoi* might face each other in battle for their respective cities. We can thus see that two types of *xenia* develop, which may be termed heroic and civic. Sophocles, living in a period in which civic *xenia* was a common practice, while working in a poetic tradition that recognized heroic *xenia* from its earliest times, could conceivably portray one or the other or could borrow elements from both to create an intermediate state.

In both heroic and civic *xenia* encounters happen by chance, but in the incidents preserved from historical times, a pattern emerges.

> Two strangers (not necessarily enemies, it must be stressed) are first brought together. The prospect of a violent exchange looms over the encounter. Violence is averted, however, mostly against common expectations, by some generous gesture.

---

53. Ibid., 2.
54. Ibid., 2.

From this common pattern, Herman decides,

> We must infer the existence of a stylised etiquette, made up of cer-
> emonials, a technical language, and a whole series of ritualistic
> devices.[55]

Among these were perhaps a mediator, oaths, the handshake, or some
type of formal agreements (*spondai*).

In Sophocles' play, we see only occasional indications of civic *xenia*.
Much more often in the work, the playwright makes use of the heroic.
Oedipus first encounters a *xenos*, a local man, in the grove of the
Eumenides. It is a telling detail that the *xenos* has no name, no identity
except as a stranger, who is to Oedipus as Oedipus is to him. Thus, their
meeting is governed by the aforementioned Homeric nicety that "all
strangers are from Zeus." It need not have fallen out that way, of
course. Sophocles could have assigned the *xenos* a name, but he preferred to keep the suggestion of *xenia* before us in the early part of the
play. Just as in the case of the inadvertent trespass into the grove, we
are reminded of the element of "accident" that Herman observes as a
commonplace in the meeting or development of *xenoi*.

Oedipus maintains throughout that he bears a gift for Athens and
that he seeks one in return. Interestingly enough, never do the words
euergētes or *euergesia* appear in the course of the drama, although the
words do appear in Sophocles. Vidal-Naquet would have us accept
that Sophocles does portray his hero as an *euergētes*, but in maintaining
this position he fails to recognize an important distinction. To the
Athenian audience, *euergesia* must have suggested a person badly in
need of help.[56] Both practical politics and drama forbid such a portrayal. Athens may find help useful, but Oedipus can scarcely persuade
the king that it is necessary, even with the discourse on the effect of

---

55. Ibid., 43.

56. Herman writes: "On the contrary, *euergesia* was unabashedly recognized
as a secular strategy in the conduct of interpersonal relations. The benefactor
put the beneficiary in a state of indebtedness, from which state the beneficiary
could only redeem himself by a display of submission and loyalty—and that
was all there was to it" (*Ritualised Friendship*, 48–49). To suggest *euergesia* in the
context of the play demands that we imagine either Theseus or Oedipus hum-
bled: neither is likely to be in that state.

time.[57] And Oedipus, it seems, would be unlikely to use the term for the favor he seeks, even if it might seem appropriate. He has avoided *hiketeia* as unworthy of his heroic status. It would follow that Oedipus would decline to use *euergesia,* which might conjure up a related image. For either Theseus or Oedipus to look on their mutual favors as *euergesiai* would be to deny their own heroic status. It is a fine distinction, but since Sophocles observed it, so should we.

There is a meeting but no mediator in the historical sense. Even the *xenos* from Colonus, who went to fetch Theseus, cannot really serve this function, since Oedipus had not announced his identity when the *xenos* left. Indeed, Sophocles falls back on the old expedient of rumor and reputation, perhaps to avoid a nuance that might imply civic, rather than heroic, *xenia.* Finally, there are no oaths or pledges: Oedipus will not hear of it, and Theseus does not really offer.

Theseus refers to Oedipus as his *doruxenos,* a term that implies some ancient hereditary alliance between the two cities of Thebes and Athens. It is nowhere else mentioned, and Sophocles probably invented it for the purpose of this play. *Doruxenia* does, however, justify Theseus' decision to use the Athenian cavalry to aid Oedipus and to recover his abducted daughters, precluding the need for some obligation created from a citizenship Oedipus never seeks or receives or from a supplication he never performs. Since Oedipus is a *doruxenos,* he can claim the same duty from the Athenian king.

It is interesting to note, in this context, that the two heroes do not really know each other. When Oedipus arrives in Colonus, he has to ask the identity of the king in the *astu,* even though, as Sophocles has made clear, he has long since known that he is in the polis of Athens. In turn, Theseus recognizes Oedipus by his ghastly appearance and by his reputation. They recognize mutual obligations on account of a pact, a preexistent system, rather than on the basis of their own personal relationship.

In short, then, we have Theseus and Oedipus already bound by *doruxenia,* which, by Sophocles' time, has lost much of its particular distinction and is really just *xenia.* Sophocles would have us take *doruxenia* more seriously, and more specifically, in this play than his contempo-

---

57. As Oedipus observes, "You will not call Oedipus a useless resident" (627).

raries do in the political world. The playwright, therefore, uses the term, in this scene of acceptance of Oedipus by the Athenian king, to recall the heroic *xenia*, of the sort found in the *Iliad*—a preexisting condition that mandates the actions of mutual gift giving, Oedipus granting the favor of his tomb, Theseus granting Oedipus' burial. The reciprocity of gift, then, confirms the relationship that Sophocles had invented between the two houses and creates continuity. Clearly, heroic *xenia* is called for, since Theseus takes on the role of hero far more than he does that of the democratic patriot frequently envisaged in Euripides. His action in calling out the cavalry to defend Oedipus and his daughters is simply arbitrary and conforms precisely to the standards of heroic behavior described by Herman and to the older concept of *doruxenia*.

Two additional features confirm the dominance of *xenia* as the governing consideration of Oedipus' arrival and stay in Athens. As Herman points out, *xenoi* were frequently responsible for specific duties toward each other. Two particular obligations were (1) providing for the burial of a *xenos* and the maintenance of his tomb (the masculine is advisable here: female *xenai* are virtually unattested, even in myth) and (2) taking care of the offspring of the *xenos*. Both occur in the *Oedipus at Colonus*. Oedipus entrusts the secret of his final resting place only to Theseus and advises that the king reveal the secret only to his own descendant. And, of course, he asks Theseus to look after his daughters. It is not the king's fault that they decide to seek destiny in Thebes.

It might fairly be objected that these last two tasks that Theseus undertakes for Oedipus smack more of civic, than heroic, *xenia*—a fair observation, yet not that remarkable. Recall Herman's statement (quoted earlier) that "the community tamed the hero, and transformed him into a citizen." For Oedipus, as Vidal-Naquet observed, his pollution makes that impossible. Yet Theseus, though he is unquestionably a hero, must perforce, as king, also be a part of his polis. The physical setting of the *Oedipus at Colonus* suggests, as Segal says, transitions and disjunctions—upper and lower worlds on a vertical plane, city and country on the horizontal.[58] On the cultural level, then, we have the heroic and the civic, with Oedipus and Theseus each maintaining as much of his heroic identity as possible. Here and only here, on the wilds at the edge of the polis (a gross exaggeration of course, as I dis-

---

58. *Tragedy and Civilization*, 368 ff.

cuss in the next chapter), can Oedipus finally be reconciled to civilization—a hero, tamed to the very minimum by the polis. Theseus, with broader responsibilities, still manifests his heroic nature, making as few allowances as possible.

So, in this play, *xenia* is to be discerned over *hiketeia,* and *empalin* is to be read over *empolin.* No matter how one tries to preserve Musgrave's emendation of 637, the effort must fail. It was no part of Sophocles' dramatic plan to civilize his hero, beyond the bare necessities for the plot. Reading the indefensible *empolin* can only confuse the issue. Sophocles knew what he wanted when he wrote *chora{i}* in the same line. He sought a geographical resolution for his hero's life, not a political one. Oedipus had to die somewhere, and for various reasons, Attica and Colonus are preferable. But Sophocles wished to emphasize that his hero was more integrally a part of the land than a part of the city.

As to a "type" for the play? Following too closely superficial points of similarity between plays can be hazardous, as Reinhardt observed.[59] Certainly, suppliant drama proved a very weak contributing element in the structure of the *Oedipus at Colonus,* offering, at best, a framework. However, that disclaimer having been made, one play, or one part of a play, does come to mind in a discussion of *xenia* and may be worth a look.

In Euripides' *Heracles Mainomenos* (henceforth referred to as *Heracles*), the protagonist, made insane by Lyssa at the instigation of Hera and Iris, kills his wife and his children. When he recovers his wits, he surveys the damage that he has done and resolves to kill himself to bury the shame. While he screws up his resolve to commit suicide, he sees Theseus coming toward him at a distance and resolves to cover his head. At this crucial juncture, Theseus arrives. The Athenian hero had come to Thebes to repay a great debt. Heracles, in the course of his twelfth labor, had rescued Theseus from the underworld, where the Athenian had gone with Peirithous, and now Theseus had come to assist Heracles, whose kingdom had been taken by Lycus, a usurper (1168). Theseus, after much discussion, manages to persuade Heracles to return with him to Athens, where he will share his home and resources with the fallen legend. Heracles agrees and returns with the king to Athens.

Here we have the same story as Oedipus', told in a different way. A hero is destroyed by the realization of the evil he has wrought. Hera-

---

59. *Sophocles,* 241 (quoted in chap. 2).

cles' desire to end his own existence in a futile but final gesture recalls both the suicide of Ajax and the self-blinding of Oedipus. His intermediate solution, his decision to cover his head at the approach of Theseus, has a dual purpose, as he notes.

> I will cover my head with something . . . For I am ashamed at the deeds I have done, and I wish not to infect him with my own bloodguilt, nor do I wish to harm the innocent. (1159–62)

Amphitryon makes the same explanation to Theseus later.

> *Thes:* Why does he cover his wretched head?
> *Amph:* He is ashamed to be seen by you; he is ashamed at the sight of his kin, at the sight of his murdered sons. (1198–1201)

Theseus will have none of it. He approaches Heracles and tells him "to show his face to his friends" (*philoisin omma deiknunai to son*, 1215). Later, he says, in words reminiscent of his welcome to Oedipus:

> Why wave me back, shaking your murderous hand? So that your polluted speech not touch me? . . . Rise, uncover your wretched head, look on me. Whoever is born nobly bears the blows of the gods and does not flinch. (1218–19, 1226–28)

Nobility, heroism, and obligation exceed the claims of pollution. Such is the way of heroes. Euripides' Theseus will not recognize pollution, and neither will his Sophoclean counterpart. In the *Heracles*, the point is driven home in the following exchange.

> *Her:* Why do you reveal my head to the son?
> *Thes:* Why not? Do you think that, as a man, you can corrupt the property of the gods?
> *Her:* Flee, unlucky man, from my unholy pollution.
> *Thes:* No vengeful spirit [*alastor*] comes to friends from friends. (1231–34)

Theseus will not be put off by his friend and benefactor's crimes. On the contrary, he invites Heracles to Athens with him.

Leave Thebes as the law demands and follow me to Athens. There
I will wash the stains from your hands, and I will give you a house
and part of my goods, and the gifts the people gave me for saving
their children (fourteen in all), I will give these to you. (1322–27)

Theseus' generosity will be repaid with

A worthy reward from the cities of Greece, the fame of helping a
noble man *(andr' esthlon)*. (1334–35)

Some parallels between Euripides' *Heracles* and Sophocles' *Oedipus
at Colonus* are easily adduced. The parallels are not exact, of course, but
are sufficient to reveal similarities. Euripides' Theseus invites Heracles
to return to Athens, where he will give him a home and part of his
goods. Compare this to the offer made to Oedipus at 637 of the *Oedipus
at Colonus*: Theseus uses the verb *katoikizō*, which literally means "to
establish an *oikos*."[60] In the next verse, Theseus states that Oedipus can,
if he wishes, accompany Theseus or remain.

Thus in both plays, hero offers hero a home. Nobility takes care of its
own. So Theseus reminds Heracles that those nobly born understand
the dangers attendant on the status, dangers that lesser men do not
comprehend. Because they endure the peril that the gods can bring,
heroes separate themselves from ordinary men on matters of pollution.
So, in the *Heracles*, Amphitryon sees the pollution rather than the hero,
as do his counterparts in the chorus of the *Oedipus at Colonus*. But Theseus looks beyond the externals in both cases and recognizes the hero
within. As Theseus reminds Oedipus, "You would have to tell of awful
works, indeed, to make me shudder" *(deinēn gar tin' an praxin tuchois
lexas hopoias exaphistaimēn egō,* 562–63). For Theseus, pollution is not
even an issue.[61]

---

60. Segal, in one of his many citations of the passage, renders the force of
katoikio as follows: "In this land I shall establish your dwelling *(oikos)* as one
within the city" *(Tragedy and Civilization,* 379). While I clearly disagree with his
use of *empolin*, his reading here is the closest one to being acceptable. Unfortunately, in his other citations of the verse, he makes it clear that he reads *empolin*
as "citizen."

61. Burian notes that Theseus maintains silence on the issue that had so exer-
cised the chorus just before the king's arrival ("Suppliant and Savior," 414–15).

The matter of sight and blindness in both works raises the possibility of an additional parallel. Theseus unveils Heracles. It is an obvious reminder and reversal of Heracles' rescue of Theseus from Hades.[62] It also serves as a gesture by which Theseus reaffirms the heroic bond between the two men, and it brings Heracles back into the light, enabling him to see. In the same vein, at the end of his life, Oedipus can move without a guide. In fact, he guides Theseus to the spot of the grave. Perhaps we can surmise that Theseus, by recognizing and affirming the heroic identity of the blind exile from Thebes, has returned to him his sight.

Burian makes the argument that, as Oedipus is received into Athens, "[the chorus'] fear of a polluted pariah is replaced by Theseus' spontaneous assertion of a common human bond between himself and his suppliant."[63] But that misses the point. These are not common men. A common man might have come to Colonus as a suppliant. The choristers are common men; the Amphitryons and Creons of the world are common men. Theseus and Oedipus are heroes, and that bond Theseus recognizes. Sophocles emphasizes no relationship so strongly in this play, not even Oedipus' love for his daughters.

---

62. Furley writes: "Theseus first persuades Herakles to uncover his face to his friend (1214 ff.). His speech invites a reading on two levels. Herakles has veiled himself to keep the pollution of murder from touching his friend (1155–62), and the surface meaning of Theseus' speech is simply a repudiation of this concern: no darkness *could* conceal the disaster that has fallen upon Herakles, and Theseus is ready to take a share of the burden. But a deeper meaning lies underneath: Theseus is inviting Herakles to choose the light of life over the darkness of death" (D. Furley, "Euripides on the Sanity of Herakles," in *Studies in Honour of T.B.L. Webster*, ed. J. H. Betts, J. T. Hooker, and J. R. Green [Bristol, 1986], 1:110).

63. "Suppliant and Savior," 415.

People and Places

Three localities effectively provide the backdrop against which the *Oedipus at Colonus* is set. At an immediate, physical level, Colonus dominates, a land of pleasant groves, shrines, and sacred districts, inhabited yet suitably remote, geographically distinct from the *astu*, Athens, but expressly under the jurisdiction of its king, Theseus. Out of view, but lurking ever prepotent on the horizon, we find Athens, the seat of the king and the *locus fixus* of political and moral authority. And still farther off lies Thebes, whose fratricidal squabbles intrude on the placid environs of Colonus and threaten both the moral and physical integrity of the *astu* and the deme. Thebes is, as Zeitlin has so well described it,[1] the "anti-Athens" of Greek tragedy, the polis in which things may be reliably and mechanically expected to go wrong, just as, in Athens, things may be expected to be set right.

For dramatic purposes, the three areas exist in contradistinction to each other. The relationship between Colonus and Athens conveys the sense of both the opposition and the symbiosis of city and country, as well as the attendant synergistic possibilities inherent in the unity of purpose between these evidently disparate elements.[2] Thebes and Athens, in turn, represent the discordant desires and purposes of the good and bad, or at least functional and dysfunctional, polis.[3] To each place Sophocles has assigned its own representative: for Colonus, first the *xenos* and later the entire chorus; for Athens, The-

---

1. "Theater of Self," 101–41.

2. Bernidaki-Aldous observes that in the opposition of city and country, "the dichotomy between *polis* and mother earth is clear. In spite of the difference, this pair of opposites—like so many others—consist of members closely akin to each other" (*Blindness in a Culture of Light,* 157). Kirkwood notes that the choral ode in praise of Colonus "contributes to a contrast, for the following episode brings the arrival of Creon and a sharp disturbance of the graceful tranquillity that characterized the preceding episode and reached its height in the ode" (G.M. Kirkwood, *A Study of Sophoclean Drama,* 2d ed. [Ithaca, 1994], 204).

3. Zeitlin, "Theater of Self," particularly 105 and 129–41.

seus; and for Thebes, Creon. In the presence of these three characters
(treating the *xenos* and the chorus as a corporate whole), in the immediate setting of the grove, with the great cities looming in the background, Oedipus reveals, asserts, and maintains his heroic identity
against all comers, allowing us to contrast or compare him to foe and
benefactor alike. In art as in life, comparison to friend and enemy,
rather than portrayal in isolation, best defines and delineates the individual. A close look at locales and characters, then, should reward our
investigation. A line of approach must be posited, even if it seems
artificial. As ever in this play, subjects and themes intertwine, rendering discreet analysis of individual components problematic at best.
Still, some order should be imposed, although the drama itself does
not always permit us to find clear, precise divisions. Colonus stands
first, then its residents. Athens and Thebes, the two great poleis, each
must be taken in their turn, and in final position are Theseus and his
Theban counterpart, Creon.

Colonus

Pride of place, by both its importance to the drama and the regional
affinity and loyalty of the author, must go to Colonus. Scholars, taking
their lead from the choral ode (668–719), have generally agreed on the
beauty of the landscape.[4] Indeed, few of the physical settings for Greek
plays have received so much discussion. And this should not surprise
us, for no locale in tragedy has been so lovingly or thoroughly portrayed. As Knox said of the choral passage in praise of Athens
(668–719),

> The ode which precedes Creon's entry sings praise of Colonus
> and of Attica . . . as Sophocles knew and loved it: the thick shade
> of trees, the nightingales in their branches, the ivy, the dew on the
> narcissus, the golden crocus, the river waters, the olive groves, the
> horses, the sea.[5]

In his splendid re-creation of the landscape of his native deme,
Sophocles chooses from the outset to emphasize the remoteness and

---

4. Jebb gives a detailed account of the play's landscape in his *Oedipus at
Colonus*, xxiv–xxx.

5. *Heroic Temper*, 154.

wildness of the place. Sensory stimulation first compels and excites the attention of Antigone. A preliminary examination discloses to her that the grove, patently a holy site, teems with laurel, olive, and grapes, and echoes with the voices of nightingales (15–18). Yet the sense of wilderness that dominates her initial description of the place is augmented and to some extent contradicted by her subsequent recognition that beyond the grove lie habitations, and she realizes that she and her father have not come to an area as remote, perhaps, or as desolate as her first impressions have suggested.[6]

In due course a local inhabitant, the *xenos* of the play, arrives. As the travelers learn from the native (36–63), the entire area is consecrated to Poseidon and Prometheus; the immediate district lies under the protection of the eponymous hero of the place, the horseman Colonus; and the particular spot into which Oedipus has wandered is dedicated to the "all-seeing Eumenides" *(tas panth' horōsas Eumenidas),* familiar to tragic audiences from Aeschylus' *Eumenides.*[7] Thus the *xenos* confirms Antigone's intuited appreciation of the numinousness of the place. Other revelations follow, as Oedipus and Antigone also discover both the sentimental and the political attachments that obtain in Colonus. The district is the *ereisma* (stay or support) of Athens, much loved by its inhabitants, and it falls under the political sway of the ruler of the *astu,* Theseus.

After the *xenos* departs to fetch Theseus, the chorus itself appears, and its members begin their search for the interloper, Oedipus, who has taken refuge just out of their sight. They supplement for the audience the earlier observations of Antigone as they communicate more vividly the sense of religious awe that the grove holds for them.

> Who was this wanderer, this old wanderer? Not a native, certainly. No native would walk upon the untrod grove or would risk offending the indomitable Maidens, whom we fear even to

---

6. The presence of nearby habitations is crucial to the atmosphere of the play. As Segal notes: "For him [Oedipus] the point of return is not a desolate island, a lonely cave, or the remote summit of a mountain but a sacred grove which serves as the border between city and wild. Like Oedipus himself, it is both part of the civic order and outside of it" (*Tragedy and Civilization,* 364).

7. Given that Pausanias 1.27.6 affirms the presence of a memorial to Oedipus within the shrine of the Eumenides on the Areopagos, it is tempting to conclude that Sophocles merely took note of the presumed sympathy between the goddesses and the exile and created a story and a setting to dramatize the union.

name. We pass them by in silence without looking, speaking, or
making any sound at all. (123–31)

Thus they reaffirm the presence of the spiritual powers latent in the
grove, as they make clear the authority that the *tas panth' horōsas
Eumenidas* command. For a better sense of the physical terrain, its
appearance rather than its importance, we must wait as first Ismene
and then the king himself appear on the scene and discharge their
respective dramatic obligations of exposition (Ismene) and the recognition and acceptance of the hero into Attica (Theseus).

After no little interval, Sophocles presents a detailed description of
the eventual resting place of the protagonist, in the choral ode that follows Theseus' reception of Oedipus into the land (668–719). Throughout these verses the description of the physical landscape dominates,
allied to the reiterated discussion of the religious awe that Colonus
and its sacred grove inspire. In the first strophe (668–80), the chorus
notes the clear voice of the nightingale, the wine-dark ivy, and the
berries in the sunless, windless glade. Mortals do not go to this place
where the god Dionysus conducts his nightly revels. In these verses
Sophocles offers a landscape simultaneously imbued with all manner
of associations with death and yet brimming with life, a place fre-
quented by the archetypal divinity of death and resurrection. The
presence of the nightingale, the bird so frequently connected with
death and mourning, confirms the evident antithesis.[8] The following
antistrophe (681–93) expands the scope of the chorus' depiction, on
both the physical and spiritual planes. On the physical plane, the choristers mention the narcissus (ever the flower of the dead) and the crocus, fed by the tributaries of the Cephisus. By so doing, they move the
physical parameters from the immediate grove to the Academy and
prepare for a broader discussion of Attica itself. On the spiritual plane,
the choristers expand the catalog of relevant divinities by mentioning
Demeter and Persephone Kore (the *megalain theain* of 683), the Muses,
and Aphrodite.

Sophocles' purpose in grouping these named divinities is not obvious, and therefore his choice requires more detailed analysis. Dionysus,

---

8. See McDevitt, "The Nightingale and the Olive," 52–54, for an excellent
discussion of the connotations of the nightingale, in Greek myth in general and
in Sophocles.

Demeter, Persephone, the Muses, and Aphrodite—why name these? For Jebb, the mention of ivy and vine was sufficient to merit the inclusion of Dionysus, and in this context he noted the association of the god with Demeter at Eleusis, in his manifestation as Iacchos.[9] McDevitt observed that the mention of Dionysus, as a god of death and rebirth, connects the strophe to the allusion to Demeter and Persephone Kore and thus presents the chthonic aspect of Dionysus, appropriate to the theme of death and rebirth that runs through the play.[10] Segal observes the chthonic and Olympian connotations of Dionysus and combines them with the Olympian aspects of Aphrodite to develop the connection with the Olympians (Zeus, Athena, and Poseidon) mentioned later in the ode.[11]

These observations are all well and good, as far as they go. Death and rebirth recur as themes in both this particular ode and the entire play. After all, the assurance of the power of Oedipus' grave to provide a blessing to the land that receives him suggests a sort of triumph over death (although a very limited one, as I discuss in chapter 6), and the reassertion of his heroic identity during the play, after his long suffering and exile, indicates a rejuvenation of spirit in the face of what was, at least, a metaphorical death. However, some difficulties with the passage have been overlooked. When the *xenos* mentions the local deities, he mentions Poseidon, Prometheus, and the Eumenides. We need not worry about the latter. Repeated mention affirms their presence throughout. But why does he mention Prometheus? The choral ode omits mention of him entirely. Also, the *xenos*, in the course of his account of the deities of the place, made no mention of Demeter, Persephone, or Dionysus. Where has Prometheus gone, and what has induced the playwright to mention the others? Is the location of the hill of Demeter Euchloos, about one-eighth of a mile north of Colonus, adequate to account for her presence? The progression of the ode suggests spatial movement in the opposite direction, toward the Academy.

---

9. *Oedipus at Colonus,* 149. Bernidaki-Aldous expounds at some length on the possible Eleusinian connections, in her epilogue "Oedipus and Demeter" (*Blindness in a Culture of Light,* 192–213). Of course, the location of his eventual resting place, near the hill of Demeter Euchloos, makes such an identification more attractive. However, we should note that the chorus is not yet aware of the site of the grave.

10. "The Nightingale and the Olive," 54.

11. *Tragedy and Civilization,* 374.

The remainder of the antistrophe may offer scope for alternative critical suggestions and may allow us to postulate an iconography of sorts.
Two other names appear with the allusion to Demeter and Persephone
in the antistrophe: the Muses and Aphrodite. Jebb connects them by
geography: the Muses have a shrine in the neighboring Academy, as
Pausanias states, and Euripides mentions Aphrodite in connection with
the Cephisus, the river described in the antistrophe.[12] However, more
may be at work here. Aphrodite, like Dionysus, Demeter, and Persephone, has chthonic associations. Thus Pausanias mentions cults of
Aphrodite Melainis at Corinth and Phokis (2.2.4, 9.27.5). Further, as
Jebb notes, she is frequently associated with Demeter and her daughter.[13] Moreover, through the story of Adonis, she is linked to themes of
death and rebirth.

Thus, with Aphrodite's inclusion we now have the collocation of
four deities, each with chthonic associations, each with personal
mythologies that incorporate the theme of death and resurrection. By
themselves, their associations with a theme so integral to the play can
easily allow their inclusion into the dramatic landscape. The presence
of the Muses on the list, however, leads the inquiry into another
direction.

Drama was an integral part of Athens' celebration of the festival of
Dionysus, the recognition by the polis that the earth had survived for
another year and that birth and renewal had once again conquered
death and decay. As a result, a reference to Dionysus alone in a tragic
context may survive as a commonplace or perhaps as a prophylactic
against that overused Attic critique "What has this to do with Dionysus?"[14] To alert his audience that, in this choral ode, he had more in
mind than simply a pro forma reference to the god (in connection to the
ivy and the vine), the poet needed to intensify the image. For in this
play, the sense of rebirth and rejuvenation, of life after life, is so critical
that the invocation of Dionysus by himself would scarcely do these
themes justice. By adding other divinities with similar associations,
Sophocles in effect amplifies the message. And by the presence of the

---

12. Jebb, *Oedipus at Colonus*, 147–52; Pausanias 1.30.2; Euripides *Medea* 835.
13. *Oedipus at Colonus*, 152.
14. For a discussion of the significance of the remark, see J. Winkler and F.
Zeitlin, eds., *Nothing to Do with Dionysus: Athenian Drama in Its Social Context*
(Princeton, 1990), 3–4.

Muses, he accomplishes something else, perhaps far more important to the poet himself.

The Muses are, for the purposes of general taxonomy, goddesses of artistic inspiration. Sophocles, by including them in a poetic landscape so evocative of death and rebirth, forces the audience to recall and acknowledge the presence of art, the conscious exercise of creative skill, in the midst of natural forces that seem to presage the eventual destiny of his hero.[15] Once we establish the presence of art in the scene, we must consequently admit the presence of the artist. In this pastoral description of his native deme, Sophocles in effect leaves his own calling card, a reminder to his audience that the poet controls the scene at hand.[16]

Against this suggestion, one might argue that the poet in reality reminds us of his existence throughout the play simply by the fact of the text itself. In response to such a potential critique, let us consider both the scene and its overall significance to the play and the Oedipus myth. As to that scene, the poet portrays nothing less than the land in which Oedipus—the exile, the incestuous parricide, the outcast; a man hopelessly defiled by his sins, irreparably scarred by his actions; the man who collapses all differentiations and embodies all contradictions—can be reintegrated into civic life from the wild.[17] He is introduced not into the town—recall that Oedipus specifically declines the opportunity to return to the *astu* with Theseus (643–46)—but at least into habitable space, if only on the (somewhat artificially created) frontier of the polis. The polis, as Herman observed, tamed the hero and made him a citizen.[18]

---

15. Segal observes something along the same lines when he remarks, "The singing nightingale in the sunless, windless grove, the beauty of the narcissus, the light of the crocus amid the dim foliage suggest a crossing of life and death not only for Oedipus and not only for Athens, but also for Sophocles' art: something in touch with the sources of vital energy that lie beyond human control, a promise of transfiguring brilliance in the midst of darkness" (*Tragedy and Civilization,* 374–75). He also notes that the presence of the Muses in the grove "alludes to the great public festivals through which the city expresses its consciousness of its civilizing functions" (376).

16. For a parallel situation, cf. Segal's discussion of Polyneices' willing acceptance of his role as a tragic hero (*Tragedy and Civilization,* 389).

17. On this question of Oedipus' collapsing of temporal boundaries, see chap. 1 and the discussions of Zeitlin ("Theater of Self," 128) and Vernant (Vernant and Vidal-Naquet, *Myth and Tragedy,* 215).

18. Herman, *Ritualised Friendship,* 3.

Oedipus cannot become a citizen, for he cannot be so tamed. Indeed, as his ferocity toward his apparently, if unconvincingly, repentant son demonstrates, even the long years of suffering have scarcely impacted on his stormy disposition. If Oedipus can exist in the polis at all, he must do so on the fringes.

Tragedy, as Euben observed, was the medium in which the mediation of conflicts between hero and polis was portrayed.[19] By portraying Colonus as the land that brings together so many deities with chthonic, resurrective, and therefore tragic associations and the divinities who sanction artistic endeavor, the poet subtly announces that he, the tragedian, has created the space in which the most intractable of tragic heroes can be reconciled to a civic life that otherwise could offer no place to him. Sophocles himself defines the terms of reunification. The chthonic deities in attendance guarantee the successful termination of Oedipus' life, but only in the narrow space that the artist provides. The artist must be present to focus the audience on the process of reintegration.

Herein, perhaps, we find an element of that compensation for the hero that critics invariably feel takes place in the play. There is no compensation from the gods, no active effort on their part to restore something to the hero that they had taken away. They had never taken away his *gennaion*, and they could never return his kingdom or his lost years. Oedipus denies even the possibility of recompense, and the words of Apollo, spoken long since, remind us that, in the long run, the protagonist can no more avoid his eventual status as a cult hero than he could his fate as a parricide, pollution, or exile. Yet recompense does exist, if not from the gods, then from the poet. The *Oedipus at Colonus* is about nothing so much as the recognition that the gaunt, hideously marred, blind exile is truly a hero. Yet no transformation takes place within Oedipus. As Sophocles shows from the initial encounter between Oedipus and the *xenos*, the hero still abides within the broken shell of the man, where he has always been, unaltered by the external forces that have battered him. What has been transformed in the course of the play is the perception that the other characters, except Theseus, have of the hero. By logical extension, the perception that the Athenian audience has of Oedipus changes as well. Yet that transformation can be

---

19. See Euben's introductory chapter to *Greek Tragedy and Political Theory*, particularly 26–38.

achieved only through tragedy.[20] The drama cannot change the hero, for he has created, through incest, parricide, and self-blinding (the latter his method of prematurely aging himself), such a twisted, skewed existence that he defies all external change, and his own self-acknowledged *gennaion* precludes any internal change.[21] But the drama can change those who witness it. We can see the hero in a truer light, define heroism in a more generous and noble manner, though only with the tragedian as our guide. The real, political world can never create a space for the heroic contradictions that Oedipus embodies; the world of tragedy can. What Pindar states bluntly of poets and athletes, Sophocles says obliquely of poets and heroes; they stand in a very special relationship to one another, one that sets them apart from the unwashed masses, and the hero needs the poet. Ordinarily, though, the hero needs the poet only to tell the story. In the case of the *Oedipus at Colonus*, the hero needed the poet to finish the story. As I observed in chapter 1, Sophocles' could simply have left the story of his Oedipus unresolved, left him to wander, blind, broken, and exiled, both literally and figuratively. But Sophocles brought him home.

In light of this asseverated importance of the dramatist, let us consider the second strophe and antistrophe of the ode. The second strophe (694–706) reminds us of the importance of the olive and of the goddess Athena to the city. The olive is called "fearful to the foes' spears" (*egcheōn phobēma daiōn*). It is unique to Athens, found neither in Asia nor in the Peloponnesus. And the patroness of the city cherishes it beyond all other plants. She watches over the olive, as the olive provides the means by which men watch over her city. In the final antistrophe (707–19), Sophocles counters the gift of Athena with the twin gifts of Poseidon, the horse (and thereby the cavalry) and the ship (and thereby the fleet).[22] The reference to the horse is easy and anticipated. Colonus, as the *xenos* informed the wanderers at the outset of the play, took its name from an ancient Athenian knight, and at the very begin-

---

20. Thus, for Vidal-Naquet, tragedy has as a primary duty the task of "expatriating" conflict and presenting the city as a unified whole, free of any divisive behavior (Vernant and Vidal-Naquet, *Myth and Tragedy*, 333).

21. In this way, he recalls Ajax, whose suicide placed him beyond time and, therefore, change.

22. For a full discussion of the possibilities entailed by the mention of Poseidon, see T. Stinton, "The Riddle at Colonus," *GRBS* 17 (1976): 323–28.

ning of the ode stands the word *euippou*, "well horsed" or "[blessed with] good horses."

The playwright offers a succession, then, of equivalents: tragedy; the olive, a symbol of peace and commercial success; and the cavalry and fleet, emblematic of military power. On this reading the poet demands the necessity of recognizing tragedy on a level with the other vital elements that preserve the state. Euben has observed wisely that the *choregos*, who produced plays, and the trierarch, who provided the means to keep a ship in the fleet, were liturgies on the same level in Athens, as though each were equally vital to the defense of the country.[23] The poet makes that very claim here, in the *ereisma* of Athens, in, as the choral ode notes at the outset, the "strongest *(kratista)* refuge of the land" (668–69),[24] where city and country meet, where olive and horse and (by connection to Poseidon) fleet flourish, where tragedy sets the conditions for the reintegration of the outcast—here, where Athens exemplifies the best characteristics of the polis.

A consequent question arises: why is the play set in Colonus? The traditional answer—that Sophocles was born in Colonus and wishes in this work to offer some homage to his native deme—is adequate in itself but not particularly inspired. Except for its connection to the poet, Colonus does not necessarily provide a good location for the setting of the play. Critics routinely disregard a problem that Sophocles' choice of setting creates, for it involves a question of verisimilitude that Greek tragedy generally requires us not to ask. Once the question is asked, however, the motives that underlay Sophocles' selection of his native deme become clearer, and our interpretation of the work becomes richer.

Oedipus has, on his own testimony, advanced very far into Attica and held converse with the local people before, yet only at Colonus does he first enter into conflict with locals.[25] This conflict in turn leads to his encounter with the king and his consequent acceptance. Critics have not on this matter suggested a problem. But something rather unique in Greek tragedy has happened here.

The Athenian dramatists routinely distort time and space. Invariably, they resort to choral passages to provide whatever indication of

---

23. *Greek Tragedy and Political Theory*, 22–23.

24. For *epaula* as refuge, see McDevitt, "The Nightingale and the Olive," 52.

25. Jebb notes that Oedipus most likely came into Colonus on the road that led ultimately to Oenoe (*Oedipus at Colonus*, xxv–xxvi).

passed time they need, be it for a king to travel from Athens to Eleusis or Marathon or for a hunted man to make the trek from Delphi to the Acropolis. Sophocles does just this in the *Oedipus at Colonus*, when the chorus sings its "battle stasimon," as Burian calls it,[26] to cover the action while Theseus and his cavalry retinue chase down Creon's henchmen and force them to yield their captives. In this play, however, Sophocles distorts space in quite a different way. Whereas the authors of most Greek plays compress the dimension, Sophocles expands it.

Sophocles presents us with a Colonus that is numinous yet vibrant, remote but inhabited. However, the remoteness is a matter of dramatic contrivance rather than fact, for in the physical world (the constraints of which drama need not recognize), Colonus stands but a mile or so northwest of the Acropolis. Sophocles embarks on this process of expanding space right from the beginning of the play. In 14–15, Antigone tells her father that she can see the towers *(purgoi)* that ring the city "far-off" *(prosō)*.[27] But according to Jebb's map, the sacred grove lies only three-quarters of a mile from the city wall, to which the audience would have doubtless made reference.[28] Towers on a city wall, while perhaps not seeming imminent, would scarcely be described as "far-off by sight" *(ap' ommatōn prosō)*.[29] Sophocles has, then, at the outset of the play, chosen to exaggerate the distance from Athens to Colonus in order to foster an illusion that Colonus lies on some distant stretch of the Attic frontier.

Later, we have another distortion. After Oedipus has successfully deflected the chorus' attempt to drive him from the land, he asks if Theseus is coming. Having discovered that the *xenos* whom he met earlier in the sacred grove has gone to fetch the king, and assuming that Theseus will certainly hasten when he learns that Oedipus has arrived, Oedipus wonders aloud who will tell the king his name, since he had not revealed his identity to the *xenos* before he left. The chorus

---

26. "Suppliant and Savior," 421.

27. "Far-off" is Ellendt's reading of *proso* (*Lexikon Sophocleum*, 669).

28. Jebb, *Oedipus at Colonus*, 281

29. At the risk of once again trying the reader's patience, a personal observation may be relevant here. I can sit in my office and see without difficulty the buildings of a mall located about four miles away. I doubt that I would describe them as "far-off," although I would not exactly consider them close. Towers located on a city wall less than a mile from the viewer would, by this standard, at least, seem rather close.

responds, "the road is long" (*makra keleuthos*, 303). This is not true in the real world, in which people like the sturdy townsman must have tracked much greater distances with ease.[30] The question remains, then, why Sophocles chose to emphasize this small but distorted point twice in the early part of the play, for it is almost certainly a matter of artistic contrivance.

A singularly unattractive possibility is, of course, that he had left his final work unfinished, not having ironed out any possible inconsistencies. This argument looks defensible, at least, in view of the somewhat puzzling details of the exchange between the chorus and Oedipus over the eventual appearance of Theseus. Jebb's explanation of the passage renders, if nothing else, a good sense of the confusion. He begins:

> 299–307 The *xenos* must have been sent to Athens before they [the chorus] came to the grove (117), and could not, therefore, know the name of Oedipus (first disclosed at 222). He could only tell Theseus that there was a blind stranger at Colonus, who hinted at his own power to confer benefits (72), and who looked noble (76). Theseus, on entering (551), at once greets Oedipus by name, though he had never seen him before (68). He had divined the identity through a knowledge of history (553)—i.e., he started from Athens on the strength of what the *xenos* could tell. And on the way to Colonus (adds Theseus) he has been made certain of the fact (554)—i.e., he had heard the name. The dramatist meant this passage to account for the instant confidence of the recognition by Theseus.[31]

And a little later, he writes:

> 301 ff. *keleuthos:* cp. 164. Some wayfarers, passing by Colonus towards Athens, may have heard the prolonged tumult of horror

---

30. Stockton points out that "a fit man in his prime whose home was only a dozen or so miles away needed four hours of brisk walking to reach Agora or Pnyx" (D. Stockton, *The Classical Athenian Democracy* [Oxford, 1990], 6). Thus, he establishes three miles per hour as his normal pace. This may be low. According to my own treadmill, I can walk four miles per hour. Of course, the treadmill allows perfect walking conditions. I have taken seventeen minutes for the mile walk from Colonus to Athens as an average.

31. *Oedipus at Colonus,* 104.

which greeted the name of Oedipus (222). As the distance to the
city is more than a mile, there will be many chances for the news
to be caught up from there lips, and carried to Theseus.[32]

As mentioned earlier, this play has been somewhat liable to criticism
generated by a belief that old age had in some way negatively impacted
on Sophocles' dramatic abilities. Wilamowitz-Moellendorf himself
defended the play against charges of hasty revision.[33] This evidently
contrived account of the circumstances that permit Theseus to recognize Oedipus instantly has been mentioned in this context, and in fact it
does look like a clumsy attempt at a facile correction of a mistake. Still,
misgivings remain. Jebb takes the spatial question at face value, as
though the mile trek from Colonus into town really constituted a great
distance. In fact, it does not. An able-bodied person should be able to
walk the distance in seventeen minutes and run it in seven. If Theseus
had ridden back, which seems likely, given that Sophocles makes a
point of declaring a cavalry engagement between Theseus and Creon's
men and suggests thereby that Theseus' retinue contained horsemen, a
return trip in under five minutes is possible.[34] At any rate, if Theseus
had, as he suggests (551–55), guessed the likely identity of the visitor,
he certainly would not have dawdled. And even if we disregard the
math, the fact remains that the distance, by the standards of everyday
travel in the Greek world, simply is not all that great. The references,
then, to people on the roads spreading rumor of the exile's arrival are
simply designed to increase the sense of distance to Athens. Segal
observes the importance of the location of the grove, on the edge of
habitable space, and the parallel to the hero.

The grove by which Oedipus enters Attica stands at the fringes of
the city but is not entirely of the wild. Like him, it has both gentle
and harsh aspects.[35]

---

32. Ibid., 105.

33. In T. von Wilamowitz-Moellendorf, *Die dramatische Technik des Sophokles*
(Berlin, 1917), 329 ff. I owe this reference to Burian, "Suppliant and Savior,"
408.

34. For a cavalry encounter and the intimation that Theseus either arrived
mounted or had ready access to horses, see lines 1059–73 and 887–89.

35. *Tragedy and Civilization*, 371.

It would not be out of place here to point out that, in fact, Oedipus had entered Attica long since. If Jebb is right, that he entered from the northwest, from Thebes, he crossed over the frontier on the road to Eleutherae and Oenoe. Hence, he had already spent considerable time in Attica. Certainly a blind man, leaning for support on his daughter, is not likely to have made good time, and besides, as they had no fixed objective, they had no reason to hurry. Oedipus arrives at Colonus by accident. Since, then, he had been in Attica for a while, why did no one report it to the king? If his fame was so extensive, as the revulsion that the chorus felt at the mention of his name would suggest, and if the hideousness of his features was so pronounced that Theseus himself suspected the identity of the traveler before anyone had actually named him, why had no one noticed Oedipus until now?

In point of fact, it is unfair to force Greek drama to consider questions of time and space as they work in the real world. But the inquiry suggests authorial intent. Sophocles had to move Colonus to the frontier in order to make it fit his story, even if in so doing he left himself saddled with distortions of time and space that the whole audience might have recognized. He wanted to create precisely the effect that Segal observed, that Oedipus ended his days stationed on the very fringes of the polis. In this way, Sophocles avoids "taming the hero" and does honor to his native deme. But this discussion has still provided at most an answer to method, not motive.

The deme makes an appearance in Greek mythology prior to that in the *Oedipus at Colonus*. Colonus was the entry point for Theseus and Peirithous' descent into the underworld. No matter how one attempts to gloss the details, the heroes embarked on a discreditable adventure. The aim of the heroes (the rape of Persephone), can scarcely be described as noble.[36] And the adventure did not come off as planned. As recorded in the most common version of the story, Theseus and Peirithous became trapped in the underworld: Theseus was ultimately rescued by Heracles, while Peirithous languished in Hades forever.

So Colonus is the site of a botched heroic venture, for which Theseus must bear at least some of the responsibility. The playwright does not

---

36. Segal would prefer that Theseus descends to Hades to rescue his friend, and that agreement is commemorated here; see *Tragedy and Civilization*, 369. Jebb hits the mark, however, with his note (*Oedipus at Colonus*, 257). Certainly, this is the version Plato has in mind at *Republic* 3.391c.

miss the opportunity to exploit the connection. Reference to the heroes' *katabasis* occurs in the messenger's report to the chorus of the last moments of Oedipus' life (1586–1666). In the course of his account, he notes the place where Oedipus stopped to allow his daughters to make final preparations for his passing.

Near the hollow where the pact of Theseus and Peirithous lies.
(1593–94)

The Greek word translated here as "pact" is *xynthēma*.

The reference and the particular word *xynthēma* suggest the additional motives for the playwright's decision to make this particular location within Attica the place in which to stage Oedipus' reconciliation to civilization. Sophocles has chosen Colonus for his setting, and Theseus for the Athenian king, with the story of Theseus and Peirithous in mind. Peter Burian elegantly entitled his essay on the *Oedipus at Colonus* "Suppliant and Saviour." Of what or of whom is Oedipus the savior? Athens, of course, is the obvious answer. But on examination, we see that Oedipus has saved Theseus as well. Oedipus has offered the Athenian king the opportunity to assert his own heroic nature by recognizing Oedipus' nature as well, by receiving the exile, by performing the function of *tapheus,* and by protecting the exile's children. And Oedipus has offered Theseus the still greater opportunity to do what he could not do for Peirithous, that is, keep his promises, in precisely the same location where he had failed earlier. The pact between Theseus and Peirithous came to naught. The agreement between Oedipus and Theseus will be kept. The city, after all, offers few opportunities for the hero to flourish. Cities are, as they must be, antiheroic. But Oedipus, merely by coming to Athens, does provide such an opportunity, and on this occasion Theseus does not fail. In short, Oedipus' arrival offers another (final?) chance to Theseus to reassert his own heroic identity.

The word *xynthema*, then, can hardly have been chosen by accident, for it has occurred earlier in the text. When Oedipus learns that he has entered the precinct sacred to the Eumenides, he refuses to leave on the grounds that he has heard the "watchword *(xynthēma)* of my fate" (46). By employing the same term in connection to the agreements made by Theseus and Peirithous, Sophocles gently reminds us that the agreements of men, regardless of the nobility of their nature, can go awry, but that the oracles of the gods do not fail, although one may not always know how they will come to pass.

The *Xenos* and the Chorus

Sophocles chose his setting with great care, to avail himself fully of the associations that Colonus held. His exploitations of those associations allowed him to demonstrate the importance of tragedy, the power of the poet, and the mutual *beneficia* required of heroes. That he employed for his chorus elders of that deme can hardly be coincidental. Furthermore, Sophocles has in effect doubled the impact of the chorus by creating a specific character, the play's *xenos*, who parallels his fellow townspeople. Their importance to the play cannot be overstated, for this is no ordinary assemblage of slaves, nurses, or miscellaneous elders. It is one of the few choruses in surviving Greek tragedy that is composed specifically of men who claim for themselves a political standing in Athens.[37]

We first meet the residents of Colonus when the *xenos* confronts Oedipus in the sacred grove. The ensuing conversation between the two men alerts us to the inconsistency between appearance and reality that marks the behavior of Oedipus throughout the play—he is beggared in appearance, heroic by nature.[38] Oedipus has violated holy ground and speaks in the grove where speech is forbidden. The *xenos* attempts to prevent Oedipus from committing sacrilege. The hero, in turn, displays his old obstinacy early.

> *Ant:* Ask him [the *xenos*] urgent questions, for the man is here.
> *Oed:* O stranger, as I learn, from her whose sight must serve both of us, that you have come to tell us what we need to know—
> *Xen:* Before you begin to question me, leave your current seat. For you walk on holy ground.
> *Oed:* What is this place? To whom of the gods is it consecrated?

---

37. Only the chorus of the *Heracleidae*, composed of old men from Marathon, comes close. The hunters that make up the chorus in the *Hippolytus* lack any real corporate identity.

38. As Burton notes, this discussion between the *xenos* and Oedipus "is a preview in miniature of the parodos and indicates the course it will take" (R.W.B. Burton, *The Chorus in Sophocles' Tragedies* [Oxford, 1980], 254).

Xen: Untouched, untrod. For the dread goddesses live here, the
daughters of Earth and Shade.
Oed: Under what name should I pray to them? (31–41)

The careful observer immediately realizes that this discussion has
gone quite contrary to the *xenos'* expectation or design. He has
instructed Oedipus to move and not to ask questions until he has done
so, since the newcomer inadvertently occupies holy ground. Oedipus,
however, instead of yielding to the *xenos'* demand, promptly ignores it
and asks a question. The *xenos'* warning, his precautionary admonition
against speech, will hardly inhibit Oedipus, especially at this late stage
in his career. As ever, given some limit, he predictably, characteristically, almost instinctively strains against it. In what better way could
the poet remind us right from the outset of the work that within the
blind, exhausted beggar, who had just so resignedly declared to
Antigone that he really needed and expected no more than a handout,
there still resides the tenacious hero who defeated the Sphinx and
strove so mightily against the oracles of Apollo?

Let us consider how the *xenos'* foiled interrogation progresses: Oedipus asks specifically which goddesses are worshiped at the place, and
when he learns that he has entered a precinct sacred to the Eumenides,
he simply announces that he will not leave. The procedure by which
the playwright accomplishes this exchange merits our admiration. For
his dramatic purposes, the poet could simply have had the *xenos* initi-
ate the discussion by announcing to the travelers that they would have
to leave the grove because it was sacred to the Eumenides, and at that
point Oedipus, relying on the terms of the prophecy, could have
refused. Instead, the *xenos* demands simply that Oedipus move before
he questions or even speaks, and Oedipus counters the opening gam-
bit, which could well be construed as intimidating, by asking two questions, in defiance of the *xenos'* command. He does this before he learns
that he has come to the place prophesied by Apollo. At the risk of pos-
ing a superfluous conjecture, the scene might have been expected by
the audience to go the other way: the *xenos,* moved by the sudden
appearance of the strangers in the sacred grove, decides for himself (or
perhaps is spurred by his fellows) to learn from the newcomers the
cause of their trespass and to correct their error. But in the presence of
a latent but overmastering authority, the *xenos* diminishes from ques-
tioner to questioned, while Oedipus, although warned to move and

keep silence, holds his ground and speaks for another 150 lines. To complete the dramatic effect, the *xenos*, who seemed so imperious at his arrival, now finds himself working as an errand runner for the stranger he originally tried to coerce. Once Oedipus declares that he will never leave the grove, the *xenos* admits that he cannot take action without the advice of the city (*poleōs dicha*, 47–48) and that he must go to seek further guidance; as we discover later (298), the same man will go to Athens to fetch the king.

At this point the *xenos* disappears, and the chorus proper soon replaces him. There has been some dispute among scholars as to the exact nature of the chorus.[39] That it is made up of men from the local deme is clear, and they unequivocally acknowledge the overlordship of the Athenian king. Beyond that, doubts and questions hold precedent over certainties and answers. What standing do the men of the chorus enjoy within the local community? Are they a landed gentry or simply aged men indistinguishable in most respects from Oedipus himself? How do they treat the blind traveler? How does Theseus deal with them, and how do they deal with the king? What dramatic function would Sophocles have them serve, and how do they compare with members of similar choruses? A close look at their actions should yield the needed answers.

As we first see them, the men of the chorus do nothing more than reprise the role of the *xenos*. They enter, seek the stranger, and, when they have discovered him, demand that he move, at least a bit, to avoid inadvertently discovering and consequently defiling the glade in which the sacrifices are offered (118–69). Oedipus complies after extracting from them a guarantee that they will not harm him (174–75). The choristers agree to his terms initially, but when from subsequent investigation they ascertain his identity, they promptly demand that he leave both the grove and the land itself (229–36). As noted in chapter 2, they have extended to the stranger a sort of presumptive *xenia*, to which strangers are always entitled as long as they do not abuse their privileges. As the choristers view the situation, however, Oedipus' mere

---

39. Burton supposes that the choristers are "simple countrymen" (*The Chorus in Sophocles' Tragedies*, 295), while Gardiner, giving greater weight to the greetings addressed to the chorus throughout the play, insists that they form a local gentry (C.P. Gardiner, *The Sophoclean Chorus: A Study of Character and Function* [Iowa City, 1987], 110 n. 38). On the whole, Gardiner's view may be revealed to be a bit more sound, although with some qualification.

name and reputation qualify as grounds to abrogate any compacts, spoken or implied. One so defiled has no right to presume anything.

Oedipus argues, convincingly, that they fear him for no reason better reason than his reputation and that they ought not for this reason alone break their earlier compact, especially in view of the favor that he offers the city (258–91). The choristers for their part consent only to leave the issue to the king, then they settle in for the far more pleasantly distasteful task of eliciting from Oedipus an account of his life.[40] In this instance, as in his earlier encounter with the *xenos*, Oedipus manages to deflect efficiently the justifiable concerns that the locals voice concerning the joint issues of trespass and pollution. The dialogue avails nothing. Though they would apparently be acting well within their rights as guardians of the place (*tēsd' ephoroi chōras*, 145) if they were to remove the intruder, both the *xenos* and the chorus discover that they are, quite simply, overmounted. In mastering the chorus at this juncture, Oedipus demonstrates the classic prerogative of the hero, to stand outside ordinary judgments of right and wrong. In fact, it is in front of this rather unappreciative audience that he first affirms the heroic nature that had lain dormant through his long years of exile. This pattern will recur later.

After the arrival of Ismene and her report of the news from Thebes, the choristers take up their now familiar role as experts in the local religion and advise Oedipus on how he can make amends to the goddesses for his inadvertent trespass. They then proceed to interrogate Oedipus about his specific sins (508 ff.), in an inquiry that Knox shrewdly observed was "almost prurient."[41] It is a telling exchange, especially given its juxtaposition to the prior discussion concerning the proper observation of religious ritual. The choristers have already heard one protestation of moral innocence from Oedipus, which he made immediately after their effort to drive him from the grove and from Attica. Now, after having demonstrated their piety and attended to their obligations to the local gods, they perform a remarkable about-face and demand, in effect, gossip. Certainly they knew the story, at least in broad outline, or they would not have attempted to force Oedipus to

---

40. Burian argues that Oedipus has won the chorus over ("Suppliant and Savior," 415, 417). Burton more correctly observes that the chorus is in fact noncommittal (*The Chorus in Sophocles' Tragedies*, 260).

41. *Heroic Temper*, 152.

leave earlier or reacted with such horror at the mere sound of his name. Theseus clearly knows the full tale of the horrors done at Thebes when he arrives on the scene, and it strains credulity to think that the chorus is less well informed. What, then, is the point of bringing up the matter? Is there really, as Gardiner has suggested,[42] a need for dramatic exposition of a story so well known in its incidentals? Why does Sophocles have the chorus behave in such a reprehensible manner?

Contrast certainly plays the key role. Our appreciation of Oedipus' stature grows, in part, in relationship to the diminishment of the stature of those around him. Sophocles sharpens our perception of the qualities of the hero all the more keenly as the other characters prove increasingly more disappointing. The choristers do not accept the hero; from them Oedipus wins no real approval. In fact, they cannot accept him, and their approval would ultimately be of no consequence, for as they explicitly state, they can do nothing one way or the other without consent of the king. To defer judgment to another scarcely qualifies as acceptance. In these passages, rather, Oedipus establishes, in his encounters with the *xenos* and the chorus, his own immeasurable superiority to the average person, in which class the choristers undoubtedly fall.[43] This is a necessary precondition of heroism, to which the poet attends with considerable alacrity. The opening of the play gave Sophocles no choice, given the visual impact that Oedipus undoubtedly had on the audience. The playwright had to make clear that the protagonist had maintained his heroic nature right from the outset of the play, then the poet had to use the subsequent encounters both to establish the magnitude of Oedipus' heroism and to portray the increasing awareness of that heroism on the part of the other characters.[44] When the choristers return to the matter of Oedipus' crimes and demand an account that can only prove redundant, they show themselves to some extent unworthy of the hero. At best, they grasp the externals of the man's life, his appearance, even his actions, which Oedipus would contend were

---

42. Gardiner, *Sophoclean Chorus*, 112 n. 40. She recognizes the inevitable contrast between Theseus and the chorus but denies its fundamental importance.

43. For the choristers as exemplars of "the average person," see Bernidaki-Aldous, *Blindness in a Culture of Light*, 164–65.

44. So Kirkwood notes that "the horror of the Colonean elders at the appearance and identity of Oedipus and at his transgression of the sacred grove emphasizes the battle that Oedipus must fight in order to vindicate himself and reveal his Beneficent Power" (*Sophoclean Drama*, 191).

external to his own *gennaion*, his own inner nobility of character. Although the choristers can feel the power of that *gennaion*, by which their own formally correct but morally inadequate religious zeal has been in a manner of speaking neutralized, they lack the heroic fiber to apprehend fully the inner power of the man. They remain fixated on the incidentals.

Having identified the choristers as representatives of the average, nonheroic person, we need still to answer the attendant question. That they are not themselves heroes is clear; but what and who are they?

We know better what is said of the choristers than who they actually are. Oedipus refers to them as the *ephoroi* of Colonus: Ellendt correctly renders this as *custos*, "guardian."[45] The term *ephor* itself can suggest governmental authority, but that possibility may not apply here. In the first place, Oedipus obviously cannot see the choristers. Thus, if they bear with them any tokens of authority, the effect would be lost on him. However, his only sure information on the locals thus far has been obtained in the course of his interview with the *xenos*. From this man Oedipus has discovered that while the *xenos* himself does not feel that he has the authority to act without the sanction of the polis, the local men do have the power to judge (*krinousi*, 79) the matters that affect the area. Of course, that power may extend only to religious matters involving the sacred precinct. Religious observance, perhaps rather than religion itself, comprises the one area in which the chorus has consistently demonstrated ample expertise.

The choristers certainly do not comprise an advisory body, at least at the highest level. Theseus takes little notice of them, and he makes his decision to receive Oedipus without asking their opinion. They do aver on their own initiative that Oedipus has, in making Theseus the offer of his tomb, spoken in the same fashion as he had earlier, but this passage (629–30) feels more like testimony than advice. Moreover, when Theseus allows Oedipus to decide whether he will accompany the king back to Athens or remain, he states, "I will appoint him [the coryphaeus] to watch over you" (*se nin taxō phulassein*, 638–39)—a royal command, not a request. Theseus then essentially repeats this message in the exchange at 652. When he asks Oedipus the reason for his unabated concern for his own safety, Oedipus replies that there are

---

45. *Lexikon Sophocleum*, 290. Gardiner argues for a more political reading (*Sophoclean Chorus*, 110 n. 38), which would suggest broad authority.

people after him. The king quickly responds, decisively but dismissively, "this will be a matter of concern for these men" *(alla toisd' estai melon)*, referring to the chorus. As far as the king is concerned, the men of the chorus are there to take orders, not to supply counsel.

The choral ode praising Colonus and Athens proves without question the choristers' affection for deme and polis alike but tells us nothing new of the choristers themselves. The *xenos* had affirmed the residents' love of their own country when he first described the locale to Oedipus. Creon's greeting in the scene immediately following does not help us much. He refers to the choristers as "noble residents" *(eugeneis oikētores,* 728). Yet this is not altogether persuasive, for Creon has reason to lie and to flatter. He can tell from the outset that the choristers fear him, and if he would avoid conflict, he must put these men at ease (729–31). Hence, his greeting may be nothing more than courtesy or, less generously, the prelude to treachery. We may see the same difficulty in reading too literally Oedipus' appeal when he realizes that his daughters are being taken and that his turn is coming: "O lords of the land" *(O gēs anaktes,* 831). A man begging for help will most likely err on the side of caution when invoking the aid of potential benefactors. On the other hand, it seems unlikely that the actors could have addressed the choristers in these terms if such address were completely incongruous. It is most likely that the choristers were well born, perhaps wealthy natives of Colonus, but with no authority whatsoever in the presence of the king.

If the testimony of the other characters does not yield with certainty a corporate identity for the choristers, do their own statements? The lone, certain fact ascertainable from the play is that they are old. So Antigone, who can see them, describes them as *chronō{i} palaioi* (112). The choristers seem to acknowledge the fact themselves when, faced with Creon's imminent approach, they comfort Oedipus by saying, "If I [we] are old, the strength of this land has not grown old" *(kai gar ei gerōn ego, to tēsde chōras ou gegēraken sthenos,* 726–27). As old men, they are perfectly placed to sing the odes on Colonus, the "battle song," the second stasimon of the play, and the lament on old age, as Burton has observed.[46]

Of the ode on Colonus, enough has been said earlier. Clearly the choral song manifested the love that the locals felt for their home, an

---

46. *The Chorus in Sophocles' Tragedies,* 251.

affection that the *xenos* had indicated previously. They sing of what is permanent and enduring in their country, possibly making an implied comparison with more ephemeral elements in the *astu*.[47] The "battle ode" and the lament on old age disclose more pessimistic aspects of the chorus and perhaps reveal, by the choristers own views on old age, something more of the greatness of Oedipus and Theseus by comparison.

The ode that the chorus sings during Theseus' pursuit of the kidnappers of Oedipus' daughters (1044–95) serves the obvious and traditional function of indicating a lapse of time. The distance to be covered was not small.[48] No difficulty obtains in discerning the meaning of the ode, which is straightforward: the choristers, unable to join the young men who aid the king in his pursuit of the Theban interlopers, imagine the chase instead and long to view their fellow citizens in battle. They mention the customary and expected deities: Ares twice, each instance a depersonalized reference to war (1047, 1065); Athena twice (1071, 1090); Zeus twice (*pantopta Zeu*, "all-seeing Zeus," 1082–83), with an ordinary reference to him at 1077; and Apollo and Artemis once each (1090–91). All except Ares are called on to aid the Athenians in their pursuit. For their part, the choristers wish for wings, in order to view the battle from above (1079–81).

The ode is straightforward yet revealing. The chorus describes "in brilliant detail the cavalry engagement."[49] A clue, perhaps, to the choral character. Were the choristers cavalrymen themselves in their younger days? Their provenience, from Colonus Hippias, might support that conclusion. In turn, this would justify an assumption that the chorus was composed of wealthy, and therefore important, local men.

Burton describes the ode, correctly, as an escape lyric, although he observes that, unlike other escape lyrics, the chorus here wishes to fly

---

47. Whitman notes that the idealized landscape described in the ode contrasts with the damage undoubtedly wrought in the course of the Peloponnesian War (*Sophocles*, 210); Burton strikes a similar note when he observes that the choristers "emphasize what in their land has resisted destruction and therefore provides a sense of permanence and a promise of comfort to the old and weary as well as a challenge to the young and vigorous" (*The Chorus in Sophocles' Tragedies*, 251–52).

48. Jebb provides an account of the proposed geography of the pursuit (*Oedipus at Colonus*, 192–95). The pursuit certainly took the Athenians to the northwest of Colonus, toward Eleusis and ultimately the deme of Oea.

49. Burton, *The Chorus in Sophocles' Tragedies*, 279.

into danger. Yet the chorus does not wish to fly so closely to danger as he thinks. The chorus would be there, but instead of saying something like "then I would teach the Thebans a lesson," in the time-honored fashion of old and garrulous warriors since Nestor, the chorus simply claims, "I'd see Theseus and the other warriors" (1055–59). The choristers real wishes are made clear at the end of the second strophe (1081 ff.), when they admit that they would like to witness the battle, not fight in it.[50] It goes without saying that this marks them as something less than heroic, in the classic sense. Indeed, coming off their dismal failure to protect Oedipus and his daughters (a role specifically assigned to them by Theseus at 652), the wish to observe rather than participate evidences, and indeed accents, the presence of a rather deficient warrior spirit. Oedipus, blind though he is, shows more heart. Of course, he has more to lose.

The ode on old age may be viewed in the same light. The chorus has one clear power as defined explicitly in the play, the right to judge matters pertaining to the sacred grove. The choristers' attempts to perform this task are frustrated by a blind beggar and a girl, and so they are forced to remand the matter to the king. The king, in turn, orders the chorus, or the coryphaeus, to look after (phulassein) Oedipus (639). But the choristers are overmastered by Creon and his men. The girls are seized, and Oedipus himself is only saved by Theseus' timely return. The choristers' description of the ensuing cavalry engagement affirms their knowledge of warfare and, presumably, their status as former warriors; but they themselves are reduced to mere observers, even in their own imagination. The weakness of their own old age has been laid bare for all to see. All that remains is to acknowledge the inevitable.

As the departure of Theseus triggered the battle ode, now the arrival of Polyneices and Oedipus' blatant discomfiture at the prospect of seeing his son serve as the excuse for the lament on old age (1211–48). Depression among the old is hardly a recent phenomenon, despite the sudden appearance of the subject in virtually all contemporary media. Homer knew of the sorrows of aging (Nestor can scarcely contain himself on the subject), and Hesiod includes old age as a child of Night.[51]

---

50. Burton states that they long to fight in the battle (*The Chorus in Sophocles' Tragedies*, 281). I find no indication of that wish, and the absence of such a commonplace desire is telling.

51. Homer *Iliad* 19.336, *Odyssey* 24.250; Hesiod *Theogony* 225. I owe these references to Burton, *The Chorus in Sophocles' Tragedies*, 286.

For the chorus, such concerns are omnipresent. To avoid being born is best, to die young a close second; but to live beyond youth is to loose all the evils: envy, civil war, strife, battles, and slaughter (1233–34). To survive to old age leaves one weak, lonely, and unloved (1236–37). In Oedipus the choristers see the worst-case possibility for themselves, a man hemmed in on all sides by misfortunes (1239–48).

Sophocles has progressed in his three choral lyrics to the point at which the lament on old age is inevitable, and it is perfectly apt for the character that he has given to his chorus. Any dramatic character may make a careful observation of his surroundings and love his country. Thus, the ode on Colonus, while perhaps slightly more effective when presented by a chorus of old men, could still have been sung by any local group of men from the area or even could have been recited by Theseus. The desire to see the battle, at root the desire simply to be elsewhere, again could have been sung by any group or any individual character who had, for any reason, been excluded from the fighting. But this lyric, the lament on old age, absolutely fits the chorus of old men. As Gardiner observes:

> So great is the strength of the alliance of old men, so deep is the chorus' understanding of Oedipus' suffering (1239), that they persuade the audience that Oedipus is not simply being stubborn and querulous in refusing to see his son, but has truly been dealt another blow by the storm of troubles that beats down old age and ends at last in death. If such words were sung by young men, they would be far less convincing; only those who have endured long life can say with authority that not to be born is best (1224).[52]

Thus the choristers establish their own identity throughout the *Oedipus at Colonus.* They observe religious usage strictly, yet their conventional sense of religion withers in the face of the militant, heroic morality of Oedipus. They are patriotic, obedient to their king, reverent to the gods, rendered impotent in military affairs by their age and infirmities, and filled with the memories and regrets of a long life. In short, they are old men, characters in a work that often reads like a meditation on old age. If they did appear to be wealthy, the *eugeneis oikētores* of Creon, their appearance created an intriguing set of contrasts to the protago-

---

52. *Sophoclean Chorus*, 114.

nist. Though coevals of Oedipus, the external circumstances of their lives would have suggested to a casual observer that they were far better or at least far better off. On closer inspection, however, they pale in comparison to Oedipus, who proves far tougher than they can imagine. It is tempting, though completely unprovable, to believe that Sophocles saw in himself the best parts of both the chorus and the hero.

Athens and Thebes

Athens provides a dual frame of reference in the play, in that it appears as the *astu* in which resides the king who also rules the deme of Colonus, while at the same time the name of the *astu* is coextensive with the polis; thus when Antigone tells her father that she knows that they are in Athens but that she does not recognize the immediate locale, Oedipus snaps, "Every passerby has told us this [that they are in Athens]" (25). Yet the walls of the city lie off in the distance. From the opening scene of the play, then, Sophocles reminds us that, while he may occasionally refer to the walled city of Athens itself as the polis, for him, as ordinarily in discussions of Attica, the writ of the polis runs far beyond the city walls, all the way to the borders. The poet's suggestion that the city extends, in effect, to the frontier, is mandated by the opposition inherent in the customary dramatic portrayals of Athens and Thebes, an opposition that Sophocles exploits to great advantage in the *Oedipus at Colonus*.[53] That dramatic opposition, in turn, anticipates (in mythological time) and reflects (in historical times) a genuine distinction between the political management of Athens and Thebes.[54]

Sophocles' portrayal of Athens takes precedence in the discussion, although an analysis of the role of Athens in isolation entails some pragmatic difficulties. Of Colonus we are overinformed: we have an extensive physical description, clues to the importance of the setting in mythological terms, and, if the soil really does produce character, a chorus of local citizens who provide ample insight into the deme. What we know of Athens, on the contrary, we know only by scattered and sometimes allusive references in the text and from the character of The-

---

53. For the terms of that opposition, see Zeitlin, "Theater of Self," particularly 102, and Vidal-Naquet in Vernant and Vidal-Naquet, *Myth and Tragedy*, 334. Later in this chapter, Zeitlin is quoted at some length on the subject.

54. Vidal-Naquet suggests that the Boeotian League reflected the ideals of Cleisthenes (Vernant and Vidal-Naquet, *Myth and Tragedy*, 334).

seus, who, as Reinhardt observed,[55] acts less as the "ideal Athenian" and more as a hero. Hence, we must resist the urge to allow him, mechanically, to typify the city.

Such caveats in place, we may proceed. The first thing we learn of the *astu* is that the towers of its walls appear in the distance (*prosō*). This is an important detail, for as we observed earlier, Sophocles exaggerates the distance between Colonus and the city proper in order to provide a sense that Oedipus has arrived on the frontier of the polis, rather than at a place that is only a short walk from the Acropolis. We also learn, shortly thereafter, that Colonus is considered part of Athens, *proprie dicta*, that is, that Colonus is only a district of the polis, even if it lies beyond the city's walls. The *xenos* confirms this fact when he notes that the men of Colonus are ruled by the king in the *astu*, Theseus. We are prepared, then, when the *xenos* decides not to risk independent action in his initial attempt to remove Oedipus from the grove. When he meets with resistance from the trespassing Oedipus, the *xenos* denies that he has the authority to remove Oedipus and states rather that he cannot act without the city's approval (*poleōs dicha*, 47–48) in the matter. He does claim that the issue can presently be adjudged by the local townsmen. When they encounter Oedipus' stiff defense, however, they opt for their part to pass the matter on to the king. We have observed earlier the general weakness displayed by the choristers. In the neglect or abrogation of their responsibilities, we see sure proof that in important questions, even of the sort that would seem to be under their clear purview, the townsmen must appeal to the moral authority of the leader of the city. Perhaps we should not judge the matter too harshly. This is clearly a special case; after all, an Oedipus does not wander into the grove every day. And yet the fact remains that the *xenos* quickly adopts the position that he himself lacks the competence that he appeared to claim at the beginning of his conversation with Oedipus, and in turn, when Oedipus resists the efforts of the chorus to drive him out, the choristers offer only token resistance before they yield to the stranger as well.

Thus, on an initial, cursory inspection, true authority, even limited to a specific area that has apparently been entrusted to the local men, resides in the *astu*, resides in fact in the hero-king Theseus. To receive or reject Oedipus demands political and moral calculation, and both the

55. *Sophocles*, 213.

xenos and the chorus lack the will or power to provide either. Sophocles thus asserts the preeminence of the *astu,* at least in grave matters.

The military situation mirrors the political and even the moral. When Oedipus' daughters have been seized and the old exile himself has been imperiled, the chorus can do no more than reiterate Oedipus' appeal for help. As he cries, "O lords of the land" *(O gēs anaktes),* presumably addressing the choristers, they offer no constructive aid but prefer to dispute with Creon the legality of his attempted abduction of the city's guests (831–32). Oedipus in turn broadens his plea, crying, O city *(iō polis,* 833). Still, the choristers prove incapable of decisive action, and at the last, when Oedipus himself is nearly taken, they resort to their own appeal, "O citizenry, O princes of the land" *(iō pas leos, iō gas promoi,* 885). At this juncture, Theseus returns from his sacrifice at the local altar of Poseidon and intervenes. He prevents Creon from taking Oedipus and forces the Theban to lead him and his men to the kidnapped daughters. As before in the matter of trespass, the choristers cannot act on their own; they await the king, paralyzed in the urgency of struggle just as they had been in dealing with the more abstract question of the reception of Oedipus.

From the outset of the work, Sophocles has laid the groundwork for this recurring motif of the reliance of the deme on the *astu.* The choral ode on Colonus and Athens helped contribute to the picture. Earlier, the ode was explained as a commentary on dramatic poetry and on the significance and importance of the drama to the polis. Rival interpretations can be posited, with no attendant diminishment of one another. (Even mediocre authors seldom present work with only one meaning.) In the initial strophe and antistrophe, Sophocles mentions Dionysus, Demeter, Persephone, Aphrodite, and the Muses. In the answering stanzas, the playwright chooses to emphasize the olive and Athena, the horse (and, by extension, the fleet) and Poseidon. If we accept Jebb's view of a geographical progression, starting from Colonus and moving out into the Academy and down the Cephisus into the wider polis, we also see progression of another type.[56] Dionysus, the Two Goddesses, and Aphrodite suggest natural forces of vegetation, death and rebirth, and procreation, and each in turn are appropriate to the wilder setting, beyond the *astu,* in which Sophocles sets his mythological Colonus. Moving from the immediate locale of Colonus out into the broader

---

56. See Jebb, *Oedipus at Colonus,* 152–53.

world, the deities of natural forces give way to gods of a different, more
sophisticated nature: Athena, with her inherent guardianship of wisdom and war, shown as patroness of the olive, which automatically
implies cultivation and hence the subjugation of the natural world; and
Poseidon, dual tamer of animals and the sea. This scheme suggests the
mutual need between the city and the country, the symbiotic relationship on which the whole of the Athenian polis thrives. But how is this
vision realized in the play? Certainly the country needs the city and
particularly the king, as is evidenced throughout. But does the city in
turn need the countryside?

Sophocles insists that it does. The grove at Colonus is the *ereisma* of
Athens, the *chalkopous odos* (57–58). So the loyal *xenos* describes his
township to an inquiring Oedipus. Do greater considerations obtain, or
does the local man merely recite a commonplace? We might be
inclined, on the basis of the previous analysis, to dismiss the claim as
hyperbole. Although the proposition seems tempting, to maintain it
would prove unwise. The flaws of the old men have been duly
observed and dissected, their weakness juxtaposed to the city's
strength, but they must have their innings as well. What does Colonus,
and by extension the chorus, offer to Athens that merits the townsman's boast?

Jebb takes *ereisma* as the "stay" of Athens, in relationship to the
chalkopous odos, the "brazen threshold" located in the immediate vicin-
ity, a connecting point between Hades and the upper world. Thus he
connects this passage to 1590, which provides a fuller description of the
"downward" (*katarraktēn*) threshold to the underworld, fixed by
bronze supports.[57] The connection is automatic in the long view but is
not at first glance obvious (the audience, presumably, had not read the
script in advance).[58] The text at 55–57 makes no reference to the upper
and lower worlds, and peculiarly, at this juncture the Eumenides are
not mentioned (although they just had been); the *xenos* names
Prometheus, Poseidon, and the eponymous hero Colonus as divinities
of the place. The *xenos* says, specifically, that "the place where you have
trespassed is called the bronze threshold of this land (*chthonos tēsde*),
the *ereisma* of Athens." In this play, *chthōn* sometimes refers to the local

---

57. *Oedipus at Colonus*, 75.

58. Segal notes the connection between the two verses and remarks upon the
vertical and horizontal nature of the threshold (*Tragedy and Civilization*, 369).
For this discussion, I prefer to concentrate on the latter.

spot but at other points clearly refers to the whole land of the polis, and the latter reading applies here, for it offers the only suitable apposite to *ereisma Athenōn* in the following line.

The *chalkopous odos* Jebb takes as "adamantine," in the sense of unbreakable or all-enduring.[59] Hence, Colonus is the all-enduring threshold of the land and the stay or support of Athens. Since *chalkopous odos* cannot yet with certainty be made to refer to the nether-world (although the association later becomes obvious), we should consider the meaning of the word in view of the fact that a threshold, that is, a transitional point on the horizontal plane (passing over for the moment the sense of vertical polarity that Jebb and Segal ascribe in light of the later reference in the text), is the stay or prop of Athens. If we pursue the notion, we see the value that Colonus offers to Athens.

A threshold allows entry or an easy manner of barring access. It focuses intrusive elements (unwanted strangers?) into a single fixed point, allowing for selection of the chosen over the rejected. The rural deme provides this service to the polis, acting in effect as a filter. Colonus, situated on the mythic frontier, offers a distance of time and space for the polis by permitting separation from the *astu* and thus the opportunity for deliberation and preparation. Of course, a threshold can be a point of exclusion, yet it serves even this function in a far less threatening manner than would a wall.[60]

As Segal has noted, Oedipus' only logical final resting place would be at an area like Colonus, which, being both remote and inhabited, could contain his gentler and harsher nature. Sophocles' late dramatic program demanded reintegration of the exile, but not too much so. Oedipus was still Oedipus, as he himself acknowledges when he declines to touch Theseus. The "stay" of Athens provided a place in the polis that could accommodate all individuals of merit and where those without merit (e.g., Creon) could be exposed and rooted out. In essence, on the basis of this "filtering" function, Athens derives some defensive benefit from the deme. One cannot of course stretch the point too far, but without question the playwright clearly posits here an inte-

---

59. *Oedipus at Colonus*, 75.

60. Gould argues that numinous sense associated with thresholds and boundaries dominates the ambiance of the play (*"Hiketeia,"* 90). This is certainly true. But the physical sense of the boundary is equally important. Otherwise, Sophocles would not have so manipulated his creation and location of the Athenian frontier.

gral symbiosis between polis and deme. So Athens, while physically distant, requires very much the native strength of Colonus and repays the debt. The power and authority of the city permeates out to the frontier, for Oedipus, the exiled hero, must find a home in the polis, though far from the ordinary comings and goings of civic life; his pollution would forbid such regular social intercourse.[61]

Essential to our understanding and appreciation of the *Oedipus at Colonus* is the recognition that, among many other issues, the poet addresses the question of what constitutes the good polis. How, exactly, should a polis behave, and who should take responsibility for that behavior? The discourse on these questions takes the form of a dichotomy between Athens and Thebes, with primary emphasis on the negative aspects of Thebes. To appreciate fully the extent of that dichotomy, we must consider the nature of Thebes as Sophocles has portrayed the rival polis in the *Oedipus at Colonus.*

That Thebes functions as a tragic, polar opposite to Athens has been well documented and need not detain us overlong. As Zeitlin expresses it,

> If we say that theater in general functions as an "other scene," . . . then Thebes, I suggest, is the "other scene" of the "other scene" that is theater itself.

She continues:

> First, within the theater, Athens is not the tragic space. Rather it is the scene where theater can and does escape the tragic, and where reconciliation and transformation are made possible.

Finally, Zeitlin concludes,

> But Thebes is also the obverse side of Athens, the shadow self . . . on whose other terrain the tragic action may be pushed to its furthest limits of contradiction and impasse.[62]

---

61. Segal, *Tragedy and Civilization*, 381.
62. "Theater of Self," 116–17. A contemporary parallel could be adduced: the television series *M*A*S*H*, which, though set in Korea, was about Vietnam.

Clearly, in the other two Theban plays, Sophocles has exploited Thebes to serve just such a purpose. The author makes use of his antipolis as the backdrop against which to portray those questions whose solutions figure so integrally in the maintenance and operation of civilized and civic society. In the *Antigone* the poet questions with unrelenting subtlety the relationship of the individual to the state—the tension definitionally inherent between the *oikos* and the polis—in terms that defy solution and offer in its place only misery and destruction. In the *Oedipus Tyrannus,* a narrowly focused discussion on guilt and innocence, knowledge and ignorance, becomes the metaphor for a larger discussion of man's relationship to fate and of the frequent irreconcilability of what Knox well referred to as "the heroic temper" (in his book by that name) with the responsibilities of civic governance. Hence, for the Athenians, perhaps the work served as a moral referendum on monarchy.

What, then, is the role of Thebes in the *Oedipus at Colonus*? How does it function as an "anti-Athens" in this particular play? Sophocles establishes that Athens can offer some type of home to Oedipus. On that point, the reasons are clear, and more than enough has been said. Athens is large enough, spatially and morally, to accommodate the exile. We should at this juncture consider how, precisely, Sophocles delineates the spatial difference between Athens and Thebes in this play. This investigation focuses on specific elements in the text that signal the antipathy between the two poleis, on a spatial as well as a political level. For the poet has drawn his picture of Thebes precisely to highlight the distinction between Oedipus' former city and his new home.

There is no clear evidence as to whether Athens had walls in the heroic period and, if so, where the walls actually stood. It does not matter. For Sophocles the walls exist, ringed by towers, seen far-off (*prosō*) from Colonus. We have already noted that Sophocles has distorted the distance between Colonus and Athens, to allow himself to observe duties of regional loyalty while capitalizing on the illustrative mythological reference of Theseus and Peirithous. He removes Colonus as far as possible from Athens, while at the same time he brings Athens out to Colonus—that is, he brings the polis to the frontier—first in the person of Theseus, and later in the presence of the king's warriors. For Sophocles, Athens' walls were purely a matter of defensive necessity rather than political utility. They exclude only the foe, not the outcast, the wanderer, the *xenos*. Perhaps that is why Antigone devotes to them no description, beyond the observation of the towers.

By contrast, one knows all about Thebes' walls without requiring much exposition. The phrase "seven-gated Thebes" is a commonplace that nearly attains the status of a cliché. For the Thebans, at least in Attic drama, the walls are the borders, if not in theory, then in practice, and Sophocles gives us a stunning example of this when he reveals the plans that the Thebans have for the disposition of Oedipus' corpse.

Ismene arrives with news from Thebes. The Thebans, prompted by an oracle, have determined that they need Oedipus back; at least, they need his tomb. Ismene and Oedipus discuss the new turn of events.

> *Oed:* So that he [Creon] may do what, daughter? Make things plain to me.
> *Ism:* So that they might place you near the land of the Cadmaeans, in order that they have control over you, but that you might not enter the boundaries of their land. (398–400)

The key verb here is "have control," *kratōsi*. It is the same verb that Oedipus employs to describe Theseus' rule of Colonus and Athens (68). Unless we imagine the unlikely scenario of the Thebans annexing some enclave in a neighboring land and stationing a battalion there on permanent foreign assignment, the place in which the Thebans will have power of Oedipus simply does not exist. The polis extends as far as its writ runs. Thus Colonus, for Sophocles' dramatic purposes at the frontier, is still an integral part of Athens. But no place can be beyond the boundaries and still be controlled by the polis. Rather, the boundary simply moves.

The polis, as customarily defined, is a city-state, that is, the city and the land that surrounds it. The land however, matters far less than the people; geography must be subordinated to politics. As Thucydides says, "men are the polis" (7.77.7). If people and their tombs fall under the control of the state, they are part of the polis.

This small but relevant detail demonstrates that Thebes and particularly its representative, Creon, do not comprehend the true nature of the polis. They assume that the polis, and certainly their own polis, is a fixed piece of land, symbolized in tragedy for all time by the massive walls and the seven gates. They believe that, if Oedipus, living or dead, can be planted near enough to the fixed border that they can keep an eye on him, he will be under their power but not in their land. This assumption underlies all the actions that Thebes takes in this play. Yet the real situation would be quite the opposite: if they have control over Oedipus (recall that the Theban plan calls for returning Oedipus, living or dead), he becomes part of their polis. This Thebes simply can never do. It is too inflexible, too parochial, and too small (to put it bluntly) to ever permit the reintegration of the exile.

Such inflexibility has been documented in the other Theban plays. Creon's autocratic dealings with Antigone evidence the pathology, as do the tumult surrounding the sudden demise of Oedipus and the attendant struggle for succession. The duties of *oikos* and polis sometimes conflict. Kings die or vanish or go mad and disable themselves. The successful polis must be fluid enough to accommodate the tensions inherent in the conflict of individual and state and to adapt to the vicissitudes of fortune without disintegrating into chaos at the sudden and unexpected development of a major crisis. Thebes fails such tests, and although one may fault Antigone for her own obsessions or Oedipus for the rage that supersedes his obligations to his people, the blame for the consequent folly that consumes the polis falls squarely on Thebes itself.

The persistent failure of Thebes to comprehend the true nature of the polis is accented, in this play, by Creon's inability to grasp both Athens' commitment to the *xenos* and the difficulty and contradictions sometimes inherent in the integration of heroes into the polis. When the Theban envoy, having failed to persuade Oedipus to return with him, consequently attempts to seize his daughter, he seems genuinely surprised that Athens would attempt to stop him. Theseus upbraids Creon for his behavior.

Now the laws to which he himself appealed, by these and no other be he judged. You will not leave this land until you have brought his daughters back. You have not acted correctly, neither with respect to me nor to your family nor to your own land. You came to a city that sanctions the right and does nothing without the rule of law, and you set aside the authority of this land, coming and taking what you wanted by force, thinking, apparently, that the city lacked men or was manned by slaves, and thinking me equal to nothing. (907–18)

Creon begs the following excuse.

> I did not consider the city unmanned or lacking in counsel, as you
> suggest, child of Aegeus. I did what I did thinking that no one
> would so eagerly come between me and my kin that they would
> use force to stop me. I knew that they would not receive an
> unholy parricide or one to whom charges of incest had been laid.
> (939–46)

Creon has a point, in that incestuous parricides are not commonly
viewed as welcome additions to a Greek city. But he has less of a point
than he hopes, for ritual pollution can be absolved by one hero acting
for another. The case of Theseus and Heracles in Euripides' *Heracles*,
where Theseus offers to purify Heracles of his sins upon their return to
Athens (1324), provides the salient example.

More importantly, Theseus insists that his city sanctions law, but
Creon cites the law in defense of his own actions. Which law, or whose,
applies? Creon argues that no state should come between himself and
his kin. Thus he attempts to collapse the boundaries between polis and
oikos, much as he did in the *Antigone*. Indeed, he manages to make matters worse by failing to recognize the autonomy of each polis. Theseus,
in contrast, insists that the polis be respected and blames Creon for dis-
gracing Thebes, his own city. Theseus is of course being polite, and
Sophocles is being ironic. In fact, as Zeitlin observed, Creon's Thebes, as
portrayed by the Athenian tragedians, usually makes just this kind of
mistake. For Creon, the Theban, there is no opposition to collapse, for the
self-contradictory nature of Thebes never recognizes such distinctions.[63]
Athens does recognize distinctions, yet it promotes unity. Thebes, in the
person of Creon, argues for unity, but in its failure to make valid distinctions, it condemns itself to repeat its dismal fate ad infinitum.

Theseus and Creon

Theseus is the king of Athens; Creon's immediate standing in Thebes is
rather less sure. He originally served as regent to Eteocles and Polyneices, but given that Eteocles has specifically cast his brother out, we

---

63. Zeitlin, "Theater of Self," 141.

may assume that Creon's regency has ended.[64] The technical specifics are subordinate to the dramatic point. For the purposes of the *Oedipus at Colonus,* Creon is to Thebes as Theseus is to Athens, and so the characters are drawn in sharp contrast to one another. From what would in the modern era be termed their management styles, we witness how the two men contribute to the sharp distinction that Sophocles draws between their respective poleis.

It would be odious to repeat the earlier discussions of the Athenian king's heroic nature, a nature that caused him to accept Oedipus without question, in contrast to the chorus, who lacked the authority or will to do so. In receiving the polluted exile into the city, Theseus has disclosed his own *gennaion.* The arrival of the Theban representative gives him the consequent opportunity to prove his worth under fire.

The manner of the two men could not be more different. When Theseus arrived at Colonus, he took no notice of the choristers, asked them no questions, and received only one piece of unsolicited input. His focus was on Oedipus, which is right and proper and after the fashion of the hero, who frequently resides above considerations of courtesy, much as he does commonplace issues of right and wrong. His first real indication that he has taken notice of the local men comes, characteristically, in a potential order. He will, if the stranger wishes to stay, appoint the local man (the coryphaeus, presumably) to watch over him. Then, assurances having been given to Oedipus that Theseus will protect him come what may, the king departs.

The advent of Creon differs considerably from that of his Athenian counterpart. His first concern is to address the choristers, flatteringly, as "noble inhabitants" (*eugeneis oikētores,* 728), and to assuage their apparent fear at his arrival. In view of their evident concern, he states that he, like them, is an old man, and he protests that his own old age ill disposes him toward violence. The first part is certainly accurate; he is, after all, Jocasta's brother and therefore Oedipus' uncle. However, his own actions will quickly disprove his attendant claim of passivity. But in his gregarious approach to the chorus, he acts like a politician—in this play, a damning indictment.

Creon does not speak to Oedipus directly until 740, after he has presented his credentials as a representative of Thebes and paid due respect to Athens. His first words to his former monarch—"O wretched

---

64. However, Creon does identify himself as *tyrannos* at 851.

Oedipus" *(all' o talaipōr' Oidipous)*—establish the tone. *Talaipōros* occurs
three other times in the play. Antigone refers to her father as *pater
talaipōr'* in 14. In 91 Oedipus calls his own existence *talaipōron bion.*
Finally, Antigone addresses Polyneices simply as "O wretched one" (*o
talaipōr'*, 1280). The last usage echoes a passage in the *Antigone* in which
Ismene refers to Polyneices and Eteocles in the dual as *to talaipōro* (56).
The word obviously recalls the dismal condition of the Theban royal
house, and Creon's use of the word to address to a man from whom he
needs a favor seems impertinent. By contrast Theseus at least waits
seven lines before he addresses Oedipus as *dusmor'* (557). The latter
term, of course, emphasizes the role that fate *(moira)* played in bringing
about Oedipus' condition.

When Theseus received Oedipus into Athens, he cited *doruxenia,*
Oedipus' attitude of respect for the city, and the boon that Oedipus
offered. In short, he was honest and concise, behaving toward the newcomer as befits both a hero *(doruxenia)* and a king *(kerdos).* Creon offers
no parallel. He seeks Oedipus under entirely false pretenses, although
many of his arguments are sound and should not necessarily be overlooked merely because we know that the Thebans have no intention of
restoring Oedipus to his homeland. Antigone's condition was
appalling, and Oedipus' ultimate claim, that the love that his daughters
received from their father has repaid all their sufferings (1617–20),
seems in retrospect unsatisfactory.

Oedipus, forewarned by Ismene and having already realized that, as
Apollo had prophesied, his destiny lies in the grove of the Eumenides,
is undeceived by Creon's offer and evident goodwill. He quickly
launches into a lengthy, bitter tirade that shreds Creon's arguments
and exposes the offer of a return to Thebes as a sham, on two fronts.
The offer cannot be genuine, in that the Thebans cannot readmit Oedipus anyway; and even if the offer were genuine, it has come too late
(776–86).

The audience may feel that the exile has made his point, but Creon,
more accustomed to the formidable wrath of Oedipus and well aware
that, for the sake of Thebes, his mission cannot fail, continues the
debate. After a brief, largely meaningless discussion, Creon plays his
trump card. He has carried off Ismene and will do the same to
Antigone, the "twin crutches" *(toutoin skēptroin)* of Oedipus' wandering (848–49). In so doing, Creon appears convinced of his own right-
eousness and invokes rather stinging arguments. When Creon first

approaches Antigone, the chorus asks his intent. Creon responds, "I will not touch this man, but she who is mine" (*ouch apsomai toud' andros, alla tēs emēs*, 830). He has laid the groundwork for this line of attack earlier, when he chastised Oedipus for leaving his daughter vulnerable to attack from any passerby. By referring to Antigone as his, he makes clear that he is invoking his right, as Antigone's oldest male relative, to look after her interest, on the ground that her father has abrogated his responsibility. In this context, we should remember that Oedipus had in fact entrusted his daughters to Creon at the end of the *Oedipus Tyrannus* (1465–66).

Creon also exploits another opportunity to attack Oedipus' behavior. In 849–55, after he has seized Antigone, he states:

> But since you wish to conquer your country and your friends, at whose charge I have taken on these duties [returning Oedipus] although I am myself a ruler *(tyrannos)*, go ahead, conquer. In time, I think, you will realize that you have not done right by yourself, not now, nor when you let your anger run away with you, in spite of your friends.

Creon here alludes to a harsh fact that many would choose to ignore about Oedipus. His behavior, as portrayed in the *Oedipus Tyrannus*, was inexcusable. Of course, apologies are manufactured. Under the terrible stress of revelation, what behavior could we have expected? In the event, Oedipus gave a virtuoso display of Knox's heroic temper, a temper that, in its utter self-obsession, took no notice of family, friends, or kingdom but rather sacrificed all on account of one ruinous moment of fatal insight, preferring a decisive act of self-abnegation to the gloomy reality to which most people must yield, namely, to live with our mistakes.

Oedipus is obstinate, vindictive, too little concerned for his daughters' real welfare, and far too quick to forget his obligations to the state he saved and governed. Yet Creon, for all that, stands revealed by their encounter as the decidedly lesser man. Two considerations prevent our granting any support to Creon's understanding of the situation, despite the apparent justice of his claims. First, of course, we know that when he claims that he will return Oedipus to Thebes, he lies. Perhaps if he had approached Oedipus with the truth—that Thebes would like Oedipus to return to a place near the borders—we could accept at least the genuineness of his offer and of his concern for the well-being of the girls, while we would know of course that his request would be denied. But he compromises any presumptive sympathy for his position by his initial lie. Second, his behavior subsequent to his kidnapping of Oedipus' daughters belies his real intentions. He may fairly lay claim to the girls, and in taking them he does nothing beyond the demands of his role as guardian. However, once he attempts to seize Oedipus himself, he reveals that his legitimate concern for the girls' welfare is only pretext. Oedipus remains Creon's real object of interest.

The chorus' shouts finally reach Theseus, who has been sacrificing to Poseidon. He returns and orders his own men to pursue the girls and their captors. He then demands an explanation from Creon for his abominable behavior in violating the sovereignty of Attica. Regardless of the specifics of *empolin* or *empalin* at 637, there can be no question that Theseus has extended his protection to his visitors. In view of the Theban's insult to Athens and Theseus himself, the king orders the restoration of the girls (at 909–18, quoted earlier). He then continues his chastisement of Creon by reminding him that Thebes would not sanction such behavior.

> But Thebes did not teach you evil. Thebes does not breed criminals, nor would she approve of your action. (919–21)

Theseus draws very clearly the distinction between Creon's actions and his own. Creon has not reckoned with Theseus, who, in the *Oedipus at Colonus*, is the law of the land. Creon's calculations are based on his expectation that the Theban polis is somehow paradigmatic. He does anticipate the strength of the hero, who guards, validates, and sometimes coerces the polis to do what is right. Creon would act, as heroes do, above the letter of the law. But he lacks the moral authority or the heroic stature to do so. We have already observed his use of outright lies to attain his own ends. Oedipus may, on occasion, fudge the truth. But the gods are on his side, in the old-fashioned sense that heroes can expect. As the gods oppose Creon, all his claims for the justice of his situation fall on deaf ears. He is no hero and cannot stand up to the heroic Oedipus or his Athenian counterpart.

Creon's failure to ascertain the heroic norm appears all the more clearly from Theseus' response.

Were I in Thebes, even with the most just claim possible, I would
never seize anyone by violence my own without the sanction of
your state or king; I should behave as fits a *xenos* among citizens.
(924–28)

Here Theseus reminds us again of the importance of *xenia*, the need for
some type of social order that can be invoked a priori to guarantee the
conduct by and toward the stranger. When the king states earlier that
"Thebes never taught you to be like this," he has already had experience of one Theban in the play, Oedipus, who appears reverent to the
gods and pays due *dasmon* to Theseus and the city. In fact, Oedipus presents himself to the king, whereas Creon seems to be avoiding him. If
Creon does not wish to see and consult the king, how can he be said to
match the standard of behavior to which Oedipus has adhered. Again,
Creon falls well short on the standard of heroism and cannot therefore
invoke heroic prerogatives in his dealings with Oedipus.

When Creon ultimately resorts to an appeal to the justice of the Areopagus and to the reputation of the city (939–59), he recites in many
respects the same complaints that Oedipus made when the chorus
attempted to remove him from the sacred grove. Again, the specifics of
Creon's behavior have betrayed him. He offers no *kerde*, no *onesis*. In
fact, he seeks rather than offering at all.

In essence, then, Creon is the perfect representative for Thebes, in
that neither quite understand the nature and role required of them. An
ideal polis extends far beyond the walls of the *astu*; an ideal ruler
understands the importance of fair dealing and the need to recognize
and cultivate heroes. The polis tamed the hero and made him a citizen.
But in the process, the polis itself had at least the opportunity to behave
heroically, even if it ultimately does not manage the feat. For it is Theseus, the hero-king of Athens, who compares favorably to the badly
misguided, overmatched, utterly unheroic representative of Thebes.

5

Prophecy and Curse

Thus far, there has been scant mention of the supernatural elements the playwright uses in the *Oedipus at Colonus*. The ensuing discussion should make good the deficiency. The role of the supernatural in the drama must be addressed, if only to deny or at least limit its importance. Such denial or limitation can never be absolute, of course. Leaving aside the more tendentious issues of curse and prophecy, the passing of the hero alone militates against such a casual dismissal of the role of the miraculous or at least the paranormal. Indeed, for some earlier critics, the representation of Oedipus' pseudo-apotheosis served as the sole excuse for the drama.[1] Although such limited views of the play have been rightly dismissed by subsequent scholars, still, at some level, every critic must take note of the divine or spiritual elements in the work. Without such an examination, a full understanding of the play will elude us.

Which elements in the play can safely be grouped under the rubric "supernatural"? Three suggest themselves immediately. First, both in the order of their presentation in the work and their importance to the plot, stand the oracles of Apollo, those that long ago had prophesied Oedipus' fate as well as those reported by Ismene in the course of the play. Next are the curses that Oedipus lays on his sons, desires that reach a state of dread certainty in his memorable encounter with his suppliant, when he dismisses Polyneices and condemns his sons to their fratricidal slaughter. Last in the play, if not in ultimate importance, come the death and disappearance of the hero from the grove into the earth itself.[2] In each or these three elements—prophecy, curse, and apotheosis—Sophocles portrays and examines the operation of primitive forces, a portrayal richly supported by the common Greek

---

1. Waldock, *Sophocles the Dramatist*, 218–20.

2. These divisions and the attendant question of moral guilt or innocence are Linforth's (*Religion and Drama*, 81).

practice of acknowledging the presence of spiritual powers at work in everyday life.

A fourth element intrudes, inextricably bound to the other three: the matter of Oedipus' guilt or innocence. For Oedipus, of course, no such question remains. No nuances of guilt or responsibility need to be explored; no account of his actions needs to be rendered to anyone. He proclaims his moral innocence early and often, to anyone who will listen. The audience for its part may withhold absolution. Dodds may be correct when he demonstrates the futility of playing "what if" with the *Oedipus Tyrannus,*[3] but in this work, mere critical fiat will not settle the matter, for the chorus and Creon both raise issues of guilt, intention, and responsibility, and neither in any sense pronounce Oedipus innocent. Theseus merely supersedes the pedestrian judgments of those fixated on their own mundane notions of guilt and innocence and acknowledges the protagonist as heroic, which is scarcely the same thing. The moral issue of guilt or innocence, in turn, cannot be held separate from the three "supernatural" elements detailed earlier. The oracle that foretold Oedipus' crimes of parricide and incest also told the hero of his eventual resting place at the grove of the Eumenides. The curses on his sons inevitably raise the question of Oedipus' own moral authority; who is he, after all, to take on the role of the gods and condemn his sons? Finally, his death or passing, in which many critics have seen an effort by the gods to compensate Oedipus for his sufferings, calls us, willingly or not, to examine once again his moral status in connection with his ultimate fate as a recipient of cult worship.

Prophecy

The matters of prophecy, curse, and final destiny divide the play rather conveniently, with prophecy offering the obvious point at which to commence discussion. Early in the *Oedipus at Colonus* we discover its importance, for his reliance on the authority and accuracy of Apollo's oracles provides the driving motivation for the hero's subsequent actions. When Oedipus discovers from the *xenos* that he and Antigone have inadvertently trespassed into a grove sacred to the Eumenides, he promptly announces to the local man that he will never leave, for he

---

3. "On Misunderstanding the *Oedipus Rex,*" 180.

has arrived at the "watchword" (*xynthēma*) of his fate (46).[4] After some additional exposition, the *xenos* leaves to fetch other members of the local gentry and to report to the king the arrival of the mysterious visitor and his daughter. Oedipus then explains to Antigone that Apollo had long ago told him of this grove (his final resting place), in the same prophecy that had predicted his "many evils" (*polla kaka*, 84–110). In that Oedipus has already lived out the other parts of the horrible prophecy, no serious doubt can be evinced that he will fulfill this final part as well, though we must compliment Sophocles for a neat dramatic twist. In his earlier career Oedipus had labored so strenuously to avoid the fate that Apollo had laid out for him, yet in so doing he became the instrument of his own destruction. In this play, however, he willingly conforms to the mandates of Apollo's oracle, while other characters attempt to contravene the mandates of the prophecy.[5]

In the course of Oedipus' exposition of past events to Antigone, we also learn of the oracle that, in his final repose, he would be a blessing to those who received him and a curse to those who cast him out.

> [Apollo] told me of this rest after many years, some haven for strangers in a far-off land, a sanctuary guaranteed at last by the awesome gods. "There," he said, "you shall end your weary life, a blessing to the land in which you dwell, but to the land that exiled you, a curse." (88–93)

The phrase "There you shall end your weary life" requires for clarity's sake some brief discussion. The statement is in indirect discourse, so the verb form is *kampsein*, the future active infinitive of the verb *kamptō*, "to bend or curve." With the words *ton talaiporon bion*, then, the poet clearly means "to bring an end to a wretched life." Ellendt renders the word *kamptō*,[6] and in a similar passage in Euripides' *Suppliant Women*

---

4. See Jebb, *Oedipus at Colonus*, 74, for a full discussion of the meaning of *xynthema*.

5. Thus Rosenmeyer writes: "From the very beginning we get the impression that Oedipus has advanced from abject resignation and self-hatred to a state of confident fellowship with Apollo. He is at harmony with Delphi, and his every action betokens an almost joyful awareness of this reconciliation" ("Wrath of Oedipus," 95).

6. *Lexikon Sophocleum*, 367.

(748), *kampsai kaka* means "to bring an end to evils." The phrase "a blessing to the land in which you dwell" also demands further explication. *Kerdē* in line 92 has been much noted already. By it, as by many other terms, Sophocles designates the benefit that the possession of Oedipus' body and tomb will bestow on Athens. *Oikēsanta*, the participle from *oikeō*, "to live or dwell," alerts the audience to the permanent status of Oedipus' occupation of the grove. In connection with the preceding line, which has already foretold the hero's death, we see that Oedipus fully understands his destiny (at least in the important particulars), at this early point in the work.[7] Oedipus knows, better than anyone, the invariable accuracy of Apollo's oracles; he knows that he will end his life in the grove of the Eumenides at Colonus, and he knows that he will be a blessing to those who receive him *(tois dedegmonois)* and a curse *(atēn)* to those who cast him out *(pempsasin)*. The sense of permanence that *oikēsanta* conveys must, in turn, indicate the importance of Oedipus' tomb. Thus Sophocles informs us at the outset of the play that his protagonist knows that the Athenians will benefit from his tomb and that the Thebans will be harmed in some way.

These small details present at the beginning of the *Oedipus at Colonus* demand our attention, for they demonstrate the degree of Oedipus' own foreknowledge of his future, the full extent of which scholars often neglect. Knox states that Oedipus "speaks with blind faith in the prophecy."[8] Bushnell in turn cites Knox in support of her own remarks.

> Although Oedipus recognizes that this is his predicted place of rest, he can only repeat the prophecy without understanding how it may be fulfilled. He does not yet see how he shall find his rest or how he may become a blessing to Athens and a curse to Thebes.[9]

The remarks of these scholars convey less than may appear. Oedipus knows he will end his days at Athens; *oikēsanta* adequately demonstrates that his stay in the grove is permanent; dead people usually reside in tombs; and he will be, as he says, a blessing to those who received him, a curse to those who cast him out. Therefore, he knows

---

7. Knox is surely wrong when he states that Oedipus, at 288, "does not know yet what advantage" he brings to the city (*Heroic Temper*, 150).

8. *Heroic Temper*, 150.

9. *Prophesying Tragedy*, 91.

the essentials of his destiny and his power, well in advance of the arrival of Ismene. He may lack certain knowledge of some useful particulars, but he has a sure grasp of the big picture. We should not be surprised at the absence of certainty as regards the details (god therein dwelling or not). No one in Greek literature or mythology ever quite knows how a prophecy will be realized; were the characters to exhibit such knowledge, the interesting parts of much mythological literature would be lost. Unlike most recipients of prophetic guidance, however, Oedipus has the general framework in place. Knox's remark on "blind faith" thus proves ill considered. Oedipus has far more experience of Apollo's oracles than Knox's remark suggests. Since the vast majority of the god's horrific prophecies have already come to pass, how blind can Oedipus' faith in the fulfillment of the last part of the prophecy be?

Within the previously well established framework of the hero's knowledge of his fate, the oracles, those that Ismene reports, arrive from Thebes. After the argument with the chorus, in which Oedipus contends that he will provide a benefit to Athens and that the gentlemen of Colonus should recognize his moral innocence, Oedipus holds his ground while the chorister's for their part agree to leave his case for the dispensation of the king. After both parties mutually consent to leave their conflict unresolved, Antigone states that she can see in the distance a woman, mounted on a Sicilian colt and wearing a Thessalian hat (311–13).[10] As the woman draws near, Antigone realizes that the newcomer is her sister, Ismene. Following a brief exchange of greetings and professions of mutual longing,[11] Ismene informs her father that she comes with news (*logōn g' autaggelos,* 334). When Oedipus asks after Eteocles and Polyneices, Ismene reports that their harmony has ended and, by inference, that the situation in Thebes has substantially deteriorated. Oedipus then commences on a lengthy speech in which he denounces his sons for failing to repay their father for their *trophē,* while by contrast he praises his daughters' persistent loyalty. He then continues,

---

10. Segal notes that the account of the provenance of the hat and the colt, as well as Ismene's sunburned appearance, indicates how extensively Ismene herself has traveled while trying to locate her father and her sister (*Tragedy and Civilization,* 365).

11. Given Oedipus' past, the exaggerated affection with which he treats his daughters tends to elicit from the attentive observer a certain discomfort, at least.

And you, my child, came hither, avoiding the Cadmeians' watch, to bring your father all the oracles *(mantei')* concerning Oedipus, and you proved yourself a trusty guardian of my affairs, when they banished me. (353–56)

The presence of the word *manteia* poses a necessary question that critics tend not to face squarely: what oracles? How did Oedipus know that any oracles were forthcoming? Jebb evades the issue.

> 354 *manteia panta* implies several oracles, given to the Thebans about Oedipus after he had left Thebes. There is no clue to their purport. . . . they are invented merely to create a pious office for Ismene. . . . the poetic legend required that Antigone should be the sole guide of his wanderings.[12]

Two objections may be raised to Jebb's explanation. To take the lesser first, poetic legend seldom "required" the playwright to do anything. Even death is negotiable, as the presence of Jocasta in Euripides' *Phoenissae* demonstrates. Such an argument carries even less weight in this play, in which Sophocles may have invented the legend entirely. If the playwright had chosen to have Ismene accompany Antigone and Oedipus from the outset, or if he wished to omit Ismene from the play altogether, nothing hindered him. Ismene's arrival, however, does offer undoubted dramatic value to the play, and that, rather than the imagined requirements of poetic legend, accounts for her presence in the play and her function as a messenger.

To raise the more serious objection, why does Oedipus mention, specifically, oracles *(manteia)*? "News," or *logoi*, which Ismene promises earlier, would have been more than sufficient grounds for the second daughter to remain at Thebes. Clearly—and remarkably, given that Sophocles has in no way prepared the ground for it—Oedipus was anticipating that the Thebans would receive additional oracles.[13] He confirms his expectation in the sequel.

Ismene duly reports that her brothers have quarreled over the

---

12. *Oedipus at Colonus*, 110.

13. It will not suffice to argue that these oracles to which Oedipus refers are those promised at the end of the *Oedipus Tyrannus*. By Oedipus' own testimony, he resided long at Thebes after Jocasta's suicide and his own self-blinding— ample time for those decrees of the gods to have been heard.

throne and that Polyneices has been exiled from Thebes and in consequence has sought military assistance from Argos.[14] Then she adds:

> [Polyneices] swears that he will make Argos lord of the Cadmeian
> plain or else raise the victor to the heavens. These are not just
> words but a dreadful fact, my father. How long until the gods
> finally have pity on you, I cannot say. (380–84)

A more precise, if less elegant, translation gives the full import of the
passage: the last clause reads, *tous de sous hopou theoi ponous katoiktiousin
ouk echō mathein*, which is more literally translated, "I am not able to say
at what stage the gods will pity your sufferings."[15] Still, the import of
the verse is clear enough: something in the oracles that she has come to
relate has suggested to Ismene that the gods will take pity on Oedipus
and relieve, or perhaps terminate, his sufferings. Oedipus, unsurpris-
ingly, jumps on this small detail.

> *Oed:* Do you believe that the gods will have some regard for my
>   condition and finally save me?
> *Ism:* That is the way I read the latest oracles *(manteumasin).*
> *Oed:* What oracles? What has been foretold, child?
> *Ism:* You will be sought, dead or alive, by the Thebans as the
>   source of their own safety.
> *Oed:* And who would gain an advantage by possessing me?
> *Ism:* They say that maintaining their power depends on you.
> *Oed:* So, when I am no more, I am a man? (385–93)

A troubling, disjointed aspect of this dialogue suggests to the attentive
observer that Oedipus already has some prior knowledge of these
events and that only the audience benefits from Ismene's report. Let us
consider the last part of the exchange: Ismene states that the country
will want Oedipus, living or dead *(thanont' esesthai zōnta).*[16] Yet Oedi-

---

14. As Whitman notes, "The latter [Oedipus] manifests no surprise when he
hears that a war for the throne of Thebes has broken out between his two sons,
Eteocles and Polyneices" (*Sophocles,* 194).

15. For *hopou,* see Jebb, *Oedipus at Colonus,* 113.

16. Linforth notes that the terms in which Ismene describes Oedipus confuse
the question, but only from the Theban perspective, as Oedipus knows full well
the source of his power (*Religion and Drama,* 84–87).

pus completely ignores the "living" part of the phrase and seizes on the
"dead." He implies here, by taking *dead* as the relevant word, what he
has already explained to Antigone at the beginning of the work: that he
knows that his tomb will be the agent by which he can bestow his
power. His response here accords precisely to the conditions set forth
in the oracle and to the sense of permanence inherent in the word *oikēsanta.*

Ismene continues her account of the situation at Thebes by reporting
to her father that Creon intends to fetch Oedipus back from Athens, in
order to place him near Thebes but not within the polis itself (396–97,
399–400). As we observed earlier, this place in which Thebes proposes
to locate the exile does not, in fact, exist. Rather, Thebes and Creon's
plan manifests on the spatial level Thebes' persistent failure to comprehend adequately the nature and function of the polis. This passage further illustrates the extent of Oedipus' knowledge. Ismene has merely
stated that the Thebans propose to place him near the land of Thebes.
She employs the verb *stēsōsi* (399)—which can be a perfectly neutral
term—in conjunction with the aforementioned desire of the Thebans to
accomplish Oedipus' return, living or dead. Oedipus responds, "How
do I aid them, lying at the gates?" (401). Oedipus, therefore, assumes
the latter option (dead) automatically, when he refers to himself "lying
there" *(keimenou)*. Only at this point in her account does Ismene mention the curse on the Thebans if they fail to honor Oedipus' tomb (402).
Hence, Oedipus does not learn of the power of his tomb from his
daughter: he assumes it, an assumption that accords with Apollo's
original prophecy.

In effect, then, Ismene's speech largely serves to confirm only what
Oedipus already knew and to perform the task of exposition for the
audience. The oracles that the Thebans have obtained reveal nothing to
Oedipus that he did not already know or at which he could not guess.
An additional factor, however, is thrown into the mix. As Bushnell
pointed out:

> This prophecy, in contrast to the older oracle, seems to offer an
> alternative for the future. . . . It seems possible that Oedipus may
> not die in the Eumenides' grove if Creon can persuade him to
> return home.[17]

---

17. *Prophesying Tragedy*, 92.

Earlier, Knox had suggested much the same thing.

> [T]he new prophecy supplements the old. . . . He sees now that the
> two prophecies are one; it is by his choice of a resting place that he
> can do what Apollo promised him the power to do, to hurt his
> enemies and help his friends. He chooses to give victory to
> Athens and defeat to Thebes when one day Theban armies invade
> Attic soil.[18]

Both of these statements demonstrate a fundamental misunderstanding of the nature of Apollo's prophecy. Apollo's oracles come to pass;
Apollo has already told Oedipus that he will die in the grove of the
Eumenides and that he will be a blessing to those who received him, a
curse to those who cast him out. Bushnell, commenting on Knox's reading, made the observation that

> What Oedipus "chooses" here is, in fact, what he has already
> decided to do: to remain in Attica, in the grove where Apollo had
> promised him rest and power. . . . That Oedipus has chosen, how-
> ever, is not enough in these circumstances, for he alone, physi-
> cally helpless, cannot prevent Creon from forcing him to return to
> Thebes.[19]

A grave difficulty attends Bushnell's conclusion, although her remarks
do afford a useful corrective to Knox. Bushnell claims that Oedipus has
"decided" to stay in Attica but that the possibility of Theban intervention into Oedipus' destiny threatens to compromise the veracity of
Apollo's promise. In reality, however, choice and decision have little to
do with Oedipus' actions. He simply acknowledges that he had arrived
in the place destined by the oracle, and he accepts at this late season the
need to conform to the will of Apollo and Zeus as expressed in the
prophecies he heard as a young man.[20] Hence concepts like choice and
decision, except in the decision to abide willingly, do not usefully
inform the discussion of the passage at all. But Knox errs more greatly

---

18. *Heroic Temper*, 150–51.

19. *Prophesying Tragedy*, 92–93.

20. It is perhaps useful, though sorely anachronistic, to think of Oedipus as
being like a good Christian, exercising his free will by willingly conforming
that will to the will of God.

in this matter. The oracle that the Thebans have received does not indicate that Oedipus can choose where he will bestow his blessing. It may appear so from the Theban perspective, but in reality the oracle first given to Oedipus by Apollo has never been contravened.[21] He will die at Colonus. He is simply in a position where he knows fully the mind of Apollo, whereas the Thebans understand it imperfectly at best. In this way, Sophocles recalls and reverses the situation of the *Oedipus Tyrannus*. In that play, Oedipus had, as it appeared, the facile answers to the various challenges that the oracles of Apollo put forth but insufficient information on which to base his actions. In this work, the same type of ignorance constrains the Thebans, who have worked out a perfectly simple, elegant, and efficient plan to avert the dire eventualities that the oracle has predicted for them, but who lack adequate information to read those oracles correctly and, as a result of their ignorance, doom their best efforts in advance.

Neither is the inability of Oedipus to resist Creon unaided truly relevant to the oracular situation. As Dodds noted, in his essay on fate in the *Oedipus Tyrannus:*

> The oracle was *unconditional:* it did not say 'If you do so-and-so you will kill your father': it simply said 'You will kill your father, you will sleep with your mother.' And what an oracle predicts is bound to happen.[22]

Just such a case presents itself in the *Oedipus at Colonus.* Apollo's oracle does not say, "if you do so-and-so, you will end your days at Colonus." Nor does it offer the alternative possibility of death at, or near, Thebes. Only from a Theban point of view does Ismene's revelation indicate the either-or situation that Knox suggests.

To continue with Dodds' view on prophecy in the *Oedipus Tyrannus,* while the fate of the hero, from Homer on, can be predetermined, his actions remain free.

---

21. As Linforth explains it: "He knows from Oracle I that if he is granted asylum in Colonus he will there end his life in peace and be buried in the soil of Colonus. He can be confident, therefore, that the terms of Oracle II [Ismene's oracle] can never be fulfilled" (*Religion and Drama,* 85).

22. "On Misunderstanding the *Oedipus Rex,*" 181.

But fifth-century Greeks did not think in these terms any more than Homer did: the debate about determinism is a creation of Hellenistic thought. Homeric heroes have their predetermined 'portion of life' (*moira*); they must die on their 'appointed day' (*aisimon ēmar*); but it never occurs to the poet or his audience that this prevents them from being free agents. Nor did Sophocles intend that it should occur to readers of the *Oedipus Rex*. Neither in Homer nor in Sophocles does divine foreknowledge of events imply that all human actions are predetermined.[23]

Another way of viewing this paradoxical relationship between destiny and will, as it applies to both the *Oedipus Tyrannus* and the *Oedipus at Colonus*, is to realize that fate remains after human actors act. Prophecy tells the future and may help shape it, but it does not create it. The prophecy of the *Oedipus Tyrannus* comes true not only despite Oedipus' actions but because of them. Naturally, Oedipus' actions and will, in conjunction with the action and will of the other characters, must work to ensure that Apollo's prophecy of a final resting place in the grove, rather than at Thebes, will prove accurate. Prophecy simply states what will be, without in any way relieving the human agent of his own privileges. Thus Knox's remark is at best irrelevant and at worst redundant. No one ever quite knows the specifics of how a prophecy will be fulfilled, in terms of what actions need to be taken to guarantee the outcome predicted by the god; but Oedipus certainly knows that he shall be a blessing and a curse and that power arises from his tomb, and that is enough.

So Oedipus does not become aware of a dual prophecy by Ismene's arrival, since no dual prophecy can exist, as Oedipus, given his vast and unfortunate experience with oracles, is positioned to know better than anyone. What, then, is the point? Perhaps it is dramatic rather than oracular. The audience learns, if they had not ascertained it from Oedipus' earlier discussion with Antigone, the nature of Oedipus' value to Athens. Moreover, the passage foreshadows the eventual arrival of

---

23. Ibid., 182. Linforth says much the same thing: "But Oedipus does not leave the accomplishment of his desire to Phoebus or to the oracles themselves. He acts in his own behalf and does all he can to bring to pass what the oracles lead him to hope for" (*Religion and Drama*, 88).

both Creon and Polyneices. In addition, Ismene's narrative alerts Oedipus to the hostility between his sons.

A full understanding and realization of the extent of Oedipus' foreknowledge refutes effectively those critics who enlist Ismene's revelations as evidence for Oedipus' growing realization of his own power. He possesses full knowledge of that power from the moment he is aware that he has arrived in the grove. Indeed, certain passages in the *Oedipus at Colonus* indicate that he may know far more than he lets on to his interlocutors—an altogether logical and defensible conclusion, which follows from the text itself. At 70–74, the *xenos* and Oedipus exchange the following words.

> *Oed:* Could one of you be sent to bring him [Theseus] here?
> *Xen:* Why? For what reason should we urge him to come?
> *Oed:* Tell him a small service may profit him much.
> *Xen:* How can he profit from a blind man? [More literally, "What profit [*arkesis*] is there from one who is blind?"]
> *Oed:* The blind man's words will be full of sight.

As so often occurs elsewhere, translation does scarce justice here. The last phrase reads, *hos an legōmen panth' horōnta lexomen*, which can be literally translated, "Whatever we speak, all we speak has insight." Clearly, Oedipus knows, or at least claims to know, the veracity of everything he says or will say. We may wonder about that, but his continuing and expanding forecasts convey to everyone the hero's own sense of his authority.

Ismene's news is not altogether without value to the old man, for, as noted earlier, he does receive one bit of information on which he can capitalize: the news of the dispute between his sons over the kingship and of the ensuing fratricidal madness that will cause Polyneices to lead an army against Thebes. Let us consider the process by which the sons' condition was stated by their sister. First, she notes simply that things are evil for them now (*deina tan keinois tanun*, 336). A strangely delighted Oedipus responds with a lengthy discourse on how his sons have failed him while his daughters have supported him and repaid their *trophe*; but as yet he offers no curse. A curse might have come at this point: Oedipus' disgust at the behavior of both his sons has been made clear. Yet no curse follows until Ismene relates Polyneices' decision to go to Argos in order to obtain allies for his march against

Thebes. Polyneices promises that he will make Argos master of Thebes or, failing that, exalt the victor. Then follows the long discussion in which Oedipus learns of the Theban plan to bring him back. Oedipus is singularly unimpressed when Ismene ascribes his newfound importance to the gods.

> *Ism:* Now the gods restore you, whom they once destroyed.
> *Oed:* It is a trivial thing to restore an old man who fell while he
>   was young. (394–95)

He reacts similarly to the information that the Thebans will suffer if he fails to receive due burial honors.

> *Ism:* Your tomb, left dishonored, is a weighty problem for them.
> *Oed:* Someone can figure that out without help from the gods.
>   (403)

The information about the Thebans' concern for his tomb, then, is of no import to Oedipus. And the gods' supposed plan to restore him matters little, in part because he knows that this "restoration" is simply part of the prophecy that he received long ago. Unlike the Thebans, and unlike even his daughter, Oedipus knows or has at least reckoned that the Theban comprehension of the oracle is imperfect. For the first time in his life, Oedipus has all the requisite information and can evaluate both the future and his own situation far better than his former countrymen are able to do. The one bit of news (*logōn*, 333) that he may not have known from the original prophecy of Apollo (as he claims a certain expanded vision, this is difficult to ascertain with certainty) is that his sons are bent on their own destruction. Ismene provides this detail, and Oedipus can thus curse both sons, for the first time (not, certainly, for the last). The specifics of those curses will be treated in the next section.

After Ismene's departure to celebrate the sacrifice to the Eumenides that the chorus prescribes, the matter of Apollo's prophecy, and with it the possibility that Oedipus knows far more of the future than he ever lets on, recurs in his interview with Theseus. In the course of his meditation on time, Oedipus states, regarding Athens and Thebes:

> Endless time begets endless days and nights, in which they will
> ruin your peaceful relations by armed invasion at the slightest

provocation. Then my sleeping, cold, hidden corpse will drink
their hot blood, if Zeus is still Zeus and Apollo, his son, is still
truthful. But it is not pleasant to speak forbidden words. (618–25)

Scholars focus on the first part of this passage. Thus Knox points out
that nothing in Apollo's oracle had suggested that Oedipus would, like
Hamlet, "drink hot blood."[24] The last part of this passage has generally
been ignored, but to do so passes over information crucial to a discussion on prophecy. The Greek reads, *all' ou gar audan hēdu takinēt' epē,*
which can be translated as, "it is not pleasant *(hēdu)* to speak words not
to be moved *(takinēt')."* Since the first part of the passage could be construed as simply a more colorful embellishment of the information
gleaned from Ismene, Oedipus must be alluding, by *takinēt',* to other
words that he has learned; in short, he suggests that he knows far more
of the future than he has chosen to indicate to any of his interlocutors,
and more than Ismene has revealed to the audience.

The poet does not let the matter rest there. Oedipus again refers to
this greater knowledge during his confrontation with Creon. When
Creon first arrives, he professes his goodwill to Oedipus and his
respect for Athens, while he appeals to the exile to return to the city
(729–60). Oedipus, in turn, having been adequately forewarned of
Thebes' intention to bury him near the frontiers but not in Theban soil,
retaliates with an extensive denunciation of the plans and motives of
his relative and former counselor. He closes the passage:

> You have come not to take me home but to station me on your
> borders, so that Thebes may be released from any trouble from
> this land. *That* is not your fate, but this is—for my vengeful spirit
> to haunt Thebes forever; and for my sons to receive just enough of
> my kingdom to die in. Do I not know better than you the fate of
> Thebes? (784–91)

The last sentence offers an instructive perspective on the whole
question of prophecy and the hero's own oracular authority. Thebes
had, of course, read the oracle of Apollo according to their own desires,
and thus, to the Thebans, it seemed possible that Oedipus could be
forced to return. Oedipus knows better, and he herein announces that

---

24. Knox, *Heroic Temper,* 153.

same destruction of his sons with which he will curse them later. In this passage, of course, the destruction is part of the greater knowledge that Oedipus can claim.[25] The last sentence reads, *ar ouk ameinon ē su tan Thēbais phronō; phronō* indicates that Oedipus knows certainly those things at which Creon can only guess. He seems, here, to appropriate to himself oracular status. For, as he points out in the next verses,

> I know these things very surely, for I have heard them from much better sources: Phoebus and his father, Zeus. (792–93)

The Greek is a bit clearer: "Have I not heard these things from those [gods] much wiser in this, Phoebus and the father of Phoebus, Zeus" *(pollō{i} g' hosō{i}per kak saphesterōn kluō, Phoibou te kautou Zēnos, hos keinou patēr).*[26] Once more, Oedipus claims the advantage of privileged communication in his interpretations of Apollo's oracles and Thebes' future. This advantage must derive from a full knowledge of the prophecies regarding himself and Thebes, before Ismene and her news of more recent oracles ever arrives.

Innocence and Guilt 1

Allied closely to this discussion of Oedipus' knowledge of the future is the question of Oedipus' guilt or innocence. The situation in the *Oedipus at Colonus* differs greatly from that described by Dodds in his aforementioned article on the *Oedipus Tyrannus*. In that work, Dodds considered and refuted three "heresies" common to interpretations of the *Oedipus Tyrannus*. One of the heresies concerned the possibility that Oedipus might have been able to avoid his destiny. Dodds remarks that Oedipus could not simply construct a list of "things not to do." He could not resolve his situation by deciding not to kill older men, marry older women, and so on.[27] As Dodds observed, the oracle did not offer an either-or proposition. As formulated in the text of the play (790–93),

---

25. Of course, he also can thank Ismene for a great deal of information on the behavior of his sons that he would have otherwise lacked.

26. Winnington-Ingram considers this entire passage to be "curse-like," in connection to the curse Oedipus lays on Creon later, at 864–70, for seizing his daughters (*Sophocles*, 258).

27. Dodds, "On Misunderstanding the *Oedipus Rex*," 180.

the oracle simply stated that Oedipus was going to commit parricide and incest.

In this play, however, we are freed from a mandated acceptance of the oracular conditions laid down in the *Oedipus Tyrannus,* partly by time and distance from the previous work, and partly by the protagonist's desire to have the chorus and the audience reconsider his earlier deeds. We may also recall Dodds' remarks (quoted earlier) that men are responsible for creating their own fate and hence bear responsibility for their own actions.

The chorus and Oedipus twice discuss his crimes, first when the chorus finds him and Antigone in the grove, and again after Ismene's arrival with news from Thebes and her subsequent withdrawal to perform expiatory rites to the Eumenides. On the first occasion, the chorus attempts to persuade Oedipus to reveal his identity. He repeatedly declines, until at last, he yields to the chorus' persistence.

> *Oed:* Have you ever heard of Laius—
> *Cho:* Oh, no!
> *Oed:* Of the race of Labdacus—
> *Cho:* O Zeus!
> *Oed:* The hapless Oedipus.
> *Cho:* Are you he?
> *Oed:* Do not be afraid of anything I say.
> *Cho:* Oh no!
> *Oed:* Oh wretched me!
> *Cho:* Oh no!
> *Oed:* O daughter, what will happen now?
> *Cho:* Go forth from our land immediately!
> *Oed:* Is this how you keep your promises? (219–27)

After the choristers reject Oedipus' argument that they would be in violation of their own promises should they expel him from the land, Antigone pleads on her father's behalf; she extracts from them an admission of their pity but no more. Then a determined Oedipus takes the offensive (258–91). The passage relevant to this discussion is 263–74.

> Where is this [Athenian *xenia*] now? First you forced me to move, and now you would drive me out of your land altogether, fearing

my name alone; I am sure you do not fear my body or my actions. For I suffered my deeds more than I did them. If there were reason to tell you of my father and mother, the cause of your fear, you would believe me. In what way am I evil? When I was attacked, I retaliated. Even if I had known it was my father, I still would not be an evil man But in ignorance I went where I went— and now I am ruined by those very things I suffered, now that all the facts have come to light.

In this statement Oedipus provides a clear affirmation of his own innocence. But Sophocles does not allow the matter to drop quietly. After Oedipus wins a reprieve from the chorus, and after Ismene's arrival and departure, the citizens of Colonus return again to the question of Oedipus' past.

> *Cho:* It is a dreadful thing, stranger, to stir up an old evil long since laid to rest, but I desire to learn—
> *Oed:* What?
> *Cho:* Tell us of the cruel, unavoidable pain that governed your life.
> *Oed:* Do not ask me (I claim this favor as a guest) to reveal my shame.
> *Cho:* I have heard the story repeated endlessly, but I would like to hear the truth. (509–18)

As noted earlier, Knox correctly described the chorus' interest as "almost prurient."[28] After a bit more persuasion, Oedipus relents and offers the chorus his view of his past.

> *Oed:* I endured things most horrible, all unwilling, but, I swear, I committed no evil deed intentionally.
> *Cho:* Explain.
> *Oed:* Thebes bound me, knowing nothing, to a ruinous marriage.
> *Cho:* Did you share a marriage bed (ill named) with your mother?
> *Oed:* It is like death to hear such things, stranger. But these two girls—

---

28. *Heroic Temper*, 152.

Cho: Tell us.
Oed: Two daughters, my ruin. (521–31)

He opposes their accusation of guilt with his own claim of moral innocence, a function of his ignorance of his real relationship to Jocasta. He
also claims that the state bears ultimate responsibility for his marriage.
After still more of the horrors of incest, the chorus turns once more to
the additional charge of parricide.

Cho: You killed him!
Oed: Yes, I killed him, but I had—
Cho: What?
Oed: A good reason.
Cho: What?
Oed: I will tell you; I killed those who would have killed me. I am
    innocent in the law, acquitted by my ignorance. (544–48)

At this juncture, Theseus arrives. And the matter of Oedipus' guilt or
innocence becomes, from the Athenian perspective, a moot point once
Theseus has agreed to permit Oedipus to remain in Attica. But the poet,
still not content to let the matter drop, returns to the question once
again later in the play. Creon, apparently foiled in his efforts to kidnap
Ismene, Antigone, and Oedipus, protests to Theseus that he had meant
no disrespect to Athens but had assumed that such a renowned city
would not harbor a man guilty of Oedipus' crimes. Oedipus retorts:

Murder and incest, deeds of horror, all those charges you name, I
endured all these evils, unwillingly; so the gods willed. . . . Tell
me, if an oracle foretold to my father that he was destined to die
by his son's hand, how can you, in justice, blame this on me[?] . . .
And if I were born doomed to misery, as I was, and I met my
father and slew him with my own hands, not knowing who he
was or what I did, how can you fairly blame me, I who did the
deed involuntarily? (962 ff.)

As to the matter of incest, Oedipus reproaches Creon for bringing up
such a shameful matter, especially as Jocasta was Creon's sister. Having dispensed with the charge (in a manner a bit facile, as we shall con-

sider later), Oedipus returns to the question of his father's murder with a hypothetical question for Creon.

> Answer one question that I will ask you: if someone should presently attempt to kill you (a just man, clearly) would you first ask the killer if he were your father, or would you punish him? (991–94)

Oedipus then praises Athens once more, for knowing how a state should behave toward the gods.

Oedipus' defense of his own actions and his assertion of his own moral innocence effectively raise those very questions that Dodds argued against even discussing for the *Oedipus Tyrannus*. Dodds would, perhaps, given his remarks on the impropriety of raising such questions in the earlier play, require us to accept Oedipus' denial of wrongdoing at face value. However, we are reminded of Ahl's shrewd observation that we may not know certainly what questions the poet would have us ask.[29] What we know and have seen of Oedipus, that walking (or limping) embodiment of all manner of internal contradictions, requires us to be very careful in examining his comments before we accept them.[30] For example, a contradiction appears immediately after his lecture to Creon regarding the appropriateness of the Theban's behavior. He states that Creon "desired to steal their [the Athenians] aged suppliant" (1008). Yet, as we have shown, Oedipus had not presented himself as a suppliant to Athens. He was properly the suppliant of the goddesses, and Theseus himself admits the distinction. But the hero could stretch the truth to serve his own needs, when necessary.

Given that the chorus and Oedipus have both opened the matter to discussion, we escape once and for all Dodds' proposed strictures on appropriate inquiry. The matter of guilt or innocence, intent or ignorance, has become part of the fabric of the play. First, we should consider the manner in which Oedipus presents his own defense. The chorus, and later Creon, lay two separate charges against the accused.

---

29. *Sophocles' Oedipus*, 5.

30. Rosenmeyer's formulation is extreme here, yet not so far off the mark: "If we drop the usual perspective according to which Oedipus can do no wrong, we must admit that his pleading is all but monstrously immoral" ("Wrath of Oedipus," 98).

Parricide takes up the much greater part of the hero's response. In his initial argument with the choristers, when they first attempt to expel him from the grove, Oedipus states at line 268 that, "were it necessary to speak of my mother and of my father," he might say much on his own behalf. He then devotes the next three lines (270–72) to a plea of self-defense against the charge that he murdered Laius, but he passes over in silence the question of his marriage to Jocasta.

Again, 250 lines later, the choristers return to their probing of Oedipus' prior deeds. In this passage, Oedipus answers the charge of incest at last, and he claims that Thebes forced him into an impious marriage: "Thebes bound me, knowing nothing, to a ruinous marriage" (*kaka{i} m' euna{i} polis ouden idrin gamōn enedēsen hata{i}*, 525–26). By this response, he casts the blame for the crime of incest directly on Thebes. Difficulties supervene his estimate of the situation, of course. No evidence is adduced in support of this remark, nothing we know of the myth from other sources suggests that it is true, and Oedipus makes no attempt to explain himself further. In point of fact, he contradicts himself a few lines further down: "would that I, much enduring, had never received that gift of the city, having aided it" (*edexamen dōron, ho mēpot' egō epōphelēsas poleos exelesthai*, 539–41).[31] We cannot really reconcile Oedipus' claim that he had received a gift from the city and his earlier contention that the polis had bound him by the marriage.[32] *Endeo,* as Ellendt rightly points out, carries with it a sense of coercion.[33] Oedipus' first response to the charge of incest and all his subsequent responses thus encourage our suspicion rather than our trust.[34]

---

31. This translation is roughly Jebb's rendering of the line (*Oedipus at Colonus,* 131).

32. The only possible resolution is, of course, that Oedipus is compelled to marry Jocasta in order to become the king of Thebes. This solution does not absolve Oedipus, for nothing compels him to take the Theban kingship, beyond his own desire; his marriage to Jocasta, then, is simply a calculated act to assist him in obtaining that desire.

33. Ellendt translates the word with the Latin *illigo* (*Lexikon Sophocleum,* 242).

34. It does no good to argue that we cannot experience the play in this manner, even if we disregard Ahl's point on permissible questions. We experience art as we experience life. When we do so, we transfer the lessons learned from life to the stage, and we all know that, once we catch someone in a lie, or even an evasion, our suspicions of that person remain heightened, more or less forever.

Oedipus' counterarguments to the charge of incest run just five lines, although he augments his response with frequent lamentations. The chorus then turns again to the more easily handled charge of murder, and Oedipus is ready, claiming justice and self-defense at two different points, at 545 and in a three-line statement at 546–48. Thus, the question of incest has received five lines, in two passages that appear mutually contradictory, while exception from the charge of parricide has received eight lines, in two admirably consistent passages of diverse provenience. Clearly, Oedipus finds the latter action easier to excuse and to explain.

In his subsequent encounter with Creon, Oedipus exhibits further inconsistency in manufacturing and maintaining his defense against the charge of incest. Creon has accused him of the now overfamiliar crimes, and Oedipus' self-exculpation should be well rehearsed by this point. So it seems, yet a glaring inconsistency in his account appears. Oedipus devotes seven lines, from 969–76, to his defense against the charge of murder, as he pleads once again his moral innocence. He then passes to the charge of incest, to which he devotes another nine lines.

> As for my mother—are you not ashamed, seeing she was thy sister, to compel me to tell the story of her marriage, which I will now talk about. For I will not keep silence, since you have brought up the matter, impious though it was. She was, she was my mother, alas; I did not know it, nor did she; and she, although she was my mother, bore me children, a shameful thing. But I know one thing for certain: you freely speak of our marriage. But I married her against my will, and I speak of these matters now against my will. (977–87)

The observant will note the incongruity. Oedipus omits specific mention of the Thebans' responsibility for his marriage (although he does claim to have married her *akōn* at 987), a culpability that he had unhesitatingly alleged earlier to the chorus. In fact, he offers no real defense at all, except ignorance of the true identity of Jocasta. Why has the suggestion of some compulsion by Thebes been dropped? As often occurs when the specifics of the *Oedipus at Colonus* are examined closely, an obvious, though dark, suggestion comes to mind. Creon, who of course lived in Thebes when the marriage took place, might know better the facts of the case than do the Athenians, who are unlikely to possess any specific intelligence about the marriage other than Oedipus' own testimony. A lie would be quickly detected. In place of a defense, then, Oedipus offers a hastily improvised attack on Creon, for the supreme impropriety of airing, as it were, the family's dirty laundry in public. And, quick as he may, Oedipus returns to the safer charge of parricide, in another nine-line passage (991–99).

Numbers are not everything, but the defense against the charge of parricide occupies twenty-two lines, incest fifteen (a good deal of which are taken up by appropriate lamentations); moreover, those arguments adduced by Oedipus in support of his killing of Laius remain consistent throughout, while his responses to the accusation of incest vary considerably, from casting blame on Thebes in a formulation that clearly implies coercion, to his own receipt of Jocasta as a gift, and finally, in his outraged invective against Creon, to his understandable, if somewhat unsatisfactory, decision that the best defense is a good offense. His remarks are clearly inconsistent and ultimately seem, when taken as a whole, a bit lame. Perhaps Sophocles himself, faced with a need to rehabilitate his hero, found the incest more problematic than the murder. This is no surprise, of course. Self-defense is instantaneous: be stricken and strike back, with no time to consider the consequences.[35] Marriage, of course, presents a separate problem and one far more difficult either to address or to dismiss. A man who has received a prophecy concerning his marriage and his future bride should be a bit more circumspect in his selection of a wife. Oedipus cannot appeal to haste or necessity in his marriage as he can in the case of Laius' death. Marriage is, or should be, a calculated, not an impulsive, act.

Yet despite the difficulties posed by the question of Oedipus' incestuous marriage, the playwright does well, ultimately, to have his hero offer any defense at all for his actions. Just as Oedipus insists on his own heroic identity, even where that identity cannot easily be detected, so too his own repeated assertions of moral innocence sway his audience, almost by pure force of personality. If we are not always persuaded by the specifics of the defense, we are nonetheless moved by the man who has withstood his awful fate. The chorus never pro-

---

35. As Knox points out: "His defense is detailed and omits no particular of the terrible events which cost him his eyes. It is a plea which the Areopagus could admit. He killed his father and married his mother in ignorance" (*Heroic Temper*, 158). Yet Knox, like every other scholar I have read, never quite mentions Oedipus' initial defense against the charge of incest.

nounces Oedipus innocent, Theseus never considers the matter, and Creon, we may safely assume, lacks any discernible sympathy for Oedipus' harsh comments on the impropriety of discussing the ruinous union in public. On the whole, detailed observation of the inconsistencies in Oedipus' differing answers to the charge of incest leaves open the disquieting possibility that Oedipus, with his shifting arguments, may be quick-witted rather than clear-sighted. However, the intensity of his conviction, and perhaps our own amazement that a man so evidently beaten by life can still maintain such ferocity, pushes us on an emotional, rather than an intellectual, level to accept his claims of heroic stature, while the well-established, veridical nature of the oracle provides sufficient justification to allow him the benefit of the doubt.[36] This ferocity, the intensity of feeling with which he defends himself even if, as seems likely, the facts resist the interpretation that he would claim, leads inevitably to the next discussion, an examination of the famous curses that Oedipus levels against his sons.

Curses

Sophocles has altered the epic version of the curses, in which those curses pronounced by the father cause the strife that destroys his sons.[37] In so doing, he very nearly eliminates supernatural elements from the play entirely. Instead, Oedipus' curse on Polyneices and Eteocles is presented as a function of intelligence and understanding, not magic.

Sophocles doles the curses out only gradually in the course of the *Oedipus at Colonus*.[38] The first suggestion of such matters within the play comes at 421, when Oedipus has discovered that both his sons have heard the oracle of Apollo, which has urged the Thebans to take possession of him, living or dead. The power of the father encourages

36. It is perhaps significant that Whitman can do no more to exonerate Oedipus than Sophocles did. In his discussion of Oedipus' defense, Whitman passes over the matter of incest completely. However, he deals at some length with the charge of self-defense and finally reaches the conclusion that Oedipus' rejection of guilt has been successful: "The gods and their gifts, the misery of his life; these are externals, and ineluctable. But he is himself, and the gods can do nothing to break the strong moral good he wills" (*Sophocles*, 203–4).

37. *Thebaid* frags. 2 and 3.

38. See Reinhardt, *Sophocles*, 205, for the significance of this "doling out" in relationship to the general action of the play.

both to attempt to capitalize on the possibilities the possession of him may afford. Outraged, the exile states,

> Then may the gods not quench their fated strife, and let the out-come of their battle for which they now are preparing their weapons rest on me; may the one who holds the scepter now lose his throne, and may the one who fled the kingdom never return. (421 ff.)

After an extensive complaint about his sons' failure to permit him to stay on in Thebes after his madness passed, Oedipus returns again to the destiny of the two and to the fate of his old city.

> No! neither shall ever have me as an ally, nor will either ever profit from the Theban kingship. That I know from the oracles I have just heard from her [Ismene] and from those old predictions about me that Phoebus now at last has accomplished. (450–54)

In these two passages we see the essential relationship of curse to oracle in the play. Oedipus pronounces what appears to be a curse against his sons in the first passage, then in the second passage he explicates the basis on which he makes his curse: his prior knowledge of their destinies via the oracles of Apollo, combined with his own insight into their characters. Oedipus, since he has known full well his own future from the initial oracle of Apollo, as shown earlier, is in a position to realize something the Thebans cannot: the oracle that Apollo gave to them will not come to pass in the manner they would have it. In turn, the data Ismene provides allows Oedipus greater certainty about his targets. Ismene has informed him that Polyneices intends, in effect, homicide or suicide. Oedipus should know that the children of himself and Jocasta will not want for determination or impulse; he can logically expect that Eteocles will display no less commitment to his own cause than Polyneices has shown on his own behalf. Therefore, to curse his sons, to wish for and predict their mutual destruction, hardly requires second sight or even an alliance with the Eumenides.[39]

---

39. Of course, Oedipus does not specifically refer to the death of his sons in these verses. Still, given that he has declared that he will side with neither and that neither will gain the *onesis* of the Theban kingship, the deaths of his sons are an easy inference.

Sophocles returns to the matter of the curse again when Creon arrives. After the Theban has flattered the men of Colonus and attempted to persuade Oedipus to return willingly, Oedipus responds with a scathing indictment of Creon's hypocrisy. He condemns Thebes for initially failing to grant him exile when he desired it, for subsequently forcing him to leave after he had ceased to desire banishment, and finally for pretending to want him back. For, thanks to Ismene's timely arrival, he knows certainly that they actually have no intention of returning him to Thebes but only of placing him on the frontier. Oedipus then tells Creon what the Thebans can expect from him.

My vengeful spirit dwelling there forever, and to my sons, this—room enough to die in. I know so much more than you about the affairs of Thebes. I know these things very surely, for I have heard them from much better sources: Phoebus and his father, Zeus. (787–93)

Once again, his curse on his sons is a consequence of his knowledge of the prophecies that he has received. The specific information that Ismene brought allows him to formulate his curses with some confidence, in that he knows the paths that his sons have already chosen for themselves. Ismene therefore has not informed him of any unknown features of his own destiny but rather has given him the means to threaten his revenge.

Having thus prepared the ground, Sophocles at last presents us with the scene that reveals the extent of Oedipus' anger and bitterness: the arrival of his son, Polyneices, sitting as a suppliant at the altar of Poseidon at Colonus. After Theseus has frustrated the Thebans in their attempt to abduct his daughters and has restored Ismene and Antigone to Oedipus, he troubles the grateful father about a small matter, the presence of a stranger who asks only a word of the Theban exile (1150–62). At first, Oedipus cannot guess at the identity of the newcomer (1166). Theseus describes him as a kinsman but not a fellow citizen, that is, not a Theban. The stranger appears to be an Argive (1167–68).[40] When Oedipus hears this, he realizes the identity of his visitor and begs the king not to force him to grant Polyneices an interview,

40. Jebb, as noted earlier, suggested that a detail of dress or appearance prompted Theseus' surmise (*Oedipus at Colonus*, 205).

while Theseus for his part reminds Oedipus that he must not show disrespect to the gods (1169–80). Antigone then begs that her father hear out her brother, for her sake, even if he does nothing else. She also points out the risk inherent in yielding to such an unruly passion as anger (1181–1204). Still, Oedipus is reluctant, and only upon a reiterated guarantee of protection from Theseus does he admit Polyneices into his presence (1208–10).

Polyneices enters and immediately bemoans the condition of his father and sisters. Unlike Creon, who seems to treat rather breezily the unfortunate circumstances of Oedipus, Polyneices has the grace, or at least the good sense, to acknowledge his own culpability in the plight of his father.

> I admit that I am the worst of men as regards your maintenance. I see that for myself. (1265–66)

Yet at the same time, he entertains some hope of redemption.

> But almighty Zeus has Compassion [Aidos] as partner in all his deeds, a sharer of his throne; father, may you be compassionate as well. For past wrongs can be repaired, but they cannot be multiplied. (1267–70)

His hopes, though, will be disappointed, for his father will not even respond. He then asks his sisters for their aid, and Antigone urges Polyneices to explain in detail his reason for seeking out Oedipus (1275–83). Polyneices, after an invocation to Poseidon as god of the place, proceeds as follows.

> Now, father, I wish to tell you why I have come. I have been exiled from the city because I claimed my right to the throne as firstborn son. But Eteocles, my younger brother, banished me. He did not earn it by defeating me in argument or in action, but simply by persuading the city. Personally, I think the cause of this [my banishment] was the curse on you. And the prophets concur. (1291–1300)

As a result of the usurpation of the throne by Eteocles, Polyneices has gone to Argos and recruited allies.

I made the best spearmen of the Apian land my allies, so I could raise a host with seven captains to lead against Thebes. With these men I shall either drive out those who persecuted me or die in a just cause. (1303–6)

Next, Polyneices explains why he has journeyed to see Oedipus.

Father, I have come to ask your help, for both myself and my allies, who now, as seven captains lead seven hosts, have invested all the plain that circles Thebes. (1309–12)

Finally, after the traditional list of the seven champions (Amphiaraus, Tydeus, Eteoclus, Hippomedon, Capaneus, Parthenopaeus, and, of course, Polyneices himself), he makes specific his request.

We all ask you to relent in your anger and favor one who seeks just vengeance from a brother who has banned me and took away my country. For if oracles can be trusted, they say that whichever side has you for an ally will triumph. (1327–32)

In return for his favor, Oedipus will be rewarded by Polyneices with a triumphant return to Thebes.

All this time, through all these appeals, Oedipus has sat and maintained his silence, a silence that seems, for one so *deinos* at speech, remarkable.[41] Finally, the chorus prompts him to speak, and he responds to Polyneices. Having started, he gives full vent to years' worth of complaints.

Evilest of men, when I ruled and held the scepter and the throne that your brother holds now, did you not drive me out, making me a man without a city, forcing me to wear these rags, the ones that you weep at the sight of now, when you have experienced the same fate that I have? There is no need to weep. I must bear this misfortune for the rest of my life, always remembering that you were the one who killed me. You cast me out. You forced me to

---

41. See especially Bushnell, *Prophesying Tragedy*, 1–4, on the significance of silence by the tragic audience as a way of withholding approbation.

partake of this diet of sorrow; because of you I have been forced to wander the world, begging my daily bread. (1354–64)

This is a formidable indictment. After he praises his daughters, whose behavior has contrasted so nobly to that of their brothers, he continues his harangue.

But you are bastards, not fathered by me. Therefore the *daimon* is keeping his eye on you; . . . (1369–70)

Then, having warmed to his task, he lets Polyneices have it with both barrels, so to speak.

You will never take that city, but first you will fall, stained by the blood of a kinsman who will be stained by yours as well. I brought such curses on you before and I call on them now as allies, so that you remember to honor your parents and not treat them badly, even if you were born of a man now blind. Your sisters did not fail me. My curses defeat your pleas and your power, if Justice, as before, still sits by the side of Zeus, according to the ancient rules.

Be off, wickedest of the wicked, bastard, and take with you these curses: that you will never conquer your homeland, nor will you ever return to the hollows of Argos, but you will die as you kill your brother, who exiled you. Thus I curse you, and I call on the fierce, paternal darkness of Tartarus, that you may dwell there; I call on the Eumenides; and I call on Ares, who inspired you both with this great hatred. (1372–92)

Now the terrible curses have been made. The dramatic moment has been seized: Oedipus has been magnified in stature, while Polyneices slinks beaten from the stage. Polyneices offers only a last few words to his sisters, but enough to ensure that his own destruction will encompass that of Antigone as well.

You daughters of this man, you have heard the cruelty of this man's curses. If his curses come to pass, and someday you return to Thebes, I beg you, by the gods, not to dishonor me, but grant me burial with the proper rites. (1405–10)

Antigone is of other mind and suggests a wiser course for her brother, but he remains fixed on his own destruction.

Ant: Retreat as quickly as possible back to Argos, and do not destroy yourself and Thebes.

Pol: Impossible. How could I ever again mount another attack, once I have backed down?

Ant: But, brother, why is it necessary for you to be vexed? What do you gain by destroying our country?

Pol: It is disgraceful to live in exile, and more disgraceful for an older brother to be mocked by his younger brother.

Ant: Do you not see that you will yourself bring to pass the prophecies of he who predicted that you will kill each other?

Pol: That he wishes: should we not comply?

Ant: Woe to me! But who will dare to follow you, once this man's prophecies have been heard?

Pol: I'll never relate them to anyone; a good general tells his men the good news and keeps the bad news to himself.

Ant: Foolish boy, is everything then decided?

Pol: It is, and do not try to stop me. I must see to my own path, now, even if it has been made ill fated and evil by your father and his Furies. But may Zeus treat you well, if you carry out your obligations to me. Now release me and say good-bye. You will never again see me alive. (1416–36)

After a few more good-byes, we reach the end of the passage and Polyneices leaves. The curses have taken final shape. But what shape, exactly, is that?

Oedipus' final curse proceeds along the lines of a prophecy. For he states that "that city [Thebes] you can never storm" and predicts that Polyneices and Eteocles will kill one another (1373–74). After all, he says, "such curses [prayers?] I sent up before" (*toiasd' aras sphōn prosthe t' exanēk' egō*). Several issues, of course, must be dealt with in analyzing these verses. To start with the most obvious, Oedipus has already prayed that his sons would kill each other. Yet he spoke this prayer only after he had received information that the brothers were already determined on civil war. Hence, (like a good Jesuit) he prays for something that he has fairly good reason to suspect will happen. Moreover, when he makes his assessment that Polyneices will never storm Thebes, we need not see quite such a mystical force involved in the prediction. Oedipus ruled Thebes for a number of years. In fact, according to the epic tradition, he actually died repelling an invasion. Oedipus says nothing on the possible success or failure of Polyneices' mission until after he has been informed of the condition and personnel of Polyneices' army. We cannot overlook the possibility that at least part of the dreaded curse is actually a military evaluation, made by a man with some experience of the specific terrain of the killing ground.

A more serious question intrudes. What "prior" curses does Oedipus refer to? Jebb defended adamantly the position that the prior curse is that within the play itself, at 421 ff., as opposed to the "epic" version of the curse, found in Aeschylus and Euripides, in which Oedipus cursed his sons before he ever left Thebes.[42] This is the clear sense of the play, and the verse at 421 has the feel of a new revelation, not a repetition. Still, doubt has remained. Knox preferred to read the line as referring to the older curses and has been followed by Bushnell.[43] Knox's view rests on the position that it makes no sense to inform Polyneices of a curse he cannot have heard before: he is, of course, not present when Oedipus utters 421 ff. Moreover, according to Knox, "those passages [421–27 and 451] are not curses (what a curse is like we can see all too clearly from 1383 ff.), they are in the first case a wish and in the second a prophecy."[44]

Knox misses two points. In the first place, the first part of his argument can simply be turned around: there is every need to tell Polyneices of a curse he has not heard before, since, after all, he was not on hand to hear it the first time. That Sophocles opts against a verbatim repetition need not trouble us; the audience would remember the specifics, and Polyneices would get the point. Rather, if Sophocles had wished the audience to think of the *epic* curse, he should have stated the matter more clearly. Moreover, the diction favors Jebb's reading. Oedi-

42. Jebb, *Oedipus at Colonus*, 230.
43. Knox, *Heroic Temper*, 194 n. 14; Bushnell, *Prophesying Tragedy*, 97.
44. *Heroic Temper*, 194 n. 14.

pus refers to *toiasd' aras: toiasd'* beyond question suggests a certain
immediacy, and *aras* poses no particularly difficult problem. Indeed,
aras is precisely the same word that Oedipus uses later, at 1385, to
describe Knox's so-called real curse.

Knox's second point in defense of his reading of 1375 is, of course,
the important one for this whole discussion: the nature of his so-called
real curses, which follow the initial imprecations against Polyneices.
Oedipus begins, "now I call [them, i.e., the *toiasd' aras* of 1375] as allies
to me" *(nun t' anakaloumai xummachous elthein emoi).* He then repeats the
grounds for his actions—a failure by his sons to honor their father, a
task that his daughters performed in their stead—and he calls on his
own deity, Dike, to counter Polyneices' Aidos (1268). Then follows the
major part of the curse.

> Be off, wickedest of the wicked, bastard, and take with you these
> curses: that you will never conquer your homeland, nor will you
> ever return to the hollows of Argos, but you will die as you kill
> your brother, who exiled you.
>
> *kakōn kakiste, tasde sullabōn aras, has soi kaloumai, mēte gēs ēmphuliou*
> *dorei kratēsai mete nostēsai pote to koilon Argos, alla suggenei xeri*
> *thanein ktanein th' huph' houper exelēlasai.* (1384–88)

We see here that, in essence, Oedipus repeats the prayer or prophecy
that he spoke earlier. That prayer in most particulars was simply a
reading of the oracles that he already knew. Hence, his certainty here
may mark not so much the greater awareness of his own prophetic
power but his greater understanding of the accuracy of all the oracles
ever uttered about his own fate and, still more, his understanding of
man's own complicity in creating his fate. For Polyneices certainly will
create his destiny. Perhaps that tendency to create one's own fate is the
daimon (family curse?) that Oedipus and Polyneices both recognize. In
1337, Polyneices has claimed that both he and his father share the same
fate: *ton auton daimon' exeilēchotes.* Oedipus later states that "the *daimon*
already has his eye on you" *(toigar s' ho daimōn eisora{i}, 1370).* The *daimon* of whom Oedipus warns his son is of course the one who curses
the family throughout: the tendency to walk squarely into trouble
when trouble has been predicted. The members of the house of Labda-

cus, male and female, share an unfortunate predilection for destroying themselves.

In reality, while there have perhaps been many oracles, there has been only one prophecy, the one that Oedipus has known about all of his adult life. Thebes and Polyneices have only learned enough of the oracle to misunderstand it and to act in such a way as to confirm the power of oracles. In this respect, of course, the *Oedipus at Colonus* mirrors and reverses the action of the *Oedipus Tyrannus*. In that play, Oedipus heard and misunderstood the oracle, thereby creating the action of the drama. Now Oedipus, hardened in faith, eager, as Knox pointed out, to be instructed in religious matters, has grasped the oracle and thus, in a sense, has stood outside or beyond it.[45] When he speaks in the accusative-infinitive discourse—instead, perhaps, of the optative—it indicates that he has developed not oracular powers but simply the far more elusive skill of accepting prophecy qua prophecy. In fact, for those who see the *Oedipus at Colonus* as the long, slow reversal of the earlier play (an attractive generalization, at least), Ismene, Creon, and Polyneices play similar roles in confirming the oracular awareness of Oedipus that Creon, the shepherd, and the messenger noted in the earlier work. Each brings to the understanding of prophecy a part that confirms a whole that was disclosed years before.

It is the final part of Oedipus' speech to Polyneices that truly seems to focus attention on the power of the curses, and the lines do seem to invoke a certain horror. Perhaps, though, the passage is more conventional and less terrifying than is usually thought. Oedipus calls on the gloom of Tartarus, that "it may take you hence" (*hōs s' apoikise{i}*). He then calls on "these demons" (i.e., the Furies) and, finally, on Ares.

Only his invocation of Tartarus seems particularly shocking in retrospect. The Furies appear in the group for a number of reasons. First, they are the appropriate avengers in any case in which a child mistreats a parent, a charge that Oedipus has made throughout. Next, they are the divinities of the place. Finally, they were, in fact, the initial confirming sign that the last part of Apollo's oracle was coming true: in

---

45. Knox writes: "The loving care with which the ritual [of purification] is described sets the tone for the religious mystery we are going to witness, and the scene also shows us the hero's docility and eagerness to be instructed in matters of religion, an attitude which will be sharply contrasted with his growing assertiveness and intractability in his relations with men" (*Heroic Temper*, 151).

essence, they provided the sign for the oracle that made the definitive-ness of the curse possible. As to the invocation of Ares, Polyneices brought that on all by himself. Contrary to his own view of the situation, no one, not even his father or his brother, has forced him to take up arms. Only his own outraged sense of honor compels him to such a suicidal undertaking. Because Polyneices is resolved on war, the god of war will perforce be inextricably involved in the brothers' fate.

The call on Tartarus, though, is perhaps a bit more disturbing. It is fitting, of course, in that Oedipus, from his greater knowledge of the oracles and his awareness of the temper of the members of his own family, knows that both sons will die at Thebes. To wish death on one's own sons strikes the reader as excessively harsh. However, his status as what Bushnell calls a "heroic prophet" allows him to predict his sons' death.[46] And no matter how dramatic or emphatic the expression of the curse, the fact remains that Polyneices takes it on himself to fulfill it.

Knox's distinction, then, between a real curse and the earlier prayers disintegrates on inspection. If anything, the curse he would adduce as "real" actually functions as a prophecy, a judgment carefully deduced by the hero himself from foreknowledge and observation.[47] The earlier, preparatory imprecations each function in the same general capacity, since in each case, Oedipus only speaks his curse on the acquisition of new data. Actually, only one "real" curse—that is, only one that does not evidently depend on some privileged information to which the hero can lay claim—appears in the work. When Creon seizes Antigone, Oedipus prays,

> May the goddesses [Furies] not prevent me from making this curse: evil man, you have taken away from me the girl who has been my eyes, now that my own eyes are gone; for this crime, to you and all your family may the Sun, who sees all things, give a life and an old age like mine. (864–70)

No prior oracular response prompts this imprecation. Oedipus offers it spontaneously, under the stress of conflict. That absence of prior oracular authority may prompt Oedipus to preface the curse by asking the

---

46. Bushnell, *Prophesying Tragedy*, 87.

47. In this connection it is useful to recall that horoscopes and the tarot operate along the same general lines.

permission of the Furies. And it strikes home, as we see from the broken Creon who remains at the end of the *Antigone.* In this curse, as well as in the curse on his sons at 421–27, optatives are the mood of choice, rather than the infinitives that recur throughout the curse delivered in the presence of Polyneices. Thus, Oedipus begs the Sun that he *doiē* to Creon a horrible fate. Similarly, Oedipus had used the forms *katasbeseian, meineien,* and *elthoi* in his first attack on his sons.

Thus we may distinguish only with great care the differentiated aspects of curse and prophecy. Some overlapping is perhaps inevitable, given the structure and nature of the play, but on the whole, we see that Sophocles never permits Oedipus to curse his sons without prior oracular authority, and in each instance, the root of that authority is Oedipus' greater knowledge of the prophecies that surround himself and Thebes.

In this context, though, we should note that a certain level of moral ambiguity disrupts our somewhat voyeuristic pleasure in seeing Polyneices "get his," as it were, and it is only our knowledge that, for the most part, Oedipus' curses are nothing more than shrewd predictions that allows us to witness the actions with an even demeanor. For us to be completely convinced that Polyneices deserves his fate, we would have to give in subjectively to the play; for on an objective level, much lacks, not least the moral authority of the one cursing.

Innocence and Guilt 2

Oedipus begs his daughters to accept, in return for the hardships that they have endured, "love" (*to philein,* 1617)—not an ignoble sentiment, yet not perhaps adequate compensation for Antigone's lost youth. Creon speaks from vested interest, but his remarks are nonetheless cogent.

> Unless I am the worst of men, I must take pain seeing your difficulties, finding you an aged *xenos,* wandering endlessly, a beggar going about with only this girl as an attendant. I never thought she would have it so tough! How far she has fallen, the poor girl, always looking after you, living in poverty, the right age for marriage but unwed, vulnerable to assault from any corner. (743–52)

Oedipus frequently argues for his right to *trophē,* the reward that a child is expected to pay for his or her nurture. The daughters, of course, have performed their tasks nobly; the sons have not. But since Oedipus has raised the issue of obligations, how did he discharge his own obligations, in light of his position as king and father? This is a fair question, if a somewhat awkward one, since Oedipus has so facilely reviled his sons for their failures.

> And my sons, who should have helped their father, did not wish to do so: for want of one small word I was driven out, an exile, to wander as a beggar for the rest of my life. These two girls, their sisters, gave as much to me as their nature allowed, food to live on, safe refuge, familial concern; but their two brothers chose the throne, the scepter, and royal power over their father. (442–49)

Indeed, repeated throughout the play are references to the sacrifices both daughters, but especially Antigone, have made on their father's behalf. But what is their return? The messenger reports the words with which Oedipus took leave of his daughters.

> As he [Oedipus] heard their sudden bitter cry, embracing them both he said, "Children, today you lose your father. I pass entirely from the world, and no longer must you look after me. I know it was a harsh duty, and yet one word alone repays all your troubles—love. And my love you have had, greater than any other's. (1610–19)

While the sentiment is certainly touching, and it may seem ungenerous to question it, a certain arrogant blindness to the consequences of his own actions marks Oedipus' claim—an arrogance that characteristically distinguishes the great and leaves the less great scurrying for protection. One senses that even Antigone, for all her devotion to her father, is, in the great scheme of things, plagued by a few doubts. She cries out:

> Woe to us! On this sad day we sisters must weep over the cursed blood of our father, the blood that runs through our veins as well—that father for whom we endured endless toil, and from

whose pain we will take unaccountable things, having seen and
suffered so much. (1670–76)

And later she says:

Night has fallen on us. Traversing what distant land or billowing
sea will we find nourishment for our bitter life? (1684–87)

Ismene responds, even more disconsolate:

I do not know. I wish that bloody death would finish me and I
could die with my aged father. The life that remains is not bear-
able. (1688–90)

Antigone (echoing, of course, the ever rational heroine of the eponymous drama) cries out,

Lead me there [to the tomb]; slay me. (1733)

We cannot help but sense a certain exaggeration in the relationships
of these characters. Granted, filial devotion is a noble virtue; in turn, a
father's love has proven more substantial than the cynical Creon may
have suspected. Still, this portrait of familial love proves far less benign
on reconsideration. Fathers die and children go on; such is the natural
order of things, and the famous story of Croesus' discussion with
Cyrus on the folly of war reminds us that the Greeks were fully aware
of the logic of this natural progression. Yet despite the fact that his
daughters had devoted so much of their lives to him, Oedipus seems to
have made little preparation on their behalf. Only at the end does he
commend them to the care of Theseus and the chorus. Theseus, ever the
generous hero, undertakes the obligation gladly. Still, this belated concern does not negate the essential validity of the point made by Creon
and Polyneices and even by Antigone: in tending his life, the daughters
have largely abandoned their own. His self-blinding started Thebes on
the course to a brutal, destructive war with Argos. His callous self-
absorption has cost both his daughters years out of their lives. It
remains to see why, exactly, Oedipus is a hero.

6

The Hero and the City

So we come to the conclusion of both the play and the life of the hero. Oedipus had outlined his destiny, guaranteed by the oracle of Apollo, early in the work. Allowed to remain in Colonus, he would prove a mighty ally to the Athenians in some future conflict. He would become, like the deme that housed his tomb, an *epaula* for his adopted city (668), and his vengeful ghost would someday drink the hot blood of slaughtered Theban adversaries (621–22). In short, upon his death he was to become a cult hero, a staple common to the stock of every Greek polis, a recipient of some type of worship, a dispenser of both benefits and hindrances, and a source of power as reliable to the polis as a good cavalry.

Several questions remain. First, what end, precisely, does Oedipus meet in the secret grove? Next, given that Oedipus has without question been acknowledged as a hero, what precisely does that acknowledgment entail? What status does a hero enjoy, in the poet's view, insofar as Sophocles defined his tragic heroes within the framework of the existing tradition? Finally, in that Oedipus' heroization has been accomplished in part by the action of the polis, and in that Greek tragedy deals tirelessly with political matters in an obliquely didactic fashion, what political lessons does Sophocles offer to the Athenians in this, his final work, the final play preserved from the great tragedians of classical Athens? The tragedian educated the polis, and the surviving Greek tragedies can all be read at some level as political discourse. Sophocles, faced with a polis in moral and political disarray as the Peloponnesian War drew inexorably to its conclusion, could scarcely have passed over the inherent opportunity to advise, admonish, and instruct his compatriots at this most critical juncture in his city's history.

The Death of Oedipus

The end of the drama refutes convincingly the suggestion of Waldock that the main action of the *Oedipus at Colonus* has, in effect, been postponed by the intrusion of a series of interruptions.[1] Without question, a playwright with any sense of conscience ought to portray the main action on stage before the audience, especially if he has engaged hitherto in prolonged gymnastics to conceal the fact that he lacked a plot. Oedipus, however, plays out the last act of both the drama and his life offstage, accompanied at first by his daughters and Theseus, and, after he dismisses his daughters, only by the Athenian king—a very private end to a public life. Our chief information on the specifics of Oedipus' passing comes from a messenger's speech. Neither the chorus nor the Athenian audience may be privy firsthand to the final secrets of the hero.[2]

After Polyneices retires from Colonus, beaten by his father's relentless anger and outrage at the treatment he had received from his sons' hands, he returns to Argos to embark on his suicidal assault against his former city. At this point, a signal from the gods, in the form of a thunderstorm, announces that the time for Oedipus' departure has come at last. The chorus marks the change (1456): "the sky rumbles, O Zeus!" (ektupen aithēr, o Zeu).[3] Oedipus quickly orders his children to seek the king and bring him back to the grove, for he has heard the final sign, the presage of his own death, which Apollo had predicted in the distant prophecies he related to Antigone earlier in the play (95). Theseus returns, interrupted once more in his apparently interminable sacrifice to Poseidon, and discovers that Oedipus must now go off to meet his fate. The king affirms his faith in Oedipus' reading of the signs of his own death, in an extremely strange and revealing comment.

> You persuade me. For I see that you prophesied (se thespizont' oro) much and did not lie. Tell me now what needs to be done. (1516–17)

---

1. *Sophocles the Dramatist*, 218 ff.

2. In fairness to Waldock, it is difficult to imagine how a fifth-century B.C. playwright could have staged the passing of the hero.

3. Burian would take this as our first indication that the death of the hero will actually be part of the drama. In his view, the prophecies of Apollo dictate only the reception of the hero into Attica, while leaving open the question of the time and circumstance of Oedipus' death (see his article "Suppliant and Savior"). However, Burian ignores the force of Oedipus' declaration to the xenos that he "will never depart from this holy place" (45), unless Burian would have us suppose that Oedipus intends to set up a campground within the sacred precinct. Obviously, if he is never going to leave the place, his death must be an event soon at hand, rather than distant and unspecified.

The passage, innocuous enough on the surface, in fact offers an evident difficulty. When, exactly, did Theseus see Oedipus prophesy anything, let alone correctly?

The verb *thespizo* appears at two other places in the *Oedipus at Colonus*, 388 and 1428. A careful examination of those passages reveals the extent of the problems created by Theseus' observation of, and reliance on, Oedipus' prophetic capacities. At 388, Ismene has begun to relate to Oedipus the content of the oracles that the Thebans have received. Oedipus asks her, "what has been foretold, child?" *(ti de te-thespistai, teknon)*. Clearly Sophocles employs the verb *thespizo* here to indicate oracular pronouncement. Likewise, in the latter passage, Antigone in effect elevates Oedipus to the level of an oracle when she asks Polyneices, "But who will dare to follow you, once this man's prophecies have been heard *(ethespisen)*." Theseus, of course, missed the exchange between Oedipus and Polyneices. In fact, he missed all save one of Oedipus' statements that could be construed as conventionally oracular. Theseus had not yet appeared in Colonus when Oedipus spoke his initial imprecations against his sons; the king was off sacrificing during Oedipus' curses against that same pair and during those he made against Creon, spoken when the Theban messenger attempted to seize him. As for the information that the Thebans would try to force or coerce Oedipus to return to their city, Ismene reported that piece of intelligence. So the king did not witness most of the direct prophesying in which Oedipus engaged, with the exception of one passage: the remarkable monologue on time (607–28).

When Oedipus attempts to persuade the king to grant burial in Colonus (although such persuasion ultimately proves unnecessary), he implies that war between Thebes and Athens threatens. Theseus asks his visitor why, exactly, the Thebans would persuade themselves to make war on the Athenians. Oedipus knows that the Thebans will seek him out and that Athens risks conflict with Thebes should they receive him. But rather than content himself with repeating Ismene's news, Oedipus uses the opportunity to posit a general rule from the specific knowledge he possesses.

> Beloved son of Aegeus, only the gods avoid old age and death. All-powerful time obliterates all other things. The strength of the earth decays, as does the strength of the body. Trust dies and distrust is born, and the same wind never blows among friends or

from city to city. For indeed, sooner or later to all the sweet becomes bitter and friendship becomes its opposite. If affairs now sit well between you and Thebes, endless Time begets endless days and nights, in which they will ruin your peaceable relations by armed invasion at the slightest provocation. Then my sleeping, cold, hidden corpse will drink their hot blood, if Zeus is still Zeus and Apollo his son is truthful. But it is not pleasant to speak forbidden words.

This passage offers the only instance in the play in which Oedipus speaks prophetically in the presence of the king, and his words have subsequently proven true. For, like the Oedipus of old, the protagonist of the *Oedipus at Colonus* has helped to create his destiny by his actions. The trouble between Thebes and Athens to which Oedipus alludes in these lines has been previewed, in effect, by the cavalry battle that Theseus and his men must fight to restore Antigone and Ismene to their father. Creon himself indicates that war with Thebes could result if the Athenians hinder the execution of his plans (1037).[4] If no conflict between the two states had existed before, one most certainly does now. Thus, Theseus has seen Oedipus prophesy truly, for conflict with Thebes has become a reality, and general war is a distinct possibility. Oedipus' reliability as a prophet has been demonstrated, though at the expense of Athens itself. We see at work here another instance of the rewriting of the *Oedipus Tyrannus* that Sophocles effects in the *Oedipus at Colonus*. In the previous play, Oedipus, not yet instructed in or convinced of the veracity of oracles, creates his destiny by avoiding it. In the latter work, by contrast, Oedipus creates his destiny by working toward it, in obedient (for him, at least) conformity to the divine will.

Unfortunately, the suspicion lingers that this reference to one event in the play carries inadequate weight to justify the king's assessment, in view of the confidence Theseus expresses in 1516–17. For the king states that he has seen Oedipus foretelling "many things" *(polla)*, and his assertion cannot be reconciled with the action of the play. Rather, for an explanation of the king's remark, we must consider the image that Oedipus has managed to create for himself throughout the course of the play. Whitman argues that the profound impression that Oedi-

---

4. This is precisely how Jebb takes *thespizonth'* at 1516 (*Oedipus at Colonus,* 247).

pus has made on Theseus causes the king to grant citizenship to the exile.[5] Most certainly Whitman errs in the assumption of an offer of citizenship, but he rightly identifies the overall effect that Oedipus had on Theseus. The king has intuited the inner worth of the hero and ratified that worth by agreeing to permit Oedipus to remain in Athens. In this subsequent passage, several hundred lines later, Theseus in effect reiterates his earlier recognition of Oedipus' inner value by acknowledging him as a true prophet, even though Theseus himself has had only limited experience of Oedipus' oracular power. Oedipus has manufactured for himself, through the nobility of his bearing, through the ferocity of his determination, through his tenacity in adverse situations, and through his general sagacity, what most other heroes in the mythological tradition manage to create through their military accomplishments: an aura of invincibility. Theseus did not witness Polyneices' dismissal and departure; the king was offstage when the rebel decided to embrace eagerly the precise destiny that Oedipus had laid out for him. The audience, however, saw and experienced the force of the old man as he drove his penitent but ineffectual son from his presence, and it is only fitting that Theseus, the one character in the play of the same nature as Oedipus, should acknowledge expressly what all must now realize. Oedipus has in fact become, as Bushnell calls him, the "heroic prophet."[6]

Oedipus had attained greatness, in most versions of the story, by vanquishing the Sphinx, using only the weapon of his mind. (In the Sophoclean version of the story, his lone battle was fought against Laius and his attendants, so while we cannot dismiss Oedipus' combat skill, it must be admitted that the exercise of that skill has proven less than felicitous.) Thus he mocks Teiresias in the *Oedipus Tyrannus* for failing to solve the riddle posed by the monster (390–92). Yet, for all his vaunted intelligence, Oedipus remains plagued with blind spots, some of which have over time proven severe. In seeking oracles at Delphi to cure a plague, he accomplished only his own destruction.[7] As we observed earlier, his facile solution to the riddle ignored the paradoxical nature of his own life. Now, however, at the end of Oedipus' life, the great hero of Athens professes that Oedipus has become a true prophet,

---

5. *Sophocles,* 193.

6. Thus Bushnell entitles her chapter on the *Oedipus at Colonus* in *Prophesying Tragedy,* 86–107.

7. See Ahl, *Sophocles' Oedipus,* 35 and passim.

not one who utters *pseudophēma* (1517). Indeed, Sophocles has elevated Oedipus to the level of a true prophet in this work for just this reason, to oppose the late Oedipus, who can deliver oracles as a student of Apollo and Zeus, to the early Oedipus, who could only manage an often facile, invariably futile resistance to the oracles of the gods.

We can pursue this matter a bit further. When Oedipus berates Creon for his hypocrisy and deceit in attempting to lure the exile back to Thebes, he claims that, "I know these things very surely, for I have heard *(kluō)* them from much better sources: Phoebus and his father, Zeus" (792–93). Ellendt rightly considers this use of *kluo* to mean the process of hearing and learning from an oracle or at least of hearing divine speech *(fando)*.[8] Yet what did Oedipus learn that has made him the accurate heroic prophet that Theseus acknowledges? No specific piece of information can be adduced from the play. Rather, the accuracy of Oedipus' curses, and thus of his prophecies, stems in part from his prior knowledge of the oracles of Apollo, and in greater part from his knowledge of the people he curses, or whose destiny he predicts. He can "read" people in much the same manner as Apollo could "read" him. For Oedipus was ultimately responsible for his own destiny: no one forced him to seek Delphi to learn the truth of his identity in the first place, and no one forced him to try to cure a plague by means of an oracle.[9] He could not, in fact, have accomplished his destiny without the inborn qualities of inquisitiveness and piety that fueled his determination to discover the truth about himself and his family.[10] Hence, when Apollo predicts Oedipus' fate, he can only do so because he understands that the components of Oedipus' character, his ambition, determination, and native intelligence, will drive him to the series of actions that form his terrible destiny. When Oedipus, in turn, predicts Thebes' fate, or Creon's or his sons', he can do so because, like Apollo

8. *Lexikon Sophocleum*, 388.

9. Ahl writes, "Oedipus' belief that consultation of the Delphic oracle was the *only* possible way to deal with the plague would have struck many of Sophocles' contemporaries as old-fashioned, not efficacious, and politically suspect" (*Sophocles' Oedipus*, 41).

10. As Vernant puts it, in his essay "Oedipus without the Complex": "Oedipus' mistake stems from two features in his character: In the first place he is too sure of himself, too self-confident in his own *gnome* or judgment and not inclined to question his own interpretation of the facts. And secondly, being proud by nature, he invariably, no matter where he is, wants to be the master, number one" (Vernant and Vidal-Naquet, *Myth and Tragedy*, 105).

in estimating the character of Oedipus himself, Oedipus knows the character of the men and the city whose destiny he is foretelling.[11] This ability, then, to put together knowledge and insight to comprehend destiny, serves as the basis for Oedipus' heroic identity.

Oedipus, identified and affirmed as a heroic prophet, has attained exactly that which he seeks from Athens at the outset: recognition of his heroism, the status he has insisted on throughout. "In Colonus I will vanquish those who cast me out," Oedipus replies to the king when the latter offers him the opportunity to leave the grove and return with him to Athens (646). And in the grove Oedipus has already done so. He proves greater than Creon, who would attempt to apply to Oedipus' behavior standards of morality and civic behavior that do not apply to heroes, and greater than his son, who would appeal to pity, an emotion to which heroes are seldom susceptible. The heroic Oedipus resides beyond either and so defeats the family and city that rejected him. Theseus had provided Oedipus the means and opportunity to conduct himself as a hero, and now the old man can leave the stage and die, his heroism a source of strength for the city that received him.

Oedipus bids the king to accompany him to his final resting place and lays on the king a final obligation. No one save Theseus can know the location of the tomb, not the citizens of Athens, not even Oedipus' own daughters (1522–29). The site of the grave must remain a royal perquisite, the knowledge of which can be handed on only to Theseus' successor. Sophocles' diction at this point reveals the distinct preference for the "heroic" Athens that he has portrayed in the *Oedipus at Colonus*. The line reads, "show it [the gravesite] to the *prophertatos*" (*tō{i} prophertatō{i} monō{i} sēmain'*, 1531–32). Sophocles uses the superlative

---

11. In that the point at issue is as much literary as theological, spiritual, or even intellectual, an illustration may be useful here. In Robertson Davies' *The Rebel Angels* (New York, 1982), the old gypsy woman tells the classicist-priest Simon Darcourt, whose tarot she has just read: "But all this is under the cloak of time and fate. You are you—if you know who that is—and I am who I am, and what happens between us when I read the cards is not what will happen with anyone else. And this is the night after Christmas, and it is already nearly ten o'clock, and that makes a difference, too. Nothing is without meaning. Why am I reading your cards at this special time, when I have never seen you before? What brings us together? Chance? Don't you believe it. There is no such thing. Nothing is without meaning; if it were, the world would dash to pieces" (225). The last observation immediately calls to mind the choral passage of the *Oedipus Tyrannus*, 899–910, where the chorus despairs of a world without oracles.

degree of the adjective *propheres*, "excelling." Hence, only to the best man after Theseus can the location of the tomb be disclosed. Jebb notes that although parallels allow the interpretation that this word refers to the elder son, the language does not preclude "pre-eminence of other kinds."[12] In fact, in that the word *son* or something similar does not appear in the verse, no notion of strict heredity obtains. Jebb suggests that this vagueness allows for the possibility that after the monarchy fails, a priest could be appointed to tend the grave, a priest who would possess the sole knowledge of the site. Yet that begs the question, On what basis should someone be chosen to tend Oedipus' tomb? *Propher-tatos* suggests the appropriate answer. Only a hero, one "most excellent," should know the location of the grave. At the end, the man who has insisted throughout on his heroic identity would prefer the company only of men who possessed the same qualities. Oedipus' choice in effect offers an indictment of the ordinary people of Athens or perhaps of ordinary people in general. One cannot avoid the suspicion that, after years of wandering in exile, forced to scavenge and to subsist, Oedipus perhaps has grown a bit weary of other people and could use the rest.

Moreover, an additional detail in the work prevents us from automatically assuming that Oedipus wishes to indicate that Theseus' own blood son succeed to his father's role as guardian of the grave. Oedipus knows that Athens is a hereditary monarchy (69), but he intentionally avoids using a kinship term here. We should recall in this connection that Oedipus has argued repeatedly, if not always convincingly, that his own sons bear the primary responsibility for their father's sufferings. The Theban exile knows from personal experience that blood relationship cannot be trusted too far.

Oedipus' request that no one know the site of his grave presents us with another difficulty, although, given Oedipus' tendency to behave contrary to expectation, not an irresolvable one. Oedipus could have joined the ranks of "oracular prophets," as Rohde called them: Mopsus and Amphilochus at Mallos, Amphilochos in Acharnania, Teiresias at Orchomenos, Calchas in Apulia, and others. As Rohde says of these,

> The notices which have come down to us allow us to hear of a few regular and permanently established Hero-oracles, but there may

---

12. *Oedipus at Colonus*, 248.

have been numbers of them of which we know nothing, and isolated and occasional manifestations of oracular powers by other Heroes may not have been entirely out of the question.[13]

These were dream-oracles. In that ordinarily incubation required the petitioner to sleep in the precinct of the grave, Oedipus, the heroic prophet, could not serve this function for Athens as long as no one knew where his grave was. For us, in our desire to understand this most incomprehensible figure, another contradiction has arisen. Oedipus did less fighting than virtually any other hero; Theseus, for his part, recognizes him at the end as an accurate prophet, not a warrior. Yet Oedipus avows and maintains that his contribution to Athens will be military, as his corpse drinks the blood of Theban aggressors (621–22). Moreover, by forbidding access to his grave, he ensures that his aid to the city will not be prophetic, unless one envisions the unlikely scenario of Theseus or his successors camping out in a remote part of Colonus, awaiting heroic inspiration. As always, the quest for absolute consistency in the case of Oedipus proves futile, although not therefore unenlightening. Oedipus is a hero on his own terms, answerable to no one else. Of course, another more cynical interpretation obtrudes. While Theseus himself, hero to hero, may have acknowledged Oedipus as a true prophet, to the masses Oedipus would always be best known for misunderstanding or misconstruing oracles. Perhaps assigning to him the conventional role of hero-prophet to the masses would have been too much of a stretch.

In any case, Oedipus departs the stage, leading the way, with Theseus and his daughters in tow. He leaves no doubt about his impending fate. In his final words he asks the chorus to "remember me, a dying man" (*memnēsthe mou thanontos*, 1555). The chorus marks the passage of time by a brief prayer that Oedipus enjoy an easy transition to the next life (1557–78). And at last, a messenger enters to report the extraordinary conclusion to the hero's life. He first states that Oedipus has in fact died (*olōlota*, 1580), then he offers a more thorough account of the circumstances of the hero's passing. His speech is the longest single uninterrupted passage in the entire play (1586–1666), and in some ways, it is the least satisfactory. He repeats the detail that Oedipus went forth without a guide. This fact, well worth noting in itself, loses some of its

13. E. Rohde, *Psyche* (1920; reprint, New York, 1972), 133.

impact because we have heard about it twice before. Oedipus earlier stated directly that he would move without a guide (1521), and he claimed that he would in fact serve as the guide for the other members of the party (1542). Still, Sophocles undoubtedly had a reason for repeating this detail, perhaps to reaffirm Oedipus' status as "true prophet," which Theseus had just bestowed.

According to the messenger, the little procession went past the local landmarks, including the previously discussed marker commemorating the pact of Theseus and Peirithous, and came to the hill of Demeter Euchloos (1590–1600). There Oedipus' daughters prepared him, and Zeus Chthonios warned him that the appointed hour was at hand (1601–6). Oedipus took leave of his daughters at last, in a passage as remarkable for its vanity and the total self-absorption of the speaker as for anything else (1611–19). As we observed earlier, in the discussion of Oedipus' own moral authority, Oedipus' conviction that love *(to philein)* wipes clean the slate for years of service simply rings hollow. He claims too much for too little. Consider the expectation of an Athenian audience.

> The *kurios* of a child or woman had authority over, and responsibility for, the dependant. He was expected to see that his dependant was housed and fed, and the dependant was expected to obey him.[14]

Theseus had previously recognized Oedipus as *kurios* to his children and had announced his intention to use his power to keep him in that position (1041). In view of these community standards, the Athenians had to conclude that, whatever his heroic virtues, Oedipus had failed miserably as a father. One wonders, in passing, if this evident failure by the hero accounts for the playwright's decision to report secondhand the hero's dismissive farewell to his daughters, rather than to stage it.

However, despite the obviously indefensible position taken by Oedipus here, the playwright does not compromise his hero. Heroes are invariably blind to the havoc they leave in their wake. The collateral damage wrought by Heracles during his varied career almost negates his unquestioned stature as humanity's greatest benefactor. Ajax abandons his wife and son; Oedipus himself in the earlier play abandons the

---

14. D.M. MacDowell, *The Law in Classical Athens* (Ithaca, 1986), 84.

city that received him as both hero and king. Nothing in the prophecy of Apollo ever demanded that he blind himself or required his abdication (although the later oracle, given to Creon, did demand that Laius' killer be driven from Thebes), and indeed Homer suggests that Oedipus never did abdicate. A virtually endless list of heroes and their unwitting, undeserving victims can be compiled, and it starts at the beginning of Greek literature, for Achilles must shoulder a fair share of the blame for Patroclus' death. Indeed, portraying a hero must invariably require portraying his victims, and not all the victims will be drawn from the ranks of the hero's adversaries.

To be fair, Oedipus did not, according to the messenger, abandon his daughters' welfare completely. At the end, when a voice had summoned him once more, he entrusted the girls to Theseus' care. Theseus in turn swore an oath to look after Antigone and Ismene, and then the daughters left the two heroes (1623–38).[15] Theseus remained with his friend until the very end but never passed on the specifics of what he saw. There was, we are told, no lightning bolt, no tidal wave, no physical sign of the passing at all. Theseus, shading his eyes against a sight no one should see, was the lone witness (1648–66).

But did he witness a death, a translation, or an apotheosis? Oedipus announced that he would die, in his last line in the play. The messenger said that Oedipus had died but admitted that he did not personally see the hero's end. Theseus, upon his return to the stage, declares that Antigone and Ismene may never see the resting place of Oedipus, but his language could be construed as a bit vague concerning the precise nature of the hero-prophet's passing.

> O children, that man told me that no one should approach the place, or speak of *(epiphonein)*[16] the holy *thēkēn,* which he occupies. (1760–64)

---

15. Theseus' oaths, alas, have a way of not quite working out. He swore a pact with Peirithous but was unable to accomplish his friend's return. And he swears an oath to look after the daughters but simply allows them to return to certain civil war in Thebes. In this regard, it should be noted that Theseus swore no oath to Oedipus concerning Oedipus' protection (650–51). One wonders if the heroic prophet knew something.

16. Jebb seems to make this passage harder than it needs to be, for he wants to take *epiphonein* as "approach with utterances." As he says, otherwise one

He later adds the detail that Oedipus is "under the earth" (*kata gēs*, 1775). *Thēkē*, in its other use in Sophocles, *Electra* 896, certainly means a grave (Agamemnon's), so it is reasonable to assume that the same meaning obtains here. Hence, Oedipus now resides in a tomb, the prophecy of Apollo is fulfilled, and the conditions necessary for his heroic career as a benefactor to Athens are satisfied. All that remains is for Antigone to create her own tragic destiny, just as her brothers and father did on separate occasions, by embarking on her suicidal journey to Thebes (1768–72).

Heroes

So Oedipus ends his days, a hero to the Athenians who have received him, a curse to the Thebans who had exiled him. Unlike most heroes, Oedipus had become famous less for his military exploits than for his intellectual capacities.[17] In the course of the play, his ability to think, to judge, and to predict has been posited, demonstrated, and confirmed, both by the participants in the drama and by the audience's knowledge of the legends subsequent to and consequent on the action of the *Oedipus at Colonus*. His final exaltation, the success he enjoys in forcing all to recognize that his inbred heroism has remained undiminished by his misfortune, should not blind us to the obvious. His flaws and virtues remain intact, and both are numerous. He sees the faults, the crimes, and the folly of his opponents, but he overlooks the ambiguities inherent in his own moral position. He unhesitatingly exposes the hypocrisy of Creon and the homicidal arrogance of his sons, yet at the same time, he has taken the youth of his daughter and contributes to taking her life as well. He merits no hagiographer; he is no saint, no symbol of suffering humanity. But he remains admirable for those qualities we have always recognized: courage, tenacity, intelligence, even ferocity. Forearmed with the recognition of both his virtues and his vices, can we then establish the rationale for Sophocles' decision to award Oedipus

---

must take it as meaning "mention to another," which he claims is unfitting (*Oedipus at Colonus*, 275). However, it fits perfectly. For anyone to approach the grave, *pelazein*, someone would have to tell its location. So the second prohibition accords well with the first.

17. The Homeric Oedipus died defending his city, while other stories showed Oedipus defeating the Sphinx in a combat of weapons, not words. As mentioned earlier, the Sophoclean version fights only one recorded battle: unfortunately, he fights it against Laius.

heroic status and to elevate him to an object of cult worship, in light of the evidence gleaned from the careers of other such cult heroes portrayed in the tragedies?

Sophocles' other works offer promising ground for our search, for he is perhaps solely responsible for making Oedipus a hero.[18] The playwright certainly has set the terms for Oedipus' heroization in this work. He portrayed his character, replete with warts, and demanded of us that we accept him as heroic. One other Sophoclean character offers a close parallel to Oedipus, one who also attained the status of a popular figure of cult, Ajax. Heracles of the *Trachiniae*, of course, poses different problems, for he was most often worshiped as a god.[19] Moreover, both Ajax and Oedipus lack immediate divine ancestry, unlike the son of Zeus. Perhaps, then, the example of Ajax offers some corroborating evidence to assist us in identifying those criteria established by Sophocles for portraying a dramatic character worthy of the eventual receipt of cult worship.

Ajax in fact has a great deal in common with Oedipus, the significant distinction between the two being that Ajax chooses a sure and final solution to the difficulties that beset him, once his heroic status has been compromised through a disgraceful revelation. His suicide differs from Oedipus' self-blinding in that, while Oedipus in a sense hurries time by prematurely aging himself, Ajax simply puts himself beyond time's reach once and for all.[20] Both Ajax and Oedipus enjoyed the cult worship of the Athenians, Oedipus on the Areopagus as well as at Colonus, Ajax on Salamis and, subsequently, as one of the eponymous tribal heroes.[21] More importantly, both men inspire a similar reaction from Sophocles' audiences. Both command our respect even while we witness, objectively and dispassionately, the folly of their actions.[22]

18. See Knox's introduction to the *Oedipus at Colonus* in Fagles, *Sophocles,* 256.

19. Pausanias makes the point that Heracles first received worship as a god in Marathon, a district of Attica (1.15.4, 1.32.4).

20. On Ajax's decision to place himself beyond the confines of time, see Whitman's remark at *Sophocles,* 199 (quoted earlier in chap. 1 n. 38). On Oedipus' self-blinding/premature aging and on his arrival, in this play, at a point where he has "caught up with himself," see Zeitlin, "Theater of Self," 129.

21. See Pausanias 1.28.7, 1.30.4 (for Oedipus), and 1.35.2 (for Ajax); see also L. Farnell, *Greek Hero Cults* (Oxford, 1921), 307–8.

22. It is no part of this work to undertake a thorough discussion of Ajax, either of the character or of the play bearing his name. That is a separate project that I will attempt later.

Of course, one great difference separates the heroic nature of Ajax from that of Oedipus. Oedipus became a hero by using his mind, Ajax, unquestionably, by using his body. Oedipus slew a monster and his father; Ajax slew men, in numbers uncounted throughout the Trojan War—Homer praises him as the greatest Greek warrior after Achilles at Troy.[23] Ajax, while not fleet of foot, presents to friend and foe alike a huge, intimidating figure, while Oedipus, even in his prime, shows the effects of having been lamed by his parents. But underlying similarities override surface distinctions. The heroic stature of both men remains intact despite their sufferings, although the means by which they solve the problems they face, and by which they attempt to master, or at least respond to, a hostile world, differ greatly. It is the similarities of the two characters, similarities that Sophocles develops so thoroughly, that suggest a reason for the ultimate cult status both men enjoyed.

A brief summary of Sophocles' *Ajax* may be useful. In that play, Ajax, angered at the decision of the Atreidae that awarded the arms of Achilles to Odysseus, plans to avenge the disgrace by destroying the Atreidae and Odysseus himself. The goddess Athena foils his plan by driving him mad, and Ajax instead slaughters flocks of animals and their guards. When he recovers from his madness, he realizes what he has done and resolves to erase his dishonor by suicide, which he eventually commits. The hero's worth and stature is subsequently affirmed by his brother Teucer and, surprisingly, by Odysseus, who generously acknowledges the greatness of his enemy, now that he is safely dead.

Ajax, though reputedly slow and rather blunt in his speech, like Oedipus offers his own perceptive analysis of the effects of time, at the beginning of his long, difficult, and evidently self-contradictory speech that presages his eventual suicide.

> Strangely the long and countless drift of time brings all things forth from darkness into light, then covers them once more. Nothing so marvelous that man can say it surely will not be.[24] (646–49)

Later, he strengthens and expands on his initial observation.

---

23. *Iliad* 2.768–69; 17.279–80.

24. The translation is J. Moore's, from *Sophocles II*, ed. D. Grene (Chicago, 1975), 31–32.

Winter's hard-packed snow cedes to the fruitful summer; stub-
born night at last removes, for day's white steeds to shine. The
dread blast of the gale slackens and gives peace to the sounding
sea; and Sleep, strong jailer, in time gives up his captor. Shall not
I learn place and wisdom? Have I not learned this, only so much
to hate my enemy as though he might again become my friend,
and so much good to wish to do my friend, as knowing he may
yet become my foe: most men have found friendship a treacher-
ous harbor. (670–83)

The similarities between Ajax's speech and the address made by Oedipus to Theseus in the *Oedipus at Colonus* is striking. Knox says of the
passage:

> Ajax comes at last to his moment of unclouded vision, in which he
> sees the world man lives in as it really is. He explores, for himself
> and for us, the nature of the ceaseless change which is the pattern
> of the universe.[25]

Oedipus' monologue on time achieves precisely the same effect, as
Knox himself shrewdly observed.[26] This clarity of insight, the ability to
comprehend the true workings of the world, suggests a greater level of
understanding than that possessed by the ordinary man and indicates a
predicate of the Sophoclean hero: a wisdom as well as a determination
that far surpasses that of the average man, a wisdom earned in fact by
suffering and experience. And in each case, time serves as an element in
which the ordinary events of the world are conducted. Unsurprising,
for *chronos* obviously governs those bound by the world. To recognize
the effects and the workings of time may therefore be posited, in Sophocles' works, at least, as a necessary precondition for the next heroic step,
the decision to stand outside of time, to resist one of the elements in
which man must live. Ajax achieves this resistance to time by his suicide, whereas Oedipus, equally eschatological in his result, accelerates
time by prematurely blinding, and thus aging, himself.

---

25. B.M.W. Knox, "The Ajax of Sophocles," in *Sophocles*, ed. Harold Bloom
(New York, 1990), 14.
26. *Heroic Temper*, 153.

Each hero, Ajax and Oedipus, makes a parallel decision as well to reject the company of other people. Like time, the presence of other people is a largely inescapable fact of human existence, but both heroes decide that they can do without others, preferring a heroic level of self-reliance. Thus Oedipus, when offered the opportunity to accompany the king back to his palace and thereby be restored to a central position in civic life, politely declines (643–46). At Colonus—that is, at a place removed as far as practicable from the *astu*, the seat of civic life—Oedipus realizes his heroic destiny as simultaneously the defender of the polis and the *alastor* of Thebes. He envisages his destiny as a solitary one; he will be accessible to no one but the king and his successors, who will seldom venture out to Colonus. Oedipus cuts himself off from the *astu*, from the polis insofar as that is possible, and even from the *oikos*. He has disavowed his sons, and he forbids his daughters to take on the customary female role of tending the gravesite of the dead, although he does allow them to prepare him for burial (1602–3).

Ajax does much the same. The event that drove him mad, the decision of the panel to award the armor of Achilles to Odysseus, heralds both the inevitable subordination of the individual to the community and the death of the heroic era. As Knox says:

> [T]he decision [of the tribunal] was to be expected. The appointment of a tribunal to award the armor of Achilles is a mythic event which marks the passing of the heroic age which Achilles dominated while he lived, an age of fiercely independent, undisciplined, individual heroism. The rewards life has to offer will no longer be fought for and seized by the strongest, whose authority is his might, but will be assigned by the community.[27]

At the end of this passage, Knox refers of course to Odysseus, the antiheroic modern man. In respect to the *Oedipus at Colonus,* as we have noted frequently, Oedipus triumphs not so much by the logic or justice of his positions as by the pure force of his will. The verbal ferocity of Oedipus matches the military ferocity of the Salaminian hero. Perhaps, in the later work, Sophocles in effect retreats from the position held earlier in the *Ajax.* The politic man should not win, should not dominate the hero. The world lost too much when it arranged itself in such a way.

---

27. "*Ajax,*" 27.

Certainly, at face value there is little difference between the deceitful Odysseus in the *Philoctetes* and the mendacious Creon in the *Oedipus at Colonus*. Might we not say that Creon represents the worst-case scenario of a mentality originally exemplified by Odysseus?[28]

Ajax to a lesser extent abandons his *oikos* as well as the polis, in this case the Achaean camp and the war effort itself. Tecmessa leaves no doubt as to her family's fate.

> For this is certain. The day you die and by your death desert me, that same day will see me outraged too, forcibly dragged by the Greeks, together with your boy, to lead a slave's life. And then someone of the lord class, with a lashing word, will make his hateful comment: "There she is, Ajax's woman; He was the greatest man in the whole army. How enviable her life was then, and now how slavish!"—some speech in that style. And my ill fate will be driving me before it, but these words will be a reproach to you and all your race. (496–505)

Like Oedipus, Ajax's first concern is for himself. Eurysaces' *trophē* will be *doulia* (499), a lot scarcely better than Antigone's. Yet just as, at the end of his life, Oedipus redeems the situation slightly by commending his daughters to Theseus' care, so too Ajax advises Teucer to look after both his family and his people (562–70, 689). And Teucer accepts his task (1168–84).

Both Oedipus and Ajax, then, possess a single-minded determination to maintain their own heroic status, no matter what the cost to themselves, to their friends, or to their loved ones. Both even call on the Furies when they curse those who have wronged them.[29] They differ only in method, Ajax opting for suicide, Oedipus for tragic endurance, which allows his *gennaion* to show through. Both men insist, in effect,

---

28. As I have long since conceived a profound loathing for the Ithacan charlatan, I note here with pleasure Farnell's sound judgment on the two characters: "we are struck with the phenomenon which the Attic drama presents, namely, that in contrast to the frequent vilification of the personages of the old epic, the figure of Aias remains noble and even sublime, while that of his old rival Odysseus is almost uniformly debased" (*Hero Cults,* 308). Odysseus' is a well-deserved fate.

29. Oedipus does so in his curse against his sons (1390), Ajax in his curse against the Atreidae (837–38).

that their own heroism outweighs all other considerations, overrides all prior claims. Knowing their own worth, they permit themselves to withdraw beyond the ordinary judgment of other people, and they insist—Ajax by action, Oedipus by declaration—that their worth be recognized. Even Odysseus must at the end of the *Ajax* admit the greatness of his adversary (1339–41, 1357). In a very real sense, then, Sophocles' two genuine heroes possess two common characteristics: an innate, instinctive appreciation of their own value, and a determination never to renounce that value in the face of any opposing claims or obligations. So they asseverate the status that lesser men must eventually recognize, and in effect, they create their own heroism. They must first of course, be men of distinction, but then they must pass through a trial and emerge with their belief in themselves unscathed. Heroes never yield; one rather suspects that the only modern leader Oedipus and Ajax could have stomached was Churchill.[30]

So Oedipus becomes a cult hero; what, exactly, does that mean? What are the predicates of existence for such a creature? Do they live after death, and if so, in what way may they be said to be alive? For Rohde, there is some continuation of consciousness after death. Thus he argues,

> The Heroes of the newly awakening creed have died unmistakably; and yet they continue to live on, though relieved of their bodies.[31]

Bowra in turn suggested that the entire play offers to Oedipus compensation in the form of elevation to cult hero.[32] For such compensation to be of value, Oedipus must of course have some degree of consciousness. Alas, no evidence supports Rohde's view of continuing consciousness or Bowra's of heroism as compensation. Linforth correctly skewers any such idea.

---

30. I am thinking of course of the famous lines from Churchill's address at Harrow: "Never give in, never give in, never, never, never, never—in nothing, great or small, large or petty—never yield except to convictions of honor and good sense. Never yield to force; never yield to the apparently overwhelming might of the enemy" Speech at Harrow School, Oct. 29, 1941. See *Winston Churchill: His Complete Speeches*, vol. 6, 1935–1942 (New York, 1974), 6499.

31. *Psyche*, 121.

32. *Sophoclean Tragedy*, 307 and passim.

And yet it is commonly said that Oedipus is glorified by exaltation to the heroic state, that he enters upon a new life of immortality, that he becomes almost a god and passes to a new state of bliss. But how are we to know this?

As Linforth further notes, nothing in the sources suggests that a recipient of cult worship "had any gratification or enjoyment" of his position.[33]

Linforth then directly addresses Oedipus' status in the play.

There is no single hint in the play that Oedipus will enter into glory after death. Neither the oracle, nor Oedipus himself, nor the divine voice which hurries him to his end, nor anyone else, envisages for him a future so shining.[34]

Linforth is quite right. Oedipus himself indicates no joy, not even consciousness, when he describes the moment that his gift of his tomb to the city will pay its reward.

Then will my sleeping, buried, chill corpse drink their hot blood.
(621–22)

There is not much personalization here, not even something as equivocal as "I will drink their blood." According to Oedipus, the only part of him that will partake of the fruits of Theban suffering is his corpse (*emos nekus*).

Clearly, heroism is not compensation from the gods, as Linforth realizes, astutely refuting the claims of Bowra.[35] What compensation accrues? Not even a sense of delight at the overthrow of enemies awaits the dead. As Winnington-Ingram notes,

It is not bliss, but power and honor that await him in the chthonian realm to which he is summoned.[36]

---

33. *Religion and Drama*, 101.
34. Ibid.
35. Linforth, *Religion and Drama*, 101–2 and n. 21; for Bowra, as observed earlier (see citation at n. 32 in this chapter), the concept of recompense occupies his interpretation of the work throughout.
36. *Sophocles*, 255.

Slatkin's suggestion, mentioned earlier, that Oedipus' arrival has challenged the Athenians to extend their democratic values of openness and inclusion might have offered a useful avenue toward understanding the mechanism of Oedipus' heroization.[37] If the city had offered refuge to the exile, they would have made themselves heroic, and the heroism that they would have confirmed for themselves would have empowered them militarily as well as morally. But as we have seen, such possibilities do not apply. The city, as represented by the citizens, did not prove itself moral or noble. Only Theseus deserves such credit, and he clearly stands far above his citizens and perhaps even above the city itself. Moreover, the citizens are deprived by Oedipus' secrecy from ever taking advantage of the benefits of the tomb. Indeed, Oedipus makes it clear that he will be of somewhat limited use, for his tomb will allow the Athenians to conquer only the Thebans (the *spartōn andrōn*, 1533–34). Oedipus will not be an oracular hero. He offers no details of the manner in which he will succor Athens, and he allows no opportunity to test the proposition in anticipation of the event. He simply asserts it, as he has repeatedly asserted his heroic status throughout the work. Perhaps Reinhardt's assessment of Oedipus' position is the best.

> But how is it that the secret has this power? What can it be, that it is capable of so much? Let us not be tempted to try to solve the mystery; it can be understood better from the significance of the work as a whole than from any single detail, let alone any external source. And whatever it may be, part of it at any rate is the knowledge of the powerful sufferer, the hero who blesses and curses, and his assimilation into an Athenian context through the cult.[38]

Oedipus is a hero; he insisted on recognition of that fact and obtained that recognition in Athens. The specifics of the workings of his heroic cult, like the precise workings of the Trinity and the reconciliation of relativity to quantum theory, remain a mystery.

---

37. See Slatkin, *"Oedipus at Colonus,"* 220.
38. *Sophocles*, 221.

Last Lessons: Political Discourse in the Play

Whatever the hero's status, the state of his perception in the grave, or his expectation of eventual worship, a lone certainty remains: the *Oedipus at Colonus* has ended, and the audience has left the theater, no doubt to discuss, debate, and quarrel over the meaning of what they have just seen, as audiences of plays always do. As part of that discussion, they no doubt considered the political aspects of the work. For in a very real sense, much more so than in most surviving Greek plays, the audience found themselves onstage in the drama. Most knew the district of Colonus, and if they could not identify firsthand with the chorus, they knew people who could. They had certainly heard a great deal about Oedipus—omitting the activity of the tragedians, Aristophanes proves that, if proof were in any way needed.[39] And Theseus was perhaps the most familiar character in Attic mythology, the alleged engineer of the unification of Attica and founder of the national identity.[40] There is no need to accept Freudian, or even Jocastan, intimations that Oedipus represents Everyman to posit with some confidence that the *Oedipus at Colonus* was, even by the conventions of Athenian drama, a very personal experience. But what did the experience show?

Greek tragedy had as its basis the worship of Dionysus, the celebration of the natural cycle of birth and death; but one of its primary functions was the political tuition of the Athenian demos. This point is easily granted and well-enough discussed of late. Indeed, perhaps it is overstressed—one wonders if the Athenians ever went to the theater to be entertained, or if they attended as many of us attend church, out of a combined sense of obligation and social ritual. Still, political importance cannot and should not be denied. Democracies, to function effectively, require an educated citizenry; education in turn requires investment; and the Athenians invested much of their resources in an education provided by tragedy. The Athenian tragedian relied on a direct subsidy from the state in the form of a liturgy performed by the *choregos*, who underwrote the costs of production in lieu of direct taxation. Thus Euben shrewdly observes,

---

39. See Aristophanes *Frogs* 1182–94, a passage discussed by Ahl in *Sophocles' Oedipus*, 8.

40. See, for example, Plutarch, *Theseus* 24.

Tragedy's importance in sustaining the quality of public life is indicated by the fact that it was a liturgy equal to the maintenance of a trireme, as if to suggest that the cultural survival of the Athenians depended on the courage of its people in confronting the risks of tragedy in the same way as its physical survival depended on its sailors' courageously meeting the risks of battle.[41]

While we need not share all of Euben's enthusiasms for the role that tragedy played in Athenian society (one rather suspects that cost played as much a role as culture in equating the trierarch with the *chorēgos*), without doubt tragedy occupied a position of central importance in Athenian public life. At the festival of the City Dionysia, the wealth, the power, and the determination of the polis were displayed for the citizens and for visitors alike. The children of men killed in battle were presented with panoplies, and the tribute extorted from dependent cities was put on display for all to see, all before visiting embassies, who would no doubt carry back with them to their own cities the intelligence that the Athenians were not to be trifled with. All these activities were undertaken in preparation for the tragic performances, and in a very real sense, all of them were made possible by those performances. Tragic education made Athens the power it was. For, as Euben also maintains—following Arrowsmith's dictum that tragedy was a "democratic *paideia* complete in itself"[42]—

> Thus citizens brought political wisdom informed by tragedy to the deliberations of the assembly, and the experience of being democratic citizens in the assembly, council, and courts to the theater.[43]

So we cannot escape the consideration of tragedy as political discourse. While undeniably a medium of entertainment, tragedy had been assigned a specific duty in the political agenda for a simple reason: it was capable of reaching a mass audience at a single sitting. The *paidea* was not of course perfect. The form limited, to a certain extent,

---

41. *Greek Tragedy and Political Theory,* 23
42. W. Arrowsmith, "A Greek Theater of Ideas," *Arion* 2, no. 3 (autumn 1963): 33.
43. Euben, *Greek Tragedy and Political Theory,* 23.

the complexity of the discourse. Nothing duller can be imagined than political didactic masquerading as drama (one thinks inevitably of Chinese opera under Mao), and nothing seems less likely to win prizes from a jury. It was understood that the messages of a play should be oblique, opaque, and apprehensible by inference and implication; the fate of Phrynichus provided a cautionary example of the risks inherent in overly frank dramatic representations of the activities of the polis. Tragedians of the time knew to employ nothing so systematic as true political theory; instead, political lessons were to be limited in number and scope. After all, at the conclusion of the play, the audience was expected to retain images rather than dialogue. It remains then to frame the specific question: what political lessons does Sophocles deliver to the polis in this, his final tragedy, and the final tragedy of classical Athens? The need for instruction was apparent: as I noted earlier, grim conditions surrounded the authorship of the *Oedipus at Colonus*. In 406 B.C., the Peloponnesian War was drawing to a close, Athens had both instigated and witnessed the fiasco of the trial of the generals after Arginusae, and the demos had, in effect, been intimidated into authorizing its own dissolution. Demagogues had wasted the city's resources, while stupidity and cruelty had exhausted and ultimately destroyed the empire. In 409 B.C., the year of the *Philoctetes*, the year after the victory at Cyzicus, a more optimistic Sophocles might have expected a recovery by his beloved polis. But in 406, common sense and poetic judgment mandated pessimism. The Athens the playwright had known was slipping away from him.

Of the varied follies perpetrated by the Athenians on themselves in the course of the long defeat, perhaps none more than the oligarchical revolution of 411 exposed the weakness of the democracy. The tale is long and ultimately unedifying, but one episode no doubt struck deeply at the core of the poet. To offer a brief summary of events, the relentless adventurer and chameleon Alcibiades, having fallen into disfavor at Sparta for, among other things, having seduced the wife of King Agis, offered to bring Persia and its huge reserves of cash to the Athenian side if Athens established a more manageable form of government, that is, an oligarchy, and rescinded the death penalty it had passed on Alcibiades. In the wake of the debacle at Syracuse and the material benefit Sparta was enjoying from its alliance with the Persians, the suggestion looked far better than it should have and found favor in some quarters.[44] Although Alcibiades failed to win much support for his own return, and although the offer of Persian aid had in fact been withdrawn, one Peisander had been recruited to persuade the Athenians to adopt an oligarchy, and ultimately they did, their resistance worn down by timely murders and beatings.[45] The key meeting was held at Colonus, in which the Four Hundred came to power, with the avowed purpose of creating an *ecclesia* of five thousand, and with the sure intent of destroying the existing constitution.[46]

No matter the strain of necessity, no matter the evident attractiveness of Persian aid, no matter the role of fear and intimidation, this was unquestionably the most discreditable episode in the long and sometimes sorry history of the democracy. To state the matter simply, they voted themselves out of existence. They betrayed themselves and their polis, yielding the one sure element in their corporate identity, the democracy, to a band of armed thugs, for Persian gold that they would never see. A drowning man will grasp even the point of a sword, but of Athens one expects better. Certainly Thucydides did; although obviously not a die-hard democrat, he maintains an unbroken antipathy to the Four Hundred, whose authority did not last out the year. The Four Hundred had come to power in part by promising to revise the citizen rolls; it was a plan they intended to abandon once they had secured their position, but to which they were forced to accede by the fleet, led by the resilient Alcibiades, who had tested the waters and decided that he was once more a democrat. The Four Hundred's successors won the historian's approval. He refers to the government that existed after their overthrow as "governing well" *(eu politeusantes),* a good mix of the few and the many.[47] For the restored government did make use of the Five Thousand and of any who had sufficient income to serve as a hoplite—property qualifications that would have suited an ardent eighteenth-century Federalist, while still maintaining some sense of the democracy.

So at Colonus the weakness and cowardice of the radical democracy

---

44. Thucydides 8.47–48.

45. Thucydides 53–54, 63.3–66.

46. Thucydides 67.3. Stockton observes that no source explains the reason that Colonus was chosen (*Classical Athenian Democracy,* 147 n. 5); meetings could be held at places other than the Pnyx, but Colonus had never served as the site of a meeting before, as far as we know.

47. Thucydides 97.2.

had been laid bare. To make the transition from Thucydides to Sophocles, from the Colonus of history to the one of tragedy, and to considering fully the political implications of the *Oedipus at Colonus,* an intermediate observation from Aeschylus will prove useful. In the *Persae,* Aeschylus had proclaimed the virtues of democratic Athens and portrayed the servile character of the failed Persian choristers, who, even though kings in their own right, remain servants of a despot. Xerxes himself does not need to render an account to his subjects for either his successes or his failures. The full contrast is revealed at 241–42. Atossa asks the chorus, "Who rules the Athenians?" The chorus responds, "Slaves of no man are they called, nor in subjection to any one man." Podlecki, in his discussion of the *Persae,* shares an insightful personal observation.

> I would be surprised if the original audience did not react like one of which I was a part in the summer of 1965 in the Odeion of Herodes Atticus in Athens, which rose to its feet *en masse* and interrupted the actors' dialogue with cheers. For here was a striking difference, as the Athenian patriots loved to be reminded, between themselves and their barbarian opponents.[48]

The *Persae* appeared in 472 B.C. and reflects the optimism of a youthful state, fresh off a decisive victory over the largest empire the Greek world knew.

To appreciate fully the difference in attitude that the events of the next seventy years engendered, and to understand the nature of the political didactic of the *Oedipus at Colonus,* we need look no further than the opening scene. At 64–69 Oedipus and the local *xenos* exchange the following words.

Oed: Do people live in this area?
Xen: Indeed, and they are named for the local deity [Colonus].
Oed: Does someone rule them, or does the word of the majority?
Xen: The place is ruled by the king in the city *(astu).*
Oed: Who rules them, with both word and strength?
Xen: Theseus he is named, the son of the former king, Aegeus.

---

48. A. Podlecki, "*Polis* and Monarch in Early Attic Tragedy," in *Greek Tragedy and Political Theory,* ed. J.P. Euben (Berkeley, 1986), 78–79.

The wording of this passage is remarkable and leads us to some
inescapable conclusions. Sophocles portrays a character, the *xenos*,
undoubtedly a citizen of Athens, who expressly denies that the people
have any political power. He does not do so by accident. The playwright had other means to communicate the same information. Oedipus could simply have asked the *xenos*, on his arrival, "Who is your
king?" Likewise, the *xenos* might have said, when he found the old man
and his daughter, "Let me go find the king and see what he has to say
about your trespass into the grove." Any number of alternatives
remain. But Sophocles virtually starts his play with an explicit denial
that Athens is a democracy. In the spirit of Podlecki's observation, one
cannot wonder if the *xenos'* remark drew scattered boos from those
members of the audience who were quick enough on the uptake to
grasp the full import of the scene.

No refuge can be found for any who would claim that the beginning
of the play offers only a meaningless commonplace and should not
granted such importance, for the remainder of the *Oedipus at Colonus*
pursues this initial theme and opposes itself to other portrayals of
"good" kings in Attic tragedies. The entire matter of Oedipus' reception into Athens rests solely on the king's decision. As I discussed earlier, this contradicts precedents found in earlier works. Pelasgos in the
Suppliants, Theseus in the *Suppliant Maidens* of Euripides, and
Demophon in the *Children of Heracles* all insist on some level of consultation with the citizens. The king adheres to a different standard of governance in the *Oedipus at Colonus*. Theseus has been specifically warned
by Oedipus that military intervention might be needed should the king
agree to receive him.

> *Oed:* Look at the matter carefully: doing this [i.e., receiving me] is
>   no small thing.
> *Thes:* Do you speak of trouble between your sons and me?
> *Oed:* Lord, they need to bring me back to Thebes. (587–89)

Shortly after this warning, Theseus leaves no doubt, in Oedipus' mind
or anyone else's, where the decision rests.

> Explain matters: without adequate information I cannot judge.
> (594)

He utters not a word that would even hint at the consultation customary between monarch and citizens, not even a pretense, just a declaration that he, the king, will make the necessary decisions and that the people will abide by them. His subsequent actions confirm his autocratic status. When he agrees to receive Oedipus, he avows as one of his reasons, among others, that Oedipus has offered "no small tribute to the land and to me" (*gē{i} tē{i}de kamoi dasmon ou smikron tinei*, 635). Sophocles' diction commands attention. The *dasmos* of Oedipus has been offered not to the polis, specifically, but to the land and the ruler, which are treated as separate but coordinate entities. An ungenerous but inevitable suggestion presents itself, that as far as Theseus is concerned, he is the polis.

Certainly the king is, as Reinhardt points out, "not the ideal democrat."[49] Rather, once he has decreed that Oedipus can stay, and after he has offered the Theban a choice between remaining in Colonus and returning to the palace, he states matter-of-factly to the coryphaeus, "I will order (*taxo*) you to guard him" (638–39). Ellendt would take *taxo* here to mean *constituo*,[50] but no justification exists. Theseus gives an order here as dismissively as he would to a young lieutenant in battle. When the king wishes to depart, Oedipus presses him for reassurance of royal protection. Theseus simply replies, "it will be a care to these men" (*alla toisd' estai melon*, 653)—a sentiment at once impersonal and regal, with no suggestion that the choristers had anything to say about their assignment.

Theseus appropriates to himself identity with the city. But what status do the citizens, that is, the choristers, claim? They acknowledge themselves to live under the rule of a monarch, yet monarchy in itself does not negate the possibility of individual action or limit the scope of individual heroism. However, in the course of the play, the choristers take no such action, nor do they display any such virtue. As I observed earlier, they appear increasingly weaker in the face of successive challenges from the strong. First Oedipus, with ludicrous ease, backs down the inquisitive *xenos* who would remove him from the grove (33–45). Next, he does the same to the choristers, whose resolve to drive the polluted stranger from their sacred site dissipates to mere sound and fury,

---

49. *Sophocles*, 213.
50. *Lexikon Sophocleum*, 715.

and very little of the latter, in the face of his tenacious opposition
(258–91). They neither enforce their original decision nor grant asylum
to the stranger; they simply kick the decision upstairs (293–94). In contemporary society, such actions cause the intelligent and observant to
lose respect for their perpetrators. One doubts that the situation differed much in fifth-century Athens or even in mythological, Bronze
Age Greece. The waffler and the coward, once he or she has revealed
the strength of his or her convictions (or the lack thereof), may be safely
ignored, which is precisely what Theseus, Oedipus, and even Creon do.

Striking confirmation comes from the text itself. When the choristers announce their determination to make no decision on Oedipus by
themselves, they declare that they will leave the matter to the "lords of
the land" (*tēsde gēs anaktes*, 293–94). Virtually the same phrase occurs
later in the text. When Creon seizes Antigone, Oedipus cries for assistance: *o gēs anaktes* (831). The remark is, in context, flattering, perhaps
unduly so. For the choristers have already indicated by their actions
and their deferral to the authority of the king that they are not the *anaktes ges.* Yet Oedipus needs their help, needs them, in effect, to display
some power, some capacity, some nobility that they denied to themselves in their dispute with the protagonist. But the choristers fall well
below expectation again, for in the face of a determined Creon they do
no more than they did against an equally determined Oedipus. They
can only cry for help. Oedipus, no doubt disgusted at their inefficacy,
broadens his appeal: *iō polis* (832). In both conflicts, the presence and
authority of the monarch alone can settle the issue. This inefficacy
would not seem so important were it not so frequently demonstrated
that these were Athenian citizens who repeatedly fail such tests. As if
to drive the message home, after numerous references to the choristers
as "townsmen" (discussed earlier), near the very end of the play the
messenger greets them by saying, "O men of the city" (*O andres politai,*
1579). Sophocles would make clear one final time, for the slower or
less perspicacious members of his audience, the precise identity of the
group that had made throughout the play such a consistently poor
showing. The contrast between the ineffectual choristers and their
bold, decisive, slightly imperious, and decidedly charismatic leader
could not be drawn more clearly or more damningly. The chorus that
represented the Athenian citizens on stage, in a manner more direct
than any chorus in any surviving Greek tragedy, had been weighed,
tried, and found lacking. All this was done at the orchestration of a

playwright charged, implicitly at least, with the education of the demos.

Tragic citizens quail at the veiled but indisputable authority of a blind old man; they jump, unconsulted, at the insistence of their king. They fail in the tasks assigned them: the guardianship of the grove (implicitly) and the guardianship of Oedipus (explicitly). They do all of this in Colonus, the spot where just five years prior to the authorship of the play, their historical counterparts had betrayed themselves and their polis. Without question, Sophocles had to consider this historical event in his selection of Colonus as the setting of the play, just as he took into consideration his own personal loyalty to the place and the mythological associations of the deme. The playwright forces the citizens to acknowledge their failures—but to what end?

Thucydides had seen the radical democracy as a disaster; he displays no fondness for the Four Hundred. Yet his views on the government of Athens after the fall of the oligarchs and the institution of the limited democracy of the Five Thousand are instructive. As observed earlier, he thought this period the best governed in Athens during his own time.[51] I have noted that the *Philoctetes* lacks any apparent fixation with old age, Athens, or farewells. Whatever lessons it harbored for the Athenians remained indirect, safely obscured in the usual pattern of inference and implication by which the cautious playwrights made their points. It perhaps reflects a period when matters in Athens did not look quite so bleak, and so it dates generally from the period that Thucydides found so attractive. But by 406 B.C., the democracy had reinvented itself in sufficient time to behave as disgracefully as it did after Arginusae.

Arginusae was, of course, a major battle fought in the Aegean near Lesbos in 406 B.C. The Athenians won a brilliant, if costly, victory over

---

51. Thucydides 8, 97.3. It is no part of my purpose to enter into the specific debate concerning what, precisely, Thucydides found so attractive, whether it was the disenfranchisement of two-thirds of the demos, as Jones reads it, or, to follow de Ste. Croix and Stockton, merely the conduct of the Five Thousand themselves—in short, whether he was attracted to the practice as opposed to the theory. In any case, Stockton is probably right in asserting that all the demos could still vote in the *ecclesia,* although office holding was restricted to the Five Thousand. Cf. A.H.M. Jones, *The Athenian Democracy* (Oxford, 1957), 41; G.E.M. de Ste. Croix, "The Constitution of the Five Thousand," *Historia* 5 (1956): 1–33; and Stockton, *Classical Athenian Democracy,* 153, 165 (who cites both of the preceding works).

the Peloponnesian fleet and killed the Spartan admiral Callicratidas. The Peloponnesians lost seventy-five ships; the Athenians lost thirteen outright, and twelve more were damaged. The Athenian *strategoi*, anxious to prosecute their advantage, left a contingent of ships to pick up survivors while they themselves sailed to Mytilene in an attempt to trap Calliciratidas' second-in-command, Eteonicus, who was blockading Mytilene with fifty ships. Eteonicus escaped with the help of a timely storm, the same storm that prevented the Athenians from rescuing their own sailors who had been trapped on the disabled ships.[52] The citizenry were outraged at the losses (around five thousand men), and the restored democracy, presented with the opportunity, obligingly ran amuck. The eight *strategoi* who had been in command at Arginousae were impeached. Of those, the six who had dared to return were tried together, by the motion of one Callixenus, a member of the *boulē*, rather than in individual trials. Callixenus and his supporters managed to dodge a countercharge of *graphē paranomōn* (illegal proposal) by threatening its author, Euryptolemus, and his supporters with the same fate as the generals. The generals were then tried, condemned, and executed. Socrates himself opposed the trial and claimed that the citizens later recognized that their decision to try the generals en bloc was illegal.[53]

MacDowell has in general terms defended the legal propriety of the action of the Athenians, although admitting the possibility that a collective action against all the generals may have been inappropriate.[54] But a consideration only of legal technicalities misses the salient point. As contemporary American jurisprudence demonstrates so boorishly on a quotidian basis, the fact that an action is legal very seldom makes it right. Arginusae resurrected the classic pathology that had brought Athens into such dire straits in the first place: the endless second-guessing of the leadership; the willingness to listen to whatever seemed good at the moment; the inability to commit to any strategy or to trust anyone, even the elected officials, for any extended period; and most of all, the ever-present, ever-dangerous requirement of radical democracy to permit anyone to have his own ill-informed say. Most important was the lack of authoritative leadership: the demos failed to produce such

52. Xenophon *Hellenica* 1.6.29–38.
53. *Apology* 32b.
54. *Law in Classical Athens*, 186–89.

leadership, and even had such a person emerged, he could only with great difficulty have prevented a demagogue like Callixenus from appealing to grief and anger instead of reason. If Sophocles shared the sympathies of Thucydides, the trial of the generals must have looked like the darkest days of the earlier parts of the war revived.

And thus Sophocles offers a stern reminder to the Athenians—one that is integral rather than appended to the other aspects of his play. All are not heroes or leaders. Perhaps all should not be. The Athenians willingly acknowledge their dependence on the king; less willingly, perhaps, they allow their inferiority to the hero, Oedipus. And Sophocles does not make either superior perfect. Oedipus' flaws remain despite his prophesied destiny. He cannot see the consequences of all of his actions; otherwise he may have gone easier on Polyneices, whose end encompasses the death of his beloved daughter Antigone. In turn, Creon expresses a valid concern when he criticizes Oedipus for his willful exploitation of Antigone's devotion. Oedipus cannot mount a real defense for incest; his effort is inconsistent and ultimately unpersuasive. And Oedipus remains embittered over Thebes' decision to cast him out, though, regardless of the situation in the previous play, parricides and regicides are not normally welcome additions to a Greek city.[55] Yet we admire Oedipus despite his flaws. No great man has ever wanted for faults or critics; rather, some inner power compels the admiration of lesser men, regardless. The flaws disclosed, the great maintain their authority throughout. The ability to maintain his portrayal of a truly heroic yet often unsympathetic protagonist, with all the difficulties his character and actions present, offers the ultimate demonstration of Sophocles' dramatic skill and political art. He never gives us an easy hero, and he certainly will not do so in his last play. The choristers, representing the audience, must acknowledge themselves lesser, the hero greater, even while confronted with persistent evidence of the hero's own inadequacy. In this play, all they need do is see Oedipus' ravaged face to be reminded of his sometimes uncontrollable passion. In acknowledging the greatness of the hero, the chorus perforce accepts a lesser, more easily malleable status.

---

55. One cannot assume that the conditions of the first play extended to the second, although that would make Oedipus' position in this work all the more untenable. After all, he himself had pronounced the decree of exile for the killer(s) of Laius (*Oedipus Tyrannus* 224–43).

Life lived in society is a series of trade-offs. The greatness of Theseus, another hero whose past is, to put it charitably, "checkered," compensates for his citizens. He leads and they follow. He does not consult. He makes no speeches; in fact he barely addresses the chorus at all. No one would confuse him with a late fifth-century Attic demagogue. In particular, no one could mistake him for a Peisander, to whom the demos had yielded without much resistance at Colonus five years before. The chorus obeys him without question simply because he must be obeyed. Commanding obedience is as integral to the king's nature as displaying obedience is to the chorus'. A temptation to view Theseus as Pericles suggests itself, yet that will not quite do. Pericles was the consummate politician; the tragedian's leader displays no political skill, no tact whatsoever. Sophocles, in his final work, prefers rather to glorify an older system, one more appropriate to the Bronze Age heroes than the civic life of the fifth-century polis. He does so consistently throughout the *Oedipus at Colonus*. *Xenia* appears as the most important social relationship. In the course of the play, Theseus is repeatedly called *anax*, the Homeric word for warrior-king.[56] The king's gesture in receiving Oedipus resembles far more closely his rescue of Heracles in Euripides' *Heracles Mainomenos* than his intervention in the *Suppliant Women*. And the action of the play, for all the reasons given earlier, takes place beyond the *astu*. The polis, as Herman observed, had tamed the hero. But in the *Oedipus at Colonus* the heroes operate in tandem as far from the constraints of the polis as the needs of the drama allow.

A final detail, the import of which Bowra duly observed,[57] although he did not pursue the matter, affirms the presence of a distinctly antidemocratic flavor to the play. The location of the grave must stay a secret, to be passed on by Theseus only when he senses his own death approaching (1530–31). The practice suggests oligarchic Thebes rather than democratic Athens. For heroes generally receive public worship. But Oedipus could not, by his own stricture. Rather, the worship that he envisions for himself recalls that of Dirce at Thebes. As Demand puts it:

---

56. See lines 549, 630, 1130, 1173, 1177, 1476, 1630, 1650; by contrast, he is referred to as *basileus* only once during the play (at 67, by the *xenos*). Clearly Sophocles wanted to emphasize the Homeric and heroic, rather than the civil or religious, aspects associated with Theseus' kingship.

57. *Sophoclean Tragedy*, 341.

The location of this tomb was known only to the Theban officials called hipparchs (cavalry commanders). The hipparch completing his term of office took the incoming hipparch to the tomb at night, and together they performed fireless sacrifices in secret, then removed all trace of the ritual and went away separately.[58]

Near the end of Sophocles' last work, he proposes an elitist cult of worship to a hero who has offered his benefits to the entire polis. No one could miss the point.

Does Sophocles, then, emerge as a closet monarchist in his final work? This is doubtful. Yet by creating a play that so vividly contrasts his heroes to the ordinary citizens, he challenges the demos to accept the opportunity for a dialogue on responsibility, duty, the need to recognize excellence over mediocrity, and the need of the polis to allow scope for heroism to flourish. The author of the last tragedy surviving from classical Athens has seen democracy for ninety years and leaves a suggestion that he is unimpressed. Like Oedipus, who permits only Theseus, and after him the *prophertatos*, to know the place of his tomb, Sophocles prefers the company of heroes.

---

58. N. Demand, *Thebes* (London and Boston, 1983), 57; see also Plutarch *De genio Socratis* 578B.

Bibliography

Ahl, F. *Sophocles' Oedipus: Evidence and Self-Conviction*. Ithaca, 1991.

Arrowsmith, W. "A Greek Theater of Ideas." *Arion* 2, no. 3 (autumn 1963): 32–56.

Asheri, D. "Studio sulla storia della colonizzazione di Anfipoli sino all conquista macedone." *RFIC*, 3d ser., 95 (1967): 5–30.

Bernidaki-Aldous, E. *Blindness in a Culture of Light*. New York, 1990.

Blaydes, F.H.M. *Sophocles*. London, 1859.

Bloom, H., ed. *Sophocles*. New York, 1990.

Blundell, M.W. *Helping Friends and Harming Enemies*. Cambridge, 1982.

Bothe, F. *Sophocles*. Vol. 1. Leipzig, 1806.

Bowra, C.M. *Sophoclean Tragedy*. Oxford, 1944.

Brunck, R.F.P. *Sophocles*. Vol. 1. Oxford, 1826.

Burian, P. "Suppliant and Savior: *Oedipus at Colonus*." *Phoenix* 28, no. 4 (1974): 408–29. Reprinted in Bloom, *Sophocles*, 77–96.

Burton, R.W.B. *The Chorus in Sophocles' Tragedies*. Oxford, 1980.

Bushnell, R. *Prophesying Tragedy: Sign and Voice in Sophocles' Theban Plays*. Ithaca, 1988.

Campbell, L. *Paralipomena Sophocles*. Oxford, 1907.

———. *Religion in Greek Literature*. London, 1898.

———. *Sophocles*. Oxford, 1879.

Carpenter, H. *The Inklings*. New York, 1978.

Colonna, A. *Sophoclis Fabulae*. Vol. 3. Turin, 1983.

Dain, A., and P. Mazon. *Sophocles*. Vol. 3. Paris, 1960.

Davies, R. *The Rebel Angels*. New York, 1982.

Demand, N. *Thebes*. London and Boston, 1983.

De Ste. Croix, G.E.M. "The Constitution of the Five Thousand." *Historia* 5 (1956): 1–33.

Dindorf, W. *Annotationes*. Oxford, 1836.

———. *Sophocles*. Oxford, 1832.

Dodds, E.R. "On Misunderstanding the *Oedipus Rex*." In *Oxford Readings in Greek Tragedy*, ed. E. Segal (Oxford, 1983), 177–88. Originally published in *Greece and Rome* 13 (1966): 3–49.

Ellendt, F. *Lexikon Sophocleum*. 1872. Reprint, Hildesheim, 1958.

Ehrenberg, V. *Sophocles and Pericles*. Oxford, 1954.

Euben, J.P., ed. *Greek Tragedy and Political Theory*. Berkeley, 1986.

Fagles, R., trans. *Sophocles: The Three Theban Plays*. New York, 1982.

Farnell, L. *The Cults of the Greek States*. Vol. 1. Oxford, 1896.

———. *Greek Hero Cults*. Oxford, 1921.

Finley, M.I. *The World of Odysseus*. New York, 1954.

Fitzgerald, R., trans. *Sophocles, Oedipus at Colonus: An English Version*. New York, 1941.

Furley, D. "Euripides on the Sanity of Herakles." In *Studies in Honor of T.B.L. Webster*, ed. J.H. Betts, J.T. Hooker and J.R. Green, vol. 1. Bristol, 1986.

Gardiner, C.P. *The Sophoclean Chorus: A Study of Character and Function*. Iowa City, 1987.

Gould, J. "Hiketeia." *JHS* 93 (1973): 72–92.

Grene, D., ed. *Sophocles II*. Chicago, 1975.

Herman, G. *Ritualised Friendship in the Greek City*. Cambridge, England, 1987.

Hermann, G. *Sophocles*. Vol. 2. London, 1827.

Hogan, J.C. *A Commentary on the Plays of Sophocles*. Carbondale, Ill., 1991.

Jaeger, W. *Paideia*. Trans. G. Highet. Vol. 1. New York, 1939.

Jebb, R.C. *Oedipus at Colonus*. Ed. E.S. Schuckburgh. Cambridge, 1903. Reprint, Cambridge, 1913.

———. *Sophocles*. Cambridge, 1900.

Jones, A.H.M. *The Athenian Democracy*. Oxford, 1957.

Kamerbeek, J. *The Plays of Sophocles, Part VII: The Oedipus Coloneus*. Leiden, 1984.

Kirk, G.S. *The Iliad: A Commentary*. Vol. 2, Bks. 5–8. Oxford, 1990.

Kirkwood, G.M. *A Study of Sophoclean Drama*. 2d ed. Ithaca, 1994.

Kitto, H.D.F. *Greek Tragedy*. London, 1939.

Knox, B.M.W. "The *Ajax* of Sophocles." In Bloom, *Sophocles*, 5–32.

———. *The Heroic Temper*. Berkeley, 1964.

———. "Sophocles and the *Polis*." In *Sophocle: Entretiens sur l'Antiquite Classique*, ed. M. Bernard Grange (Geneva, 1982), 1–27.

Lehman, D. *Signs of the Times: Deconstruction and the Fall of Paul DeMan*. New York, 1991.

Linforth, I. *Religion and Drama in the "Oedipus at Colonus."* University of California Publications in Classical Philology, no. 14. Berkeley, 1951.

Linwood, W. *Sophocles*. London, 1846.

Lloyd-Jones, H. *The Justice of Zeus*. Berkeley, 1971.

Lloyd-Jones, H., and N. Wilson. *Sophoclea*. Oxford, 1990.

Lloyd-Jones, H. *Sophocles*. Vol. 2. Cambridge, Mass., 1994.

———. *Sophoclis Fabulae*. Oxford, 1990.

Longo, O. "The Theater of the *Polis*." In Winkler and Zeitlin, *Nothing to Do with Dionysus*, 12–19.

Macdowell, D.M. *The Law in Classical Athens*. Ithaca, 1986.

Masqueray, P. *Sophocles*. Paris, 1924.

McDevitt, A.S. "The Nightingale and the Olive." In Bloom, *Sophocles*, 49–57. Reprinted from *Antidosis: Festschrift fur Walther Kraus zum 70*, ed. R. Hanslik et al. (Vienna, 1972), 49–57.

Murnaghan, S. *Disguise and Recognition in the Odyssey*. Princeton, 1985.

Musgrave, S. *Sophocles.* 2 vols. Oxford, 1800.

Norwood, G. *Greek Tragedy.* New York, 1960.

Parker, R.T.C. *Miasma.* Oxford, 1982.

Perotta, G. *Sophocles.* Messina, 1935.

Podlecki, A. "*Polis* and Monarch in Early Attic Tragedy." In Euben, *Greek Tragedy and Political Theory*, 76–100.

Reinhardt, K. *Sophocles.* Trans. H. Harvey and D. Harvey. New York, 1979. Originally published as *Sophokles* (Frankfurt am Main, 1933).

Reisig Thuringus, C. *Oedipus Coloneus.* Jena, 1820.

Reynolds, L.D., and N.G. Wilson. *Scribes and Scholars.* 2d. ed. Oxford, 1974.

Robert, C. *Oidipus: Geschichte eines poetischen Stoffs im grieschischen Altertum.* Berlin, 1915.

Rohde, E. *Psyche.* 1920. Reprint, New York, 1972.

Rosenmeyer, T.G. "The Wrath of Oedipus." *Phoenix* 6, no. 3 (1952): 92–112.

Schnedwin, F.W., and A. Nauck. *Oedipus auf Kolonos.* Berlin, 1878.

Schneider, T.H.G. *Sophocles.* Weimar, 1825.

Scodel, R. *Sophocles.* Boston, 1984.

Segal, C.P. "Time, Theater, and Knowledge in the Tragedy of Oedipus." Edited by B. Gentili and R. Pretagostini. In *Edipo: Il Teatro Greco e la Cultura Europea.* Rome, 1986.

———. *Tragedy and Civilization: An Interpretation of Sophocles.* Martin Classical Lectures, vol. 26. Cambridge, Mass.: 1981.

Slatkin, L. "*Oedipus at Colonus:* Exile and Integration." In Euben, *Greek Tragedy and Political Theory*, 210–21.

Spatz, L. *Aeschylus.* Boston, 1982.

Stanford, W.B. *Aeschylus in His Style: A Study in Language and Personality.* Dublin, 1942.

Stinton, T. "The Riddle at Colonus." *GRBS* 17 (1976): 323–28.

Stockton, D. *The Classical Athenian Democracy.* Oxford, 1990.

Vernant, J.-P., and P. Vidal-Naquet. *Myth and Tragedy in Ancient Greece.* Trans. J. Lloyd. New York, 1990.

Verrell, A.W. *Euripides the Rationalist.* 1895. Reprint, New York, 1962.

Von Blumenthal, A. *Sophocles.* Stuttgart, 1936.

Waldock, A.J.A. *Sophocles the Dramatist.* Cambridge, 1951.

Weinstock, H. *Sophocles.* Leipzig, 1931.

Whitman, C.H. *Sophocles: A Study of Heroic Humanism.* Cambridge, Mass., 1951.

Wilamowitz-Moellendorf, T. von. *Die dramatische Technik des Sophokles.* Berlin, 1917.

Winkler, J., and F. Zeitlin, eds. *Nothing to Do with Dionysus: Athenian Drama in Its Social Context.* Princeton, 1990.

Winnington-Ingram, R.P. *Sophocles: An Interpretation.* Cambridge, 1980.

———. *Studies in Aeschylus.* Cambridge, 1972.

Wunder, E. *Sophocles.* London, 1855.

Zeitlin, F. "Theater of Self and Society in Athenian Drama." In Euben, *Greek Tragedy and Political Theory*, 101–41.

Index

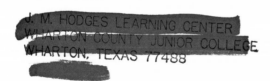